Future *in*-Formation

Choosing a Generative Organizational Life

Ron A. Carucci and Josh J. Epperson

With a foreword by
Teri Ann Drake
Senior Vice President, Creative
Hallmark Cards Inc.

Outskirts Press, Inc.
Denver, Colorado

Future In-Formation
Choosing a Generative Organizational Life
All Rights Reserved.
Copyright © 2008 Ron Carucci & Josh Epperson
V3.0 R1.2

Outskirts Press, Inc.
http://www.outskirtspress.com

ISBN: 978-1-4327-3206-6

Library of Congress Control Number: 2008935237

Outskirts Press and the "OP" logo are trademarks belonging to Outskirts Press, Inc.

PRINTED IN THE UNITED STATES OF AMERICA

"This is just who I am"… "My job would be so much easier if everyone else just got it"… "If they could only see where they need to change"… Sound familiar? Have you privately – or publicly-expressed such frustrations? If so, then Future *in*-Formation is for you. Though, if you are unwilling or unable to redefine the *"how"* you lead, rethink the *"who"* you lead, or rephrase the *"they"* into *"me"*…it will be a waste of time. Future *in*-Formation is titled as such because leadership…good, sustainable leadership, is defined by constant change and evolution. No matter how good of leader you may be today, tomorrow will be different. No matter how well you lead yourself, your team, or your peers today…tomorrow *"they"* will be different. This book is not a quick read. It should be a reoccurring read for any leader to continually remind yourself to reassess, readjust, and renew what it is *you* need to do to be an effective leader at work, in your community, and at home.

Mindy Simon
Vice President, Information Technology
ConAgra Foods

Ron and Josh's insightful grasp and articulation of what they aptly name "generative leadership" is desperately needed in today's business climate. Their work is an inviting oasis within today's corporate world, where relational "heart and soul" are all too often sacrificed on the altar of short term "efficiency". If you're a leader aiming to create enduring greatness within your organization, you must engage with the truth Ron & Josh unfold in this book!"

Peter Ash
CEO, NDG Financial Corporation

The book is an inspiration! It will give all those yearning for greater experiences of community and their organizations a stark look into the path toward greater wholeness and health. No leader will walk away from this unchanged. It's a wonderful invitation to all that your story is meant to become, and a guide for making that story become a reality. Way to go little brother!

Diane Van De Ven
U.S. Federal Government, and Ron's sister

I love this book! The human work of organizational leadership turns out to be the heart and soul of leaders who unleash generativity through healthy relationships in their organizations. And they are usually the ones who get the results. The ideas in this book need to get under your skin where they can incubate and grow. Carucci and Epperson tell moving stories, set forth powerful concepts of leadership, and walk leaders through a series of inquiries and self-reflections that can take you to new levels of generative leadership. Every page has nuggets of wisdom and launching pads for transformation.

Brian K. Rice, President
Leadership ConneXtions International

This is a very timely book on a timely topic. After working with Ron and Josh the past couple of years, I'm convinced that they have their fingers on the pulse of helping organizations become more generative – and realizing the environments and results we all say we want. I heartily endorse this book and hope that you will find their insights as helpful as I have.

Kevin McCuistion, Director
Microsoft

At first glance, this book appears to be a powerful tool for leaders of organizations. But really, its use is universal. The principles are relevant to everyone who is committed to transformational change in their personal and professional world--from the custodian/janitor to the CEO (sometimes the same person). It starts with the power of one and demonstrates how to gather and harness the synergy of the collective. I highly recommend this book to anyone who aspires to lead sustainable change.

Stacey Easterling
Program Executive, The Atlantic Philanthropies

Brilliant work by Epperson and Carucci. This book skillfully takes a deep understanding of relationships and applies it to business practices and systems. In so doing, it allows us all to see a new way forward – one that includes you and I as *the* important piece in the ever-changing business puzzle.

Joel VandenBrink
Good friend, and Founding Brewmaster Two Beers Brewing Co.

Carucci and Epperson's philosophy, frameworks, and questions accurately position the meaning of organizations in a personal context, and then boldly challenge each of us to be accountable to live generatively for those we lead. You can't read this material and remain indifferent to how you lead. This book is a must for anyone, but leaders in particular, with the courage and desire to (happily) live.

Lawler Kang,
Speaker, and best-selling author, *"Passion at Work: How to find work you love and live the time of your life"*

Great job! My read on the book is very positive. At first, I thought, "Why so much build up and reminders of the past, and of the need to change?" I was impatient and eager to get to the meat of the book. Then I realized the build up actually opened my mind, and made me crave the need to see and understand differently. Practical and relevant examples and thorough explanations make this book great for a visual learner and busy executives responsible for leading change in their organizations. We need to make changes in our organizational patterns to invoke significant change in our leadership and in our society. To settle for the alternatives would be disaster. This book can help us all get the job done."

James R. Jackson
Plant Manager, MillerCoors

How uplifting to read a book about organizations that uses words like "belief," "hope," "openness," "humility" and "accountability." The sustainability of the projects we support in developing nations is dependent upon our understanding the motivations of individuals that benefit from them. The same can be said for any organization looking to operate sustainably. We recognize that as an organization, we are successful because of the *combination* of contributions by our staff, board and volunteers – individuals who each have unique talents and motivations. Anyone who wonders about just how that works needs to read this book. And if you doubt that it works that way, read it slowly, and read it twice.

Marla Smith-Nilson
Executive Director, Water 1ˢᵗ

The breadth and richness of your future is determined by your willingness to name and understand the effects of degenerative patterns in your life and organization. Ron and Josh are a coalescing force in *Future in-Formation,* summoning us to journey into new patterns of thinking and behavior that offer a generative resonance of transformation. This is a compelling, succinct, and provocative book worth reading and applying to our places of influence and leadership—basically everywhere.

Jon DeWaal,
Good friend, and Jonathan DeWaal Painting

Ron Carucci and Josh Epperson's thought provoking book provides a blueprint for leading and becoming a positive force within our own lives and within our organizations. A cautionary note: the tasks proposed in this book are not for the weak. Future in-Formation first invites the reader to think along with the authors, but then presents a series of challenging questions which can only be answered through hard work and soul searching. Having watched Ron Carucci and Josh Epperson at work, I am convinced that the readers' own unique answers to these questions can transform those who have the courage to face them.

Melodie Blacklidge, M.D.
President, Medical Staff
Cincinnati Children's Hospital

Part analysis, part workbook, and part story, *Future In-Formation* is a multi-faceted, slightly-in-your-face dare to its readers to lead organizations of great generativity. If you know either Ron or Josh, then you are well aware that you couldn't have finer guides for this journey. If you don't know Ron or Josh, then you truly must read this book to find out why I'm overjoyed to call them friends and colleagues in seeking generative change.

Tim Soerens
Good friend and pastor of Dust Church in Seattle

for

Mariette and Albert
Jill and Gregg

mothers and fathers whose lives
first revealed to us what it means to
choose a generative life.

in loving memory of

Jeffrey McKinstry
who lived an exemplary generative life
on behalf of thousands

GRACIOUS ACKNOWLEDGEMENTS

Writing a book about living a generative life is hardly an endeavor that happens without the help and support of many people. We have learned so much from this experience, far beyond what we'd ever imagined. The truly creative process that this authoring encompassed never once happened in vacuum. It is the result of numerous generative fingerprints that have touched us both forever.

Each of you is an exemplary generative colleague and friend…with our deepest thanks…

Teri Ann Drake – Thank you for living generatively in front of the world. Your leadership is uncommon, and the power of your voice lends a great gift to this work. Thank you for supporting this cause by the example you set, and the compelling beginning you've created to the book.

Michael Russell – your brilliance and mastery never cease to astound us. All of us at Passages Consulting remain grateful and in awe of what you can do with words and ideas.

Mindy, Eric, JoAnn, Ryan & Ulrich – what a privilege to have such amazing colleagues to spend our days with. Doing the noble work of inspiring and guiding transformative change in the world is a spectacular experience for us for which we're grateful. Mindy & Ulrich – thanks for the original conversation back in the "old days" in Denver that spawned the dream, and the original "list" of organizational patterns we believed could be "decoded." Eric & Mindy – an extra thanks for getting into the mud with us and pitching in on the stories! When you decide to stop consulting, you can write screen plays!

Tom Ryan – thanks for helping us editorially and finding some cool quotes; and for helping us find what writing Stories from the Future in community could look like. You are a treasured colleague and friend.

Blaine Hogan – your artistry is breathtaking. You gave us the experience of loving a book cover. More importantly, you took what was in our soul and translated it into a magnificent piece of art with which to introduce the world to this book. Thank you for allowing your imagination to stir you in the middle of the night!

Our clients – for allowing us the privilege of coming alongside you and joining your journeys of great change and pursuits of noble aspirations. For all that you have taught us, especially on these pages, we thank you. May these stories honor you as curious and courageous leaders.

And to all of you who are determined to bring a generative organizational life to the worlds in which you reside, may you find inspiration and insight for the story you are writing in the words that follow. And for even considering such a daunting endeavor, we applaud you.

Josh Epperson & Ron Carucci
Seattle, WA
July, 2008

"The self is not something ready-made, but something in continuous formation through choice..."
John Dewey

TABLE OF CONTENTS

FOREWORD

"This book is an invitation to your own story."

When I read these words in Ron and Josh's introduction to *Future in-Formation*, I was hooked! I love a good story. As a child, I was intensely curious and a voracious reader. Stories helped me understand the world around me. In college, I was committed to telling stories through my illustrations and design work. Later on, great storytellers such as Isabel Allende, Carmen Agra Deedy, and Bruce Springsteen gave me a wider window into how people think, feel, and interact.

My professional life has been all about stories, too. Storytelling is at the heart of Hallmark's business. We hear every day from people around the world who tell us how much the people in their lives mean to them: The woman who found a box of cards in the attic ten years after her mother passed away—and in them discovered the first chapter of her parents' love story. The soldier in Iraq who delighted in the funny cards and messages his family sent when he needed a good laugh—and their love and support. The thousands of individual stories we hear inspire us to create products that speak to the genuine emotions and relationships people share.

There is another story that intrigues me. It is the story of how people bring their individual gifts to work every day in pursuit of a shared and greater good. Sometimes the most important questions as this story unfolds are the most simple.

Why are we here?

What do we stand for?

Where are we going?

My job, and *every* leader's imperative, is to make the answers to these universal questions come alive for others. That is no small task, which is why I found this book's focus on "generativity" so compelling. Ron and Josh explore the attitudes and behaviors that can generate health, growth, and adaptability in an organization and lead to a more sustainable future. As I read, I kept thinking about how I could be more actively generative in my role today.

I am honored to lead the world's largest creative community, a diverse and imaginative group of individuals who conceive, design, write, and illustrate the millions of products Hallmark creates for its consumers. Hallmark Cards is built on the idea of enriching lives by helping people connect and communicate with one another. To do this consistently and with integrity, I firmly believe we have to start by looking honestly at the ways we relate to each other at work.

Do people understand the company's mission and purpose? Do they genuinely feel a part of something bigger, something worth working hard for to achieve? Is everyone given a chance to bring the best of themselves–all their talents and strengths–each and every day? How do we treat each other along the way and how does it affect what we do?

In answering these questions, I go back to some fundamental leadership beliefs that help me navigate in both good and challenging times.

I believe people come first.

In my world at Hallmark, this is all about trusting in people's creative spirit and doing all I can to help them unleash their unique gifts. Recently my team and I spent some time thinking about a vision for the Creative group that could serve as our North Star during inevitable times of change. We wanted our storyline to include words that reflected both who we are and who we aspired to be. Energized. Worldwide. Imaginative. Insightful. Innovative. Fast. Flexible. Fun. Those words come alive only when people are trusted and encouraged to be their true selves.

I believe great communication is built on trust.

Trust begins with the truth. People who trust each other tell the truth in plain language, which can lead to healthy debate and better solutions. Telling the truth is key. Equally important is *acting* on the truth. I work on being fully present, and with the demands of business today, it's hard work. Being fully present means giving my complete attention to another person, listening respectfully to his or her point of view and asking questions to check my understanding. When I have lunch with individuals or join small groups to discuss our goals, my intent is to be fully present with them, not to check my Blackberry, not to worry about my next meeting, but to listen actively and respectfully to what they have to say. True power doesn't come from position; it comes from telling and acting on the truth.

I believe good leaders are both lifelong students and enthusiastic teachers.

I've been fortunate to have many mentors throughout my eighteen-year career with Hallmark. They have given me the gift of their experience and wisdom. They have been honest, provocative, and encouraging with their feedback and generous with their time and teachings. I have in turn looked to mentor others with that same openness and to share what I have learned (or am learning). I do this through exchanging personal stories, passing on a new book on leadership, or attending a class or workshop together with emerging leaders. Of course, it takes time above and beyond what typical leaders expect to spend their day doing. We can always make excuses for not going these extra miles when presented the opportunity. When I have this dilemma, I remember one of my favorite quotes on leadership by John Gardner:

"Each of you has within you more resources of energy than you have ever tapped, more talent than you have ever exploited, more strength than has ever been tested, more to give than you have ever given. As individuals you must understand that about yourselves, and as leaders you must understand it of others."

I believe in leading with purpose, on purpose.

I feel blessed to work for a company whose vision is to create a more emotionally connected world by making a genuine difference in every life, every day. Yes, it is an ambitious goal, but it is also a noble one that unites everyone at Hallmark and gives meaning to what we do.

All worthy goals are aspirational, but is ours attainable? We have faith that it is, because we sense we have only scratched the surface when it comes to ways to meet needs like hope, love, support, and meaningful connection. These human needs are constant and powerful and inspire us as we reflect with pride on almost one hundred years of our company's history and look to the future we are creating today.

I realize that many of my executive peers running large enterprises, or large portions of enterprises, may read these words and think, "Sure, I'd love to have time to inspire people like that, but I have to make this quarter's numbers." I can fully appreciate the tug of war between focusing on maximizing people or maximizing profits. It is sad to me that we tend to see these two important aspects of business as though they were diametrically opposing forces. They are absolutely compatible and, in fact, one cannot be achieved without the other.

The idea of leading with purpose on purpose got personal for me recently when I spent several days away with my senior leadership team focusing on ways we could positively influence and inspire our staffs. First we needed to be a positive influence and inspiration for one another, though. We talked honestly about our strengths and weaknesses. We shared our concerns and our hopes as we looked ahead. We talked about the children in our lives and the world we wished for them. We finished the sessions exhausted but exhilarated and united in our belief in what we do and why we do it.

When it came time for me to close the session, I looked around the room and saw talented and dedicated professionals, but I also saw mothers, fathers, aunts, and uncles who wanted to be a part of something good, something that would play a vital role in the lives of their nieces, nephews, sons, and daughters.

I said to them, "We are working together for a purpose greater than the next product line or program launched. We are here to ensure the next one hundred years for Hallmark. In our moments working together, we are creating a tomorrow we can be proud of for the children in our lives and all of their future global friends as they engage with our brand long after we are gone."

Our CEO, Don Hall Jr., summed it up in a message to everyone at Hallmark:

"We are in a life-affirming business, and the possibilities are everywhere."

And so our story goes on…

And your story? My hope for you is that you will write it with purpose, on purpose. More so, that you will face realistically the potential negative consequences if you forfeit the opportunity to do so. If there was ever a time in our world's history when we as business leaders needed to be more deliberate about the experiences we shape *of* our organizations, and *for* our organizations, it is today. There are many reasons to be pessimistic: Economic downturns. War. Globally competitive threats we've never considered possible. Unforeseen personal tragedies. Even in the most dire of life's moments, we still have choices. This isn't pie-in-the-sky leadership. This is sound business practice. If those we lead are to take cues from us (and they will), what cues would we want them to take? When our frustrations and cynicism get the best of us, we watch the energy dissipate from our organizations. As leaders, whether we like or not, we set the pace and trajectory of our organizations. It's a daunting responsibility, but it comes with the territory. If you take that responsibility seriously, then the concepts on the pages ahead will bolster your leadership and your organization in very important ways.

As Ron and Josh say, it's your story to write. I believe *Future in-Formation will* open your thinking and challenge you to consider ways to improve relationships and experiences in your organization now and for the future. It will open up pathways to performance levels that will make a genuine and positive difference. It will inspire you to put "generativity" in motion. I intend to keep learning from the ideas in this book, and I invite you to do the same.

With my very best regards,

Teri Ann Drake
Senior Vice President-Creative
Hallmark Cards Inc.
Kansas City, Missouri
July 2008

INTRODUCTION

L
ittle books are an interesting phenomenon. They have emerged as their own veritable literary sector, especially in the business community. They are appealing because our first thought when we see them is, "Great– it's an easy read and I can get through it quickly." Often little books nobly attempt to distill large and complicated concepts into digestible and accessible chunks so the reader doesn't have to struggle too much intellectually. They prevent busy readers from having to get bogged down in very sophisticated theories that only pile on more complexity to the already-too-byzantine, multifarious lives we face in organizations. Quite frequently little books use stories or parables to convey the beauty and simplicity of otherwise intricate hypotheses. Sage narrators cast into idyllic situations convey the author's ideas through the voices of characters in the stories. The stories carry readers through the character's experiences of tragedy and triumph. Ultimately some important epiphany of learning serves to transform the community in which the story is unfolding. We like these little books because they offer us practical advice and hope for our own transformational experiences. These works come full of great bite-sized information. Readers are invited to mine wisdom from others' experiences, picking and choosing what they believe applies to them. They boost our confidence that we, like the characters in the story, can effect great change in the lives of those around us. They make us believe we can realize noble performance gains on behalf of the organizations we serve. For all of these reasons and more, little books serve a great good on our literary landscape.

This isn't that kind of little book.

This little book will not simplify an important concept and distill it into smaller, digestible chunks. We hope it will take existing small thinking and expand it to much wider and broader views, views of your future vistas you never imagined. Dreams you've only read about in parables of an organizational experience for you and those with whom you work. While we do hope to take what we feel are highly transformative concepts and make them accessible to you, we don't want to do it at the expense of making it sound easy, or worse, by inviting you to contort yourself into the image of the character in the parable to make the concepts work. No great transformational effort would ever be described with ease or contortion as its basis. And we would like to boost your confidence, indeed your conviction, about your influence over the organization, the team, the family, the community over which you preside, but not at the risk of naiveté or arrogance. And finally, we do indeed hope to invite you to a very important unfolding story. But not someone else's story. Not a set of fictitious characters from whose voices you have to extract wisdom.

This book is an invitation to your own story.

Your story, as you well know, is full of twists and turns. There are many plots and subplots. There are many characters. There are heroes and villains, and on any given day, you could be either. There are great climatic crescendos of progress and there are tragic setbacks. There is nail-biting suspense and mystery. There is comedy. There are epic scenes of good battling evil and grand, dramatic escapade. There is boredom. And more than anything, there is a next chapter.

There is an unfolding future that has not yet arrived, for which you are preparing. Your future is *in- Formation*, and your future will shape *you,* regardless of how intentionally or accidentally you choose to shape it.

For every one of us and the communities in which we work, there is a *not yet* to our story that is moving toward us. This book is about getting you ready for it.

We are making some assumptions about the next chapter of your story that we ought to let you in on. Some of these assumptions include the following:

- You desire to play a main character in your organization's story. You have a vested interest in seeing to it that the next chapter of the story is an inspirational success, not leaving to chance that which you could influence for good.
- You are familiar with the very complex, even mysterious nature of your and your organization's story and accept the fact that attempting to oversimplify it risks trivializing, even compromising it.
- You believe there are many coauthors of the story unfolding around you, and that coalescing those authors into a holistic and healthy story would be better than having them at odds, writing a fragmented and toxic story. For the purpose of this book we will describe the differences between these two types of stories as the difference between a *generative* and a *degenerative* story. While you may not be entirely sure how to do this, we assume on some level you are not indifferent, that you have a clear preference for a generative story.

If you can accept these assumptions, then let's move ahead.

This little book also comes undergirded with five basic beliefs about organizations and communities and how they change. We'll do a crash course in these beliefs to enable your time with the material to be as productive as possible.

1. Organizations are dynamic and open systems, never static, always *in-Formation*.

That organizations must continually adapt to dramatic shifts in markets, technologies, and ever-increasing customer demands is hardly a new idea, yet the ability of most organizations to actually adapt to shifting contexts lags way behind the volume of knowledge available about how and why to do so. Macro economic trends in Asia influence the cost of goods sold from a plant in North Carolina. Increasing costs of jet fuel disable the movement of imports and exports around the globe. Unexpected natural disasters can cost a nation a decade of growth. The need to pay attention to the dynamic nature of our contexts, interpret the meaning behind the multiple forces that influence that context, and translate information that is always *in-Formation* into wisdom and eventually foresight will become a key predictor of an organization's competitive sustainability. To make these translations *systemically,* viewing all the interacting parts of the organization as interconnected and interrelating, will truly separate the gold medalists from the also-rans. Exceptional organizations understand they are more than their organization charts. Rather, they are communities of diverse, even contradicting, people, functions, and ideals. They are collections of paradoxes and endlessly complex. An organization's reciprocal influence on and from the context in which it resides demands a tolerance for ambiguity and the courage to act opportunistically.

The greatest essence of systems is indeed the aspect of openness, the vastness that makes uncharted waters both intimidating and invigorating. Openness allows the community to be influenced by its outside world and to influence its outside world. When defining a system as the human body, this open design can be illustrated by one's capacity to breathe. When defining a system as a community or an organization, this open design can be illustrated in its capacity to understand what its customers want (outside-in), and its ability to create products or services for its customers (inside-out).

By an open system design we are referring to an organization's structure, processes, culture, work, people, and leadership capacity. Moreover, we are referring to how those components combine to form the future of an organization for better or worse as they interact with the context in which the organization resides. To most leaders, viewing their organization systemically is not intuitive. It is much easier for a leader to see the static view of the organization chart, policy manual, or values statement–some artifact whose intention is to reflect the essence of a specific component of the organization. Holding all of the inter-relating components in view enables leaders to plan change more effectively. With the whole system in view, they are far more likely to consider broader implications of possible changes than if they only viewed the organization in static bits and pieces.

An open system alone is not a sufficient enough framework to summon a generative future *in-Formation*. As we see time and again, because the simple fact that organizations are *able* to create products their customers want doesn't mean they *choose* to do so. The same is true for the individual. An individual may know that it's healthy to exercise regularly, but may not choose to. The element of choice is key to a system's capacity to change.

Most leaders would agree that greater organizational health leads to greater performance; however, this belief doesn't appear to have penetrated organizational behavior beyond tacit acknowledgment that it would be "nice to do." Go into any multinational corporation and ask the marketing people how well the sales forecasts enable them to perform effective product positioning. Next ask the salespeople how responsive they think marketing is to their needs to capture new customers. Check in with forecasting and ask how well they feel manufacturing's ability to produce goods on time, on budget, is relative to their forecasting, and then ask manufacturing how accurate they feel the forecasts are, and then, just for fun, ask logistics about how well they are able to accurately palette, ship, and deliver the right products to the right customers based on both forecasting and manufacturing's ability to fill the orders on time and accurately. For the finale, go back to manufacturing and forecasting with the views of logistics and see if they care. Degenerative choices are rampant in any complex system. The question begging to be answered is "Who is calculating the cumulative cost of these choices? More importantly, who is curious about the implications of different choices?

An acute understanding of how systems cooperate within themselves is key to promulgating generativity. Ultimately, generativity is a *choice*, and the place where generative choices are lived out is within the context of relationships.

2. Any sustainable transformative experience happens in the context of human relationships.

One very cynical leader once commented to us, "Organizations would work so much easier if it weren't for having to deal with the people." Like many leaders, this executive had often repeated the obligatory "people are our most important asset" doctrine to countless crowds of his organization, obviously without much credibility. His true colors showed in the end when it came to relationships. He had very few relationships of substantive meaning. He was a lonely man, and his company eventually filed for Chapter 11 before being taken over in a hostile bid, then broken up and absorbed into a competitor's portfolio with superfluous pieces sold off.

Indeed, we are suggesting there is a direct correlation.

To extract the formation of the human experience from the formation of an organization, and ultimately, its *trans*formation, is as ludicrous as attempting to extract heat from boiling water. But so often we try in vain to neutralize the unpredictable, messy, sometimes painful element of humanity in an attempt to control our environments. As noted above, such vanity has a severe cost.

Outside of human relationships, there is no transformation.

Of course this creates a conundrum for many of us. Sure, we all love the great benefits of relationships—the sense of belonging, the pleasure of regard, the experience of intimacy, the validation of our voice, the comfort of encouragement and spurring on after disappointing setbacks, and the warmth of a safe place and kind gesture. But how many of us would say we enjoy the risks associated with these benefits? The reflection of our own shortcomings. The rejection of our ideas and hurt feelings from callous indifference. The painful reality of our capacity to hurt, or worse, retaliate. The need to navigate intractable conflicts of ideology or values. The complexity of balancing the needs of one relationship against another. The insidious experience of envy–the kind we invite, and the kind we receive. The fear, and ultimately the devastating reality, of loss. The irony of relationships is that it takes all of these experiences for transformation to occur. Without insult, there is no need for forgiveness. Without doubt, there is no opportunity for reassurance. Without honest feedback, there is no provocation to desire more. Without conflict, there is no innovation. Without difference, there is no enjoyment of distinction. And without distinction, there is no discovery of real unity.

Relationships are the building blocks of systemic transformation, and their power is discovered only when people within organizations transcend the superficial social constructs, pleasantries, and courtesies that too easily masquerade as authentic relationship. When humans risk forging ideas, crossing boundaries, and facing the future together, change happens.

Dow Chemical launched a brilliant marketing campaign titled The Human Element that beautifully describes this phenomenon. This is the text of that campaign, but we'd recommend watching the video to experience its true impact.

For each of us there is a moment of discovery. We turn a page. We raise a hand. And just then, in the flash of a synapse, we learn that life is elemental. And this knowledge changes everything. We look around and see the grandness of the scheme. Sodium bonding with chlorine. Carbon bonding with oxygen. Hydrogen bonding with oxygen. We see all things connected. We see life unfold. And in the dazzling brilliance of this knowledge, we may overlook the element not on the chart. Its importance so obvious, its presence is simply understood. The missing element is the human element (Hu), and when we add it to the equation, the chemistry changes. Every reaction is different. Potassium looks to bond with potential. Metals behave with hardened resolve. And hydrogen and oxygen form desire. The human (Hu) element is the element of change. It gives us our footing to stand fearlessly and face the future. It is a way of seeing. It gives us a way of touching. Issues. Ambitions. Lives. The human (Hu) element. Nothing is more fundamental. Nothing is more elemental[1].

Most leaders are baffled when attempts to change their organizations fail. While most would concur that they have experienced more failure than success when it comes to change, still, they begin with the expectation of a positive outcome. So why is it that some change efforts stick better than others? We asked a number of our clients this question, and to a person, they all said the same thing. "It all comes down to the people." We would say that it all comes down to *the relationships among the people.*

You need only to reflect on some of the most profound changes you have experienced in your career, and we'd bet that there are faces of important people attached to each one of them. It was in the context of important relationships that such a transformative experience was possible. And, it is hoped, there are those in your organization who, when inventorying their own transformative experiences, would have your face come to mind.

3. There is greater good organizations can create with and for their members.

Any well-trained MBA student will tell you that from the outset of their business education, the mantra "companies are in business for one reason: to make money" is drummed into them. Newly minted management consultants are deluged in the same propaganda-like messages. For some, the message is met with an anticlimactic "of course that's what they exist for." For others, there is a strident resistance to the implied capitalistic greed inherent in the corporate machinery that this purpose perpetuates. But what if the binary trap, like most binaries, were dangerously false? What if it were possible for these economic enterprises to exist both for the purpose of generating economic results as well as other good? Indeed, we believe that many are rejecting the superficial either/or thinking and are desperate to discover the great good our corporations can do beyond producing economic results. The quarter-to-quarter bloodletting to eek out shareholder returns has gutted our corporate community of its once high-spirited essence. It has rendered it with a soulless reputation, not only from those outside it, but even from those within. Too many members of our corporations come to work robotically frozen, disconnected from any sense of meaning or mission. But when ignited toward a greater good, when a fundamental belief in the organization's mission for something greater than economic gain is harnessed, people's frozen hearts thaw and a passion to contribute is kindled.

C. K. Prahaldad, for example, suggests that the role our corporations around the world can and should play in social transformation is profound. He believes, and proves, that the eradication of global poverty can be achieved in large measure through a shift in focus and belief by global enterprises to see those at "the bottom of the pyramid," the world's poorest, in a dramatically different light. "What is needed is a better approach to help the poor, an approach that involves partnering with them to innovate and achieve sustainable win-win scenarios where the poor are actively engaged and, at the same time, the companies providing products and services to them are profitable. If we stop thinking of the poor as victims or as a burden and start recognizing them as resilient and creative entrepreneurs and value-conscious consumers, a whole new world of opportunity will open up." [2]

Why do annual United Way campaigns or similar charitable endeavors within corporate communities unleash a mysterious force of goodness, where people are naturally drawn to rally for some greater collective pursuit? Could it be that embedded within the human spirit is a fundamental desire not only to see a greater good pursued, but also to actually *participate* in that pursuit alongside fellow members of a

7

community? Our belief is that this latent force lies within each of us and is waiting to be unleashed at any time. All it needs is a worthy and credible reason to ignite, and it spreads magically with the might of a rogue wave or a desert windstorm. And while the great causes we adopt in our corporate communities–walks for breast cancer, marathons for children's hospitals, fundraisers to build housing for underprivileged families–are all inspiring and laudable, our belief is that this latent force can be tapped for many more causes than just those that appeal to our altruistic sense of injustice or compassion. Indeed, it is our contention that the very missions of our corporations, the markets they exist to serve, the innovations they aspire to achieve, the social sustainability and global coalescence they aspire to effect, and yes, the profits they seek to generate, can all be worthy provocation of that inner force to rouse great good.

What if that's how our organizations functioned *routinely*?

What if that boundless spirit to passionately pursue something greater than the ordinary were the norm of our corporate experience instead of the exception? Our hunch is that it is not only possible, but for our corporate enterprises to continue to thrive in the coming decades, it is necessary.

4. Great performance and healthy (generative) organizations are directly correlated.

This may seem like the best of "Captain Obvious," but sometimes the obvious isn't. No one would argue that organizations in which people naturally thrive would most likely outperform, especially over time, organizations where people barely survive. Time and again, studies on organizations bear out this fundamental truth. The question is, for all the literature that demonstrates the competitive advantage that culture has on performance, why don't organizations pay more attention to pursuing it more persistently? Since Kotter and Heskett published *Corporate Culture and Performance* in 1992, we've seen repeated proof of their thesis that organizational culture influences economic performance, for better or worse. Kotter and Heskett[3] talk about the characteristics of unhealthy (degenerative) organizations and include traits such as arrogance, inward focus, and bureaucracy. There may be reasonable explanations for why organizations display these traits based on history and strategy, but in the long term, they will inevitably undermine both ability to change and performance. As Kotter and Heskett say, "Only cultures that can help organizations anticipate and adapt to environmental change will be associated with superior performance over long periods of time." Firms that valued their customers, stockholders and employees highly and worked to create a healthy environment for both employees and leaders showed dramatic results. Healthy (generative) firms increased revenues by an average of 682% over the eleven-year period Kotter and Heskett surveyed, as opposed to unhealthy (degenerative) firms, which increased revenue by only 166%.

More recent research both supports Kotter's and Heskett's conclusions and underscores that it is a global phenomenon. According to a study conducted by Booz Allen of 1,100 companies in all industries operating in Finland[4], 41% of the Finnish-owned companies are healthy in our sense of the word, while only 30% of the non-Finnish companies are. The results of the study are based on 1,100 profiles from companies across a broad spectrum of industries in Finland. Booz Allen found that the healthy Finnish companies "possess a greater ability to execute strategies, are more effective at decision making, and have more gradual advancement paths that better develop employees as they move upward. Overall, the majority of Finnish companies, as a result of their healthy organizational structure, rarely second-guess their decisions and are able to quickly translate important strategic and operational decisions into action. Finnish companies are also more likely to deal successfully with discontinuous change in a competitive environment compared to their international counterparts."

Regardless of the study, the question for any leader who presides over part of, or an entire enterprise, is how to build a sustainably generative organization in which superior performance and thrilling colleague and customer experience are the consistent standard to which everyone enthusiastically aspires.

5. Transformation is multidimensional and never finished.

Darwin's famous observation about survival has returned to prove itself time and again. Though often misquoted as "Only the fittest will survive," what he actually said was, "Only those most adaptive to change will survive." The implication is that adaptation is never finished; rather it is a perpetual process. We never "finish" surviving. It is our belief that healthy organizations are in perpetual formation on three different levels. First, there is formation happening *intrapersonally,* or "within." People's self-perceptions, skills, aspirations, desires, insecurities, and motivations are constantly maturing and refining. True, for some, personal growth becomes an arrested process, leaving one exposed to great consequences both professionally and personally. Nonetheless, healthy formation for an individual is a lifelong endeavor.

Second, formation is happening *interpersonally,* or "between." Any experience of personal change within an individual will be lived out only in the context of relationships; therefore there must also be formation happening *between* individuals. One leader we've worked with had made extensive effort to be more inclusive and engaging with her team after being given a great deal of feedback about needing to let go of control. After much work and reflection on why she had such strong needs for control, revealing some traits of perfectionism, self-doubt, and fear of failure, she began to liberally include others in her decision making, inviting their input and participation in key aspects of the organization. To her dismay, people didn't eagerly jump into the action and play. They sat back and didn't offer much. The leader became discouraged, confused by why no one was taking the opportunity to participate after giving her feedback on her need to include them more. When queried, the team members said they didn't know how to participate. They'd learned how to accommodate her well, nod their heads, execute her directives, and comply with her requirements. But now they had to learn an entirely new way of interacting with her, and they didn't know how. Suddenly, her invitation to be more engaging meant they had to be more engaged. Her delegation of more decision rights meant they had to be more decisive. One set of intrapersonal changes *within* this leader set in motion the requirements for another set of intrapersonal changes *within* those on the team, and a third set of changes *between* the leader and her team.

Finally, formation is happening *systemically,* or "among" members of an organization. As noted above in our discussion on open systems, the components of an organization are always interacting with one another, and formation in one area of an organization almost always requires formation in another. Leaders who are going to lead transformation effectively must always keep these three levels–within, between, and among–in mind at all times, balancing the intensity and velocity of formation, and *trans*formation under way in each. If any one of these levels finds itself outpaced by another, the hope of sustainable transformation is threatened. Keeping them synchronized and integrated is the key to realizing any hope of lasting change.

In his classic text, *Crossing the Unknown Sea; Work as a Pilgrimage of Identity,* David Whyte poetically describes the interdependence of these forces.

The core act of leadership must be the act of making conversations real. The conversations of captaincy and leadership are the conversations that forge real relationships between the inside of human beings and their outer world, or between an organization and the world it serves...out of this conversation we create a directional movement in the world that not only ensures our survival but creates exhilaration, the wind on our face, an immersion in the present whilst we simultaneously experience the joy of speeding toward our destination.[5]

Simply stated, he beautifully illustrates our ability to connect our inner transformation with our communal transformation, and embrace the delight of the adventure now while always accepting that we are audaciously pursuing an unknown future.

Blending Art & Practice

As the pages ahead unfold, you will begin to realize that generative organizational life is both subjective and objective. As beauty is in the eye of the beholder, so is much of the generative experience of organizations, and yet the results those organizations produce are objective and concrete. It is the blend of the intangible with the tangible that join to birth generativity. Art connotes mystery; practice connotes discipline, and both are required to pursue generativity. There is an element of mystery in the human spirit when coalesced into the work of transformation, and there is a significant degree of discipline–practice–to awakening and sustaining such transformation. No different than virtuoso violinists or Olympic gold medalists must invest tireless hours into their discipline, generativity is in large measure the result of deliberate and focused pursuit. There is the mystifying awe that arouses our souls when we watch the result of such sweat equity. When we gaze at the beauty, precision, and breathtaking results of the Olympian or prodigy, we are struck silent by how effortless it looks. Somehow it "just happens." When generative life is at its best, it feels much the same way. But Olympians or prodigies do not rest on their laurels, relying solely on their natural gifts; rather, as they invest diligently into their development, so too must leaders who wish to build generative organizations invest in the endeavor. Accept responsibility for the elements over which you have control and surrender the elements over which you don't. Leave those to the mystery of what happens when our humanity reaches for its zenith and finds it. Embrace the demand of the rigorous practices needed to realize a generative organization, and abandon yourself to art that stirs up the passions of those within your organization to journey with you.

Averting the Plague of Defection

Everywhere we go, we hear executives complain about turnover and wanting better retention of their employees–the "people are our most valuable asset" mantra. HR executives are completely confounded by the mass exodus they are facing in their corporations from the trigger-happy employees who seem to leave at the slightest unforeseen speed bump. Could it be that employees are arriving in organizations *expecting* to jettison at the first hint of discontent? Younger employees are especially prone to jump ship when they feel their voices are unwelcome or they are told to "wait their turn" to play. Intolerance for organizational nonsense is escalating rapidly and so is the bill for replenishing the supply of increasingly difficult-to-find employees.

Have you become intolerant enough of the nonsense that is driving people out of your organization? Or worse than those quitting and leaving, have you become intolerant enough of the performance deficit being gouged by those who have quit and *stayed?* We hope so.

Generative organizational life is vital to the people in your organization, and if you ask them, you know they will verify it. In our work with clients, we repeatedly see the impact of degenerative behaviors and actions on human beings. People work ridiculously long hours at great personal cost, are frustrated by reward decisions that don't make sense to them, and are demoralized by curt communications that overlook their contributions and focus instead on minutia. As Gary Hamel points out[6], the biggest obsession of managers in the past hundred years has been to get more out of people, but the way in which this has been done has been so soul-killing that companies virtually guarantee they will never get what they're looking for. Hamel puts it eloquently when he says, "Vassals and conscripts may work hard, but they don't work willingly."

We have seen that, to a large extent, managers have played a parental role in regard to their employees, employing a variety of controls and withholding information. Hamel points it out as do we in our recent book, *Leadership Divided*, and we all know that children eventually tire of their parents' tutelage and leave the nest. The metaphor is apt: many younger employees and junior leaders are impatient with the old structures they find, and they respond to degenerative behaviors by actively seeking generative environments elsewhere. Here is a very telling posting to a Yahoo answer board in reply to the question "Why did you leave your job?

> Tomorrow is my last day at my current job. I'm moving from a company of 1,000+ people to one of less than 100. The pay will be the same so it's not about money. I'm leaving for a variety of reasons, though. Here's my list:
>
> 1) I don't have much faith in the direction of the company. We're in a fiercely competitive market, and I don't see much of anything new to differentiate our

upcoming new products.

2) The chain of command in my particular group is not providing any direction for the group. We're floundering. Communication is practically nonexistent, and the whole direction is not to identify and solve problems but to cover up and hope it goes away.

3) I'm bored. I've been doing similar tasks for eight years now, and it's getting repetitive. I want to do something different that I will find stimulating for my mind.

4) Moving to a smaller company will have its challenges, but everyone there will have to produce. No one can hide. This happens a lot in a larger company in my experience, and it's frustrating to see how many people produce absolutely nothing. Also there will be less bureaucracy in a smaller company, which should make it easier to get things done.[7]

The disenchantment of employees, especially younger ones, threatens companies with a plague of defections, as talent literally refuses to accept degenerative environments and leaves. Most of these defections are completely preventable. The old adage is true that "Employees don't quit their companies, they quit their bosses." A recent survey[8] of more than 1,000 respondents found that the following:

- 30% left their jobs to seek new challenges or opportunities that were lacking with their previous employers
- 25% left because of ineffective leadership
- 22% cited poor relationships with their managers
- 21% said their contributions were not valued

What's the price tag for replacing disgruntled employees with new ones? According to the U.S. Department of Labor Turnover Worksheet[9], which calculates both the direct and indirect costs of unwanted turnover, looking only at *voluntary* turnover, the invoice in 2007 to American corporations was in the neighborhood of $386 billion.

Pause for a moment of silence and let that staggering number sink in.

In one midsize professional-services firm we know with annual revenues of about $3B, it calculated its annual turnover costs at about $195 million. That's 6.5% of its profits down the drain. In a 2002 study, KPMG estimated that annual turnover costs in the supermarket industry were $5.8 billion, where hourly workers' average tenure is less than a year. Most experts estimate the turnover cost to be around 150% of an exiting professional's annual salary. For long-tenured and highly skilled professionals, it can range as high as 180%. This means that for a company with 100,000 employees and a turnover rate of 10%, conservatively assuming an average annual salary of $40,000, the cost of turnover is $400 million.

You do the math.

If you aren't wondering about the hundreds of better ways to spend that money, you should be. Creating generative environments that value contributions, foster healthy relationships, meaningfully engage people in ways that inspire and provoke passion, and realize the highest levels of achievement and satisfaction ultimately is the result of intentional choice. To us, that means all of the problems cited above that contribute to the plague of defection are avoidable. Corporately, we can create communities that vanquish such destruction, and frankly, we must do so with all due speed.

Continuing to export a cadre of increasingly dissatisfied and despaired people from our organizations will only perpetuate the dilution of gifts and capabilities within our communities, but our *trans*-organizational capacity will weaken as well. If we are already losing competitive ground in the West as it is, the trending plague of defection will only accelerate our competitive decline and, more tragically, our societal and relational decline.

We simply must stem the tide and reverse the hollowing out of our organization's hearts by regenerating life and meaning into our workplaces. We hope this book will both provoke you to want the same, but also give you some compass headings for where and how to begin.

Now that we've set the stage, let's get going. We hope that your time with this material is wildly transformative for you and those with whom you share the experience of organizational and community life. Wrestle well. Struggle mightily. Hope hard. Desire deeply. Act courageously. And dream big. Your future and the future of your organization are worth it.

Your story's next chapter is about to begin.

Make it good.

Anticipating with you,

Josh & Ron

The First Half
Understanding the
Generative Organizational Life

PART ONE

The Theory of the Case

"They saw themselves as part of–not apart from–the problem they were trying to solve. Their fundamental orientation was that more than one future was possible and that the actions they and others took would determine which future would unfold. They did not believe they had to wait passively for events to occur. They believed they could actively shape their future.

They understood that one reason the future cannot be predicted is that it can be influenced."

Adam Kahane, *Solving Tough Problems*

The Theory of the Case

Everyone knows that organizations have lives and personalities of their own. Combinations of cultures, processes, structures, and people coalesce into an entity that has a distinct "look and feel," creating a unique corporate personality. Like human personalities, companies display great variety, from forces for good at one end of the spectrum to pathologies at the other. The convergence of distinguished abilities, track records, anomalies, and aberrations creates measurable patterns over time that can both contribute to and constrain performance.

The culture of organizations reinforces this personality by effectively limiting the ability of people within the enterprise to choose between alternative behaviors. Social relationships within a company have their own structures based on rules, language, styles, tacit assumptions, and definitions of reality that groups use as starting points for interactions. According to Schein[10], culture is in essence a "residue of success" within the company, a repository of all the elements that enabled both the company as a whole and individuals within it to successfully overcome challenges. Culture has its own personality and is very resistant to change. It can outlast product lines, services, the founders of the company, its managers, and virtually all other physical attributes of the organization. Just as with the deepest elements of our individual personalities, some of the most basic elements of company culture are unspoken rules that are not discussed but are nevertheless felt by people within the organization. Managers reinforce these rules because they have come to see them as appropriate, and they effectively become the guardians of the company's personality.[11]

Though personality is resilient, organizations are anything but static. Constantly changing market conditions mean that organizations are essentially always *in-Formation* as they adapt to their context. Most leaders see these patterns of formation in their symptomatic form: "We're too slow" or "We're not caring for the customer anymore" or "We've lost our edge" or "We're too siloed" or "We used to be considered a top-notch employer; everyone wanted to work here." Underneath these symptoms, though, lie potential toxins that can undermine and eventually ruin the company.

Ironically, we often associate the word *information* with a static commodity–data we can collect, compile, analyze, and then mindlessly fasten to people and problems. The dangerous assumption behind the act of fastening information to people or problems is that the information is true simply because we fastened it. The truth is that good *in-Formation* is dynamic, moving, has multiple interpretations, and is ultimately the provocateur of rich dialogue and relationship. In short, it is *in motion*. Being *in-Formation* presumes intentional adaptation to shifting contexts. It acknowledges that information must constantly be examined in ever-changing lights with fresh eyes, eyes that are themselves in perpetual formation. Organizations whose organic and vibrant beginnings give way to rote machinery–the migration from dynamic to static, from *in* Formation to information–face the peril of decline should they fail to resist the seductive allure of the predictable, routine, and comfortable. There are many examples of companies that have remained vibrant and continually revitalized themselves over time. Jim Collins identified eighteen of these visionary companies, citing household names like Wal-Mart, IBM, Disney, and Citigroup, which outperformed rivals for decades.[12] The Walt Disney Company is an example worth noting. Disney was founded in the 1920s by brothers Walt and Roy Disney, who began with a small animation studio producing cartoon shorts. After a few miss-starts (including the loss of Disney's first commercially successful character, Oswald the Lucky Rabbit, in a contract dispute), Disney introduced Mickey Mouse in 1928. When the studio began producing feature-length films in 1937, its first release, *Snow White and the Seven Dwarfs,* was the highest-grossing film of all time until 1939's *Gone with the Wind.* In 1954, Disney became one of the first American theatrical TV producers to show recent films on television. The company diversified into theme parks in 1955 and cable networks in 1981. After surviving a hostile takeover bid, Disney launched Touchstone Films in 1984 and had a major success with the subsidiary's first picture, *Splash.* The company also entered the lucrative video game market at the same time. Disney's 1991 film *Beauty and the Beast* is the only animated film nominated for the Academy Award for Best Picture, and *The Lion King*, released two years later, is the highest-grossing traditionally animated film in history. Today, the Walt Disney Company is the third-largest media and entertainment company in the world, with $65 billion in revenues and a broad range of some of the most lucrative entertainment properties, including the *Pirates of the Caribbean* franchise and Hannah Montana.[13] Throughout its eighty years, Disney has been a potent creative force, always finding new ways to reach audiences and yet never losing a palpable connection to the style of its founder.

A company like Disney illustrates that the right kind of connection to the initial creative spark is vital to the long-term health of an organization. Unfortunately, the pathologies in the personalities of many companies display destructive patterns of rigidity and stasis that are more about mechanical imitation than a constructive link to the past.

We see just how entrenched these patterns are when leaders attempt to change them.

Ironically, most organizations use the word *trans*formation to describe what they hope to accomplish with regard to their pursuit of change and a different future. In its literal sense, the word means to cross multiple formations, to transcend the process of formation to realize an exponential degree of change. Of course, the word then also presumes there is a process of formation already in place to transcend. But if an organization has become static, like inanimate information, then there is no formation process to transcend, thus making *trans*formation unachievable.

Generativity & Degenerativity

When organizations focus on their future, they summon change. The patterns of the organization's personality are then exposed by the way in which it sets direction and allocates resources, because these are processes in which the need for change is inherently implied, even exposed. Accordingly, patterns that become threatened fight for their survival. Organizations that have enjoyed the comfort of market dominance through scale and mass, and behave with indifference to shifting customer demands, find it difficult to adjust when new competitors enter their markets. Organizations that have enjoyed the ability to attract the best and brightest "top-of-class" employees find it difficult to adapt to changing market demographics when their workplaces change from environments rewarding personal achievement to cutthroat, everyone-for-himself places that lose focus on serving and retaining customers. The big three US automakers, GM in particular, are perhaps the most glaring examples of former titans accustomed to dominance in their industry who have found it hard to react to competition. Their past successes seem to have made it particularly hard for them to adapt, leading to their current decline.

The once-arrogant GM has suffered a long, slow slide in its ability to compete and has finally ceded US market dominance to Toyota, even though it continues to produce more cars worldwide in absolute numbers. The company sought to emulate the factory conditions of its competitors in its Saturn division, but has never been able to repurpose this success into the larger enterprise. GM has attempted over time to diversify, first into auto financing through GMAC, and then into home mortgages through GMAC's Ditech division. The recent subprime mortgage crisis, coupled with GM's long history of under-funding its pension liabilities, and its eroding market share have combined to form a bleak outlook. One would think that a car that used either less gas or none at all would be a lifesaving *coup* for GM, but the company has seemingly ceded the hybrid car line to both Toyota and Honda. GM actually put an electric car on the road ten years ago, but then shelved the idea and adopted the strategy of suing states like California over emissions standards as a course of action more likely to yield profit! [14] It is difficult to imagine how a company in this mindset can again become a market leader. Certainly, the way GM has sought to write its future speaks volumes about its personality. This is true of all organizations; as they attempt to change and place their bets accordingly, they reveal a lot about who they are.

The hypothesis of this book is that the patterns of organizations can fall into two categories:

Generative **patterns** – are those that continue to generate health, growth, and adaptability. These are patterns that generate new and helpful realities. They are self-perpetuating, in a sense, but with a unique degree of intentionality on the part of the organization. For generativity to remain sustainable, the frequent adaptation to new opportunities must be responded to with unambiguous standards that clarify what will be required for the organization to remain generative. The harsh reality and risk, then, is that generativity left unattended can lead to degenerativity over time, and in fact, often does. There are some generative patterns that run so deeply into the DNA of an organization that they can be largely self-sustaining as long as they remain protected from other degenerative patterns that would seek to undermine them. In other cases, generative patterns require routine attention to keep them thriving, especially when they are new to the organization and exist in a context of counteracting degenerative patterns. For example, a hospital system deeply committed to patient care and enhancing human life can survive economic stress from patient volume decline because nurses, doctors, and administrators have figured out how to work collaboratively to contain costs and stay focused on the health of their patients. If the norm has been established that relationships, even with inherent conflicts, are to take priority over departmental rivalry, then the patients (whose satisfaction is always most predicted by their experience with their nurses, not their doctors) will clearly express satisfaction and will refer others to the care of that same system. When generative patterns are fragile, however, external forces can deliver a painful blow and dislodge generativity. That same healthcare organization whose once-generative pattern of providing quality care in an environment of decapitated fees and HMOs loses this patient focus as it cedes to cost containment in a fee-for-service environment. Trust erodes as nurses and doctors find themselves in intractable conflicts over role clarity, accountabilities, and the definition of what "quality care" is. The re-introduction of patient care as a core value is very fragile, as it must contend with the physicians' resentment of their loss of personal income and self-involved focus on ensuring they get control of their time and get what they believe is their fair share of the pot. The downward spiral from generative to degenerative can often be imposed, in part, by external forces. The opportunity to adapt is missed as people struggle to cling to the familiar routine of past success. Once people dig their heels in to avoid adapting to shifting contexts, the entrenchment serves as a self-perpetuating device to unwittingly redirect the organization from a generative to degenerative posture, in this case from caring for patients to caring for self. In this case, the pursuit of a shared future is almost futile when individual resentment and demand have superseded the ability to even conceive of anything "collective" in the organization. Generativity is meant to serve as a coalescing force that enables the pursuit of a shared and sustainable future. The excessive presence of degenerative self-interest routinely undermines an organization's ability to deliberately move forward and choose a new future. Generativity creates centripetal force, while degenerativity creates centrifugal force.

Degenerative **patterns** – are those that generate slow, destructive decline. A generative posture is one that gives meaning and unleashes passion, contrasted to a degenerative posture that takes energy and suffocates desires. If generativity leads to transformation, then degenerativity leads to trans-*erosion,* the decline of multiple intersecting components of an organization or community. Once fragmentation begins in a specific area of an organization's life, it can quickly generalize to the broader organizational context, much the way a localized virus can spread to the entire immune system of the body. Once in place, degenerative patterns require as much, if not more, effort to sustain. To be fearful, contemptuous, self-involved, or complacently apathetic is not only exhausting, but can also siphon energy away from the core work of the organization. The speed at which these destructive forces can travel is often quicker than we imagine, and they are transported on the cynical perspectives of those prophets of doom that now can declare their shaming and punishing pronouncements of "See, I told you this would happen." The painful reality of degenerativity is that needed capacity and resilience for change is hemorrhaged and the requirement of transformation becomes more acute, while the resources to pursue it become more scarce, and yet not impossible to achieve. A nonprofit community organization that, through poor strategic choices, got itself into severe debt and faced dissolution found a way to redirect itself through several courageous and difficult choices. First, it was able to name that its debt had become the sole focus of its work, far afield from the mission on which the organization was founded. Second, it was able to tolerate the loss of key leaders who were prime carriers of the fear, self-contempt, and pessimism that pervaded the organization, despite being viewed as indispensable. The fear caused senior leadership to believe that if these leaders were to exit the organization, all could be lost, yet it was their very departure that opened the opportunity to invite in generative leaders who could help the organization pave the way to new postures of belief, organizational self-honesty, and a return to a focus on its core mission. Needless to say, this transition came at a painful cost, but ultimately the future of the organization remained hopeful and vibrant despite a protracted season of degenerative behavior.

The most odd and tragic aspect of degenerativity is the extent to which organizations accept its presence as a given. Over time, degenerative postures seduce communities into believing that "this is just the way things are," and that any attempt to change would be futile. The slow death of an organization over several generations of management becomes so commonplace that people stop questioning it. Ruthless competitive sabotage between rival divisions is accepted as standard fare on the menu of daily routine. Indifference to customer dissatisfaction, conventional. Dismissive and condescending reactions to new ideas, expected. Putting spin on the truth to avoid conflict and accountability, customary. Vitriolic ranting from the sidelines in the name of "speaking truth to power," reasonable. And ultimately, apathetic eye rolling in response to the battle cry for change becomes a time-honored tradition.

It does not have to be that way. We can stop turning a blind eye to the degenerative diseases around us and call ourselves to more. We don't have to mindlessly digest the nasty noxious morsels of negativity we so reflexively stomach as "the best we can do." Nonsense. We can do far better. Let's see how.

Adaptive Formation and Generativity as Essential Elements to Transformation

The dynamic reality of generative and degenerative patterns in an organization is this: they need one another for an organization to ultimately pursue its greatest degree of generative health. Just like the body needs a taste of a virus to build antibodies and resistance, so organizations need to contend with the degenerative patterns that are present, to ultimately build the generative capacity to pursue a common future. The *elimination* of degenerativity isn't the goal, and nor is it even possible. Struggling with degenerativity openly and honestly in the pursuit of generativity is the goal. Here's the paradox: you have to treat your organization's degenerativity *generatively.* You have to see it not as the unwelcome intruder that needs to be expelled, cured, or annihilated, but rather the unpleasant guest who, through greater hospitality, becomes enjoyable and congenial. It is the need to embrace the opposition that degenerativity offers that ultimately helps an organization build generative muscles. Too often, the misguided notion that it can be eradicated leads organizations to adopt the very degenerative postures they are seeking to change. Great campaigns are launched "against" certain organizational nemeses, and the ruse of a noble witch hunt is nothing more than the shift of degenerative poisons from one application to another. For example, "bureaucracy-busting" campaigns tend to become bureaucracies themselves as the work of taking inventory of minutia activity and forcing compliance with changes takes on a life of its own. Similarly, the ultimate goal of cost-cutting initiatives ought be greater stewardship of an organization's resources. Although cost-cutting efforts are a good pursuit when costs have exceeded available revenue, sadly, cost-cutting efforts too often yield mistrust, selfishness, and in the extremely degenerative case, corruption, as people conclude that the only way to survive an environment of scarcity is to take what is not theirs.

The martial art Aikido has much to teach about the movement from degenerative to generative postures. Aikido is a Japanese martial art developed by Morihei Ueshiba as a synthesis of his martial studies, philosophy, and religious beliefs. Aikido is often translated as "the way of unifying (with) life energy" or as "the way of harmonious spirit." Ueshiba's goal was to create an art that practitioners could use to defend themselves while also protecting their attackers from injury. While there are many interpretations of the art today, most have concern for the well-being of the attacker.[15] The paradox of a martial art having as its goal a peaceful resolution to conflict, with opponents standing side by side versus head to head at the conclusion, is an illustrative example of translating degenerative (violence) into generative (peace).

The experience of the Office of National Drug Control Policy (ONDCP) in combating teen drug abuse is also a good example of treating degenerativity generatively. ONDCP was charged about ten years ago with developing an anti-drug media campaign aimed at young people. The idea was to reduce drug abuse through multimedia advertising—television, radio, and print ads. The way ONDCP originally set up the program was to convince people to be "against drugs." The campaign focused on all sorts of horrible things: addiction, how even drugs perceived as "mild" could lead inevitably to consumption of more dangerous drugs, how whole groups of people could be roped into drug use, and so on. If you looked at how horrible drugs are, you'd "just say no," right?

After spending a billion dollars over six years, ONDCP was faced with a complete failure. The media campaign was not only ineffective in reducing drug use, but it was also actually accused of causing greater harm than good. Critics claimed that the campaign gave young viewers the impression that drug use is so common among peers that they might as well join in. Others pointed out that some of the claims in the ads were so exaggerated that young people assumed they were being lied to. Finally, groups in the psychological community pointed out that telling someone they must not do something is almost like daring them to do it; some will do it precisely because it is forbidden.

ONDCP's initial failure illustrates the futility of campaigning "against" a perceived nemesis, even when it is something as indefensible as drug use. Ironically, their solution illustrates the power of addressing something degenerative in a generative way. ONDCP accepted that their "just say no" campaign was fruitless and then let go of it. They engaged a new media company as thinking partners and went back to the drawing board. True, their aim remained curbing drug use in young people, but they crafted a completely different approach to the problem by looking at all their data again from scratch and trying to see beyond old solutions. This review yielded a crucial insight: the real enemy ONDCP was fighting was *influence*. Whether it was peers, drug pushers or even ONDCP's own painfully bad advertising making ludicrous comparisons between drug use and terrorism, influence was itself the enemy. ONDCP realized that if you change the influences upon young people, you might be able to change their behavior. Essentially, ONDCP was abandoning the fight *against* something and trying to use influence to create something *different, for* something. This is at the very heart of generativity. ONDCP changed every television, radio, and print ad it had been running and instead launched a campaign on living "above the influence." The change in attitude reflected in the ads was nothing short of astonishing. In only four weeks, awareness among young people of the new campaign was more than 68%, and interaction with it was viral. Even ONDCP's harshest critics are now admitting that the new campaign appears to be changing young people's attitudes in a way the old approach could never do. In essence, instead of giving young people something to say "no" to, it gave them something to say "yes" to.

Examples like this one strengthen our belief that the more dynamic, or *in-Formation* an organization remains, and the more it pursues generative postures, the more *trans*formation it will achieve. By contrast, the more static, or informational, an organization remains, and the more it allows degenerative postures to fester, the more incrementally, at best, it will see change. See figure 1.0 for this causal model.

Figure 1.0 How Formation and Generativity Lead to Sustainable Transformation

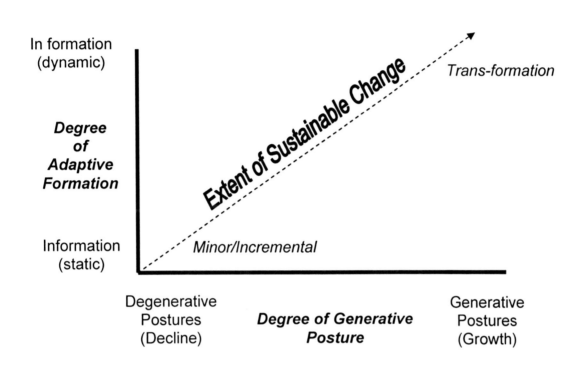

We will look at how these generative and degenerative patterns can appear in the context of future formation, most often manifested in strategic change processes such as strategic planning, resource allocation, R&D and new product commercialization, organization design, and geographic expansion, etc. They could well appear in numerous organizational contexts, but we will specifically examine how the act of planning for future outcomes uniquely exposes the opportunity to migrate to generative patterns, or for the purpose of this book, what we will call *postures.*

PART TWO

Curiosity and Inquiry: Asking Questions to Choose a Generative Posture

"The important thing is not to stop questioning. Curiosity has its own reason for existing. One cannot help but be in awe when he contemplates the mysteries of eternity, of life, of the marvelous structure of reality. It is enough if one tries merely to comprehend a little of this mystery every day. Never lose a holy curiosity."

Albert Einstein

PART TWO

Curiosity and Inquiry: Asking Questions to Choose a Generative Posture

A posture connotes choice, a stance or position that one adopts with intentionality. As an organization's living personality is a result of its choices, so too are its postures, both generative and degenerative, derivatives of that personality. Generative postures more often tend to result from deliberate choices. By contrast, degenerative postures are often the result of a default choice not to adapt or simply to ignore the need to choose something different. Organizations that refuse to deny themselves the comfort of success and routine today end up having to deny the often grim results of their choices tomorrow.

You need look no further than today's headlines to find degenerative examples of companies that made a series of decisions that became progressively harder to reverse. Countrywide Financial, for example, is the largest issuer of mortgages in the US and is squarely in the center of the subprime lending crisis. Countrywide was founded in 1969 by CEO Angelo Mozilo with a mission to help people achieve their dreams of home ownership. The company was moderately successful during the 1970s, but an initial public offering was disappointing. This story changed dramatically between 1982 and 2003. *Fortune* described Countrywide as the "23,000% stock," since the company actually managed to deliver a 23,000% return on investment in that period, beating return figures for Wall Street monsters like Wal-Mart and Berkshire Hathaway.[16] Countrywide was a pioneer in the subprime mortgage market, vastly increasing the ability of Americans to finance houses, despite huge increases in home prices during that period. The company actively decided to court households with less-than-perfect credit and offered either low or no down payment. Mozilo portrayed this strategy as both a public service to help homeowners as well as a goldmine to investors who would benefit from tapping the huge subprime market. There were clearly risks, however. Countrywide was doing business with an increasingly large number of mortgagees who were considered bad bets by traditional banks. The company managed the risk two ways. On one hand, Countrywide aggressively marketed adjustable-rate loans, locking in low "teaser" rates for the first three years, then using the increased value of the borrower's house to refinance before the rate went up and exceeded the borrower's capacity to repay. The company virtually guaranteed itself a lucrative business in refinance fees, since none of its many adjustable-rate mortgagees wanted to pay the higher rates that kicked in after three years. On the other hand, the bank managed risk by packaging the loans it originated for sale as mortgage-backed securities. These securities were resold and packed with other real estate securities, and Countrywide effectively diluted the risk of default by its borrowers, spreading the risk across the holdings of virtually every institutional investor in the US and many abroad as well. The entire setup was predicated on the constant increase in value in the US housing market. Perhaps ominously, the long-term strategy simply did not allow for a sustained market downturn. In June 2007, US housing prices began exactly the sort of sustained downturn Countrywide dreaded. Within only two months, several US subprime mortgage issuers went bankrupt.

By that time, Countrywide had issued fully 17% of all mortgages in the United States. In August 2007, Fitch, Moody's, and Standard & Poor's credit-ratings agencies downgraded Countrywide's bonds to near junk status. The cost of insuring its bonds rose 22% overnight. By early 2008, Countrywide's stock had lost 90% of its early 2007 value, and Bank of America agreed to step in and buy the company in a deal expected to close at the end of 2008. CEO and founder Angelo Mozilo appears to have been aware of the looming crisis. Between 2005 and 2007, he sold virtually all of his Countrywide holdings, reaping $291.5 million in profits. His prescience in selling his stock was not reflected in any changes in Countrywide's lending practices, and in hindsight, he appears as an almost Ken Lay-like figure, cashing out because he knew his company's house of cards was about to collapse. Although a class action suit has been filed against him, nothing has come to light as of this writing that would indicate Mozilo broke the law. For our purposes, it is safe to say that he appears to have led his company into a degenerative posture, and it seems that he was unable to make any changes to avoid calamity, even though the timing of his stock sales suggests that he was aware of increasing risks.[17][18][19]

None of us ever thinks we will be "that front-page news organization." Until we are.

There are also examples of companies in generative postures for long periods of time, essentially as part of their organizational personalities. Marriott is worth noting as a particularly good generative example. The company was founded in 1927 by J. Willard Marriott as a nine-stool A&W root beer stand called The Hot Shoppe in Washington, DC. Marriott observed his customers keenly and noted, even back then, the premium people were willing to place on speed. He introduced curb service, making his stand the first true "fast food" establishment in the country. He expanded his operation to Baltimore in 1934 and eventually took The Hot Shoppes (the future Marriott Corporation) public. Marriott was constantly interested in new businesses, however, and in 1937 he invented in-flight catering for the nation's embryonic passenger airlines. The Hot Shoppes diversified further into food service contracts with the US government during World War II and with schools starting in 1955. Marriott moved into the hotel business in 1957, the theme park business in 1976, and the vacation timeshare business in 1984. Over time, the company spun off its food service and hotel businesses at a profit, and today it divides its activities between lodgings and timeshares. [20] Throughout, Marriott had (and his family still has) a fascination with creating new ventures that reflects the generative posture of the company.

Our work across many industries affords us "free passports" to cross organizational borders most insiders would not be granted. As such, our ability to see transcendent patterns gives us a unique vantage point as outsiders. We see many patterns that replicate themselves throughout various organizations regardless of maturity, industry, geography, or demographics. We have selected ten of those patterns to highlight in this conversation. It is our belief that each of these by themselves offers profound opportunity for transformational work. This list of postures is not conclusive by any means; in fact we're certain there are others. We have chosen the postures that we experience most frequently within the organizations we work. It is also important to note that although there may be a relationship among the postures, not all of them are demonstrably visible in every organization. As such, the migration from just one of these degenerative postures to its generative counterpart could herald a change in performance of great significance.

We present the postures in the form of questions rather than labels to highlight the importance of personal exploration and collective curiosity. Generative patterns are not places at which an organization merely arrives. In fact, we would argue that once an organization believes it has cornered the market on some special quality or attribute, it has begun a slow death march toward a degenerative perversion of the very characteristic it worked so hard to realize. The Countrywide example we cited illustrates this pattern. To be clear, the beauty of the special attribute we're talking about is quite genuine and to be highly regarded. The problem is that when regard turns into reverence and reverence turns into entrenchment, the organization has lost its ability to adapt and consequently cannot experience the transformation it requires, so what once was a competitive distinction becomes a white elephant weighing down an organization's ability to respond and perform. A global technology company's passion for quality became deadly bureaucracy. A global retail manufacturer's keen ability to compete on cost through decentralized operating companies became a weak portfolio of second-rate brands and wasteful duplication. The aggressive pursuit of market domination and market share that one day results in massive success eventually turns into complacency and lackluster quality. The deep communal loyalty engendered by tribalism within many African nations turns to hatred and genocide when those nations must compete for limited resources. The devotion of a faith community's historical values-based ideals becomes hostility and segregation the moment someone who differs with those ideals attempts to enter the community. Any generative aspect of a community has the gruesome potential for degenerativity embedded within it.

We have already mentioned GM as a company whose personality has not served it well in this connection, but let's look more closely at Saturn for an example of this last point. The Saturn division was launched by GM specifically to address issues of both poor product quality and labor unrest that plagued the company in the 1980s. Then-CEO Roger Smith recognized the inroads Japanese manufacturers were making in both quality and work practices. Smith formed a series of joint ventures with Japanese companies so GM managers could work alongside Japanese counterparts and then take their experiences back to GM. Smith knew that the GM bureaucracy, firmly entrenched in the arrogance born of a past when the "GM way" dominated the auto industry, was able to effectively kill any innovation that might have come from these joint ventures. The GM CEO countered the opposition by simultaneously launching the Saturn Corporation, in which these managers could institute the Japanese system in a fresh non-GM environment. Saturn was, and still is, moderately successful as a stand-alone within GM, but the net result for the company was disappointing. Profits remained inconsistent and GM's market share continued to fall.[21] Examples like this one are endless, and you can likely add your own organizations to the list. The hallowed attributes of our organizations, in the absence of constant nurture and adaptation, can become the toxic killers that cripple competitive distinction and ultimately the future.

Generativity as a Means to Meaning

At the core of an organization, and the core of human beings, lie deeply important questions of meaning, purpose, and relationship that define the posture an organization takes. Here is David Whyte again, as he makes this point so well:

"The severest test of work today is not of our strategies but of our imaginations and identities. For a human being, finding good work and doing good work is one of the ultimate ways of making a break for freedom...the workplace carries so much of our desperate need for acknowledgment, for hierarchy, for reward, to be seen, and to be seen as we want to be seen, that we often overreach ourselves, and

our passionate and often violent inner needs suddenly break through the placid professional exterior.[22]

Whyte's notion is that we experience direct connection between the work we do and our sense of importance and well-being. The fundamental questions of significance and value are ever-present within us and always being worked out in the context of the workplace.

Unfortunately, these questions are all too often ignored or dismissed as esoteric, irrelevant, or "soft." They are the very questions, however, that properly addressed can help an organization achieve unimagined levels of performance and satisfaction. When we deny the space for the members of our organizations to freely and boldly explore their deepest questions of participation and significance, we cut them off from their greatest contributions. We misguidedly assume that our corporations, our communities, and our agencies are devoid of soul and thus can run themselves robotically. Even Henry Ford, the implementer of the modern assembly line, said, "I know there are reservoirs of spiritual strength from which we human beings thoughtlessly cut ourselves off . . . I believe we shall someday be able to know enough about the source of power and the realm of the spirit to create something ourselves. I firmly believe that mankind was once wiser about spiritual things than we are today. What we now only believe, they knew."[23] No executives worth their salt would claim that we can wind organizations up and let them just go until they need rewinding, so it behooves leaders to ask courageously and answer honestly the deepest questions of their organizations' postures, especially when working to summon a future of strength, innovation, and sustainability.

Navigating the Journey

Now that we've laid out the theory of the case, we thought we'd offer some important thoughts on how the rest of the book is constructed to help you make the most of your time with it.

The ten questions of posture are in the next chapter, the heart of the book. Each posture contains both a generative and degenerative anchor to it. Like the equalizer on a stereo that makes adjustments between treble and bass, so do these continuums offer degrees of each anchor, establishing a blend of both generative and degenerative postures. To look at our communities, indeed life, honestly, we must acknowledge that there is no reality that is purely good or purely bad. To suggest these are "either/or" polarities would be to oversimplify their dynamic nature.

After some brief exploration about what each question looks like in both its generative and degenerative forms, we will invite in the voices of the people from your organization who have experienced both natures of each posture. You will hear their stories, and they will seem strangely familiar. Perhaps you will locate your own voice among them. After each story, we will invite your reflection through some pointed questions that direct your attention to your own experiences of these postures, experiences that you have both received and caused. We have left space right in the book for you to write your notes and thoughts. Use these spaces as a journal and a drafting table. Let the ideas and visions that simmer within find life right on these pages as the blank spaces form an actual blueprint for your story's next chapter.

Finally, to help ensure your blueprint translates into your actual story, for each posture we will invite you to the story of your future. Each "Story from the Future" segment is us handing you the quill to pen how you hope to see that particular posture unfurl within your community. Once again, use the provided blank spaces to compose the narrative that has too long remained privately in your mind and heart. Let these pages serve as the midwife of the organization you have long dreamed to birth. Our hope is that through the voices of those with whom you work and the dreams they provoke within you for your future, you will become intimately familiar enough with each posture to be able to work with it on a holistic basis. In so doing, you will "rehearse your future" by writing yourself into the story that you most desire to see come true rather than the default story that, too often, becomes the one we look back on and ask, "How on earth did I get here?"

Later, at the end of Part Three in figure 2.0, we will summarize the degenerative and generative postures that accompany these questions. Finally, we will offer some compass headings for navigating toward a more generative future and away from the destructive patterns that may be lurking surreptitiously just around the bend of your next major decision. Use these continuums as a diagnostic device, plotting your organization on each of them. Use the plot points to determine the degree of generative or degenerative capacity present as you summon your future.

Part Four will coalesce the ten postures into four categories and show how they work together in a dynamic and interactive way. Parts Five and Six will serve as your mechanisms to plot your course forward, translating the "rehearsed future" of your story into concrete transformation. In essence, the first half of the book helps you understand the generative organizational life, and the second half is the process of building yours.

Our last piece of advice is this: pay close attention to how you are intellectually and emotionally metabolizing this material. Our intention is for it to get into your skin, perhaps even *under* your skin. It may unseat long-entrenched beliefs about yourself, your colleagues, and your organization. At times it should irritate you, and we hope at times it inspires you. Take special note of where it rouses your passion and desire, where it inflames your core convictions about what you believe ought to be. Where does it cause you to grit your teeth and under your breath firmly say, "Yes?" Those places are telling you something very important. They are summoning you to a future your story feels compelled to investigate. Consume yourself with curiosity and explore. What could be waiting for you may be nothing short of miraculous.

Howard Thurman so aptly said, "Don't ask yourself what the world needs; ask yourself what makes you come alive. And then go and do that. Because what the world needs is people who have come alive."

Our deepest hope is that awaiting you on the pages ahead is the discovery of what makes you and your organization come more fully alive.

When you discover it, you will indeed be choosing a generative organizational life.

The Ten Questions

"Our mind is capable of passing beyond the dividing line we have drawn for it. Beyond the pairs of opposites of which the world consists, other, new insights begin."

Hermann Hesse

The Ten Questions

There's an old adage that goes something like, "There are no dumb questions, just dumb answers." Respectfully, we disagree. Indeed, we've heard some very dumb questions, and they all have something strangely familiar in common. Regardless of how they are asked, they remove, not expand, the element of choice from those being asked the question. The one asking the question has already decided what the answer should be, retaining the choice for themselves about what comes next.

For many of our clients, dispensing information in the form of answers is second nature. Day in and day out, extremely difficult questions are brought to them. In many instances they are the bottom-line decider. Because of their hub-and-spoke, center-of-everything position within the organization, these leaders are constantly required to be the "final answer." At least that's the posture they have come to regularly display as a result of being continually reinforced in such a role. For example, one of our clients was faced with the need to revamp the company's business strategy to keep up with the changing environment resulting from an unforeseen competitor move. It was very apparent to us that the company's typical "all-knowing" big-kid-on-the-block mentality wasn't going to serve it very well for this challenge. In many respects it was going to have to *learn* its way through the transition versus *knowing* its way through it, a very different posture for its otherwise "We always have the answer" countenance. We remember looking across the table at our client and saying, "Sharon, what do you do when you don't know?"

Her response was fascinating. She replied, "It doesn't happen. I am just more confident."

We responded, "Oh, so you mean you just make stuff up?" We all laughed. It was a funny moment indeed, yet very telling about the way this client feels compelled to never be seen as unknowing. If she doesn't have the answer, the business is in trouble. True, it is important for leaders to be prepared to respond to unexpected circumstances; however, in the extreme, if that becomes the leadership posture one regularly assumes, you in fact weaken, not strengthen, your capacity to adapt. Rather than acquiring new knowledge and insight, you are creating and reinforcing "templates" by which to regurgitate and recycle solutions regardless of the presenting problem. This is not a posture of inquiry, but rather a counterfeit posture of retrofitting static information onto dynamic challenges.

I (Josh) remember a difficult time in my own life, when I was at the crossroads of some very complex decisions and questions, and a similar scenario unfolded. I took a walk just to clear my head of all the clutter. I sat down for a moment to reevaluate the situation and was suddenly struck by a new perspective on answers and questions. The voice in my head said, "If you don't care about their questions, why should they care about your answers?" In that moment, I didn't necessarily know what I should do any more than before I started my walk, yet that moment forever transformed me. I realized that answers, often dispensed at the absence of questions, can have an extremely degenerative effect because great insights, when imposed rather than invited, are usually rejected with a posture of defense or resistance. A question, on the other hand, can have a very generative effect, because it is invited and is met with a posture of curiosity and openness. This is typically the case, because questions have the ability to take into account others' views and secondly give those involved the opportunity to participate in the pursuit of answers versus being forced into being passive recipients of potentially irrelevant and intrusive answers or information. It becomes a generative interaction because all are invited to engage with a posture of exploration. In short, questions include; answers potentially exclude. When seeking transformation, the inclusion of those being transformed is essential if the transformation is going to stick.

Our philosophy behind Future *in*-Formation is that it would invite and involve more of you to the posture of a near-anthropological dig into your own future. As an anthropologist approaches a dig site with a balanced hypothesis of anticipation and openness, so too do we hope you will approach the edge of your future with a similar stance of expectation and wonder. This approach may seem a bit backwards from bestselling business books that laud a handful of answers to questions you may or may not be asking. We pose ten questions instead of ten answers. These questions have both generative and degenerative possible responses. As we have repeatedly said, generativity is a choice, and with choice comes the possibility of both healthy and unhealthy actions.

One important point to these questions: you will not answer them one time and be finished. Neither will you answer them all at once. These are questions that need to continually reappear in your life through every season of change and growth. Some seasons will focus on some questions, other seasons will focus on new questions. One year's answers may become your next year's challenges. That is the beauty and difficulty of pursuing a generative organizational life. Once you begin, you are never finished. So as you locate your story in the context of these questions and the vignettes that accompany them, expect that you will find stronger resonance with some than others as you begin to form your own path to the future. What will be especially important for you to notice is when you are avoiding the painful reflection of yourself in the degenerative stories. While it will, of course, be easier for you to identify how those stories remind you of *others* in your life, you may want to wonder about who might be reading some of those stories and be reminded of *you*. Yes, it will pinch, but better for you to wonder about it first than to be blindsided by having someone else point it out for you.

We hope these questions will invite your participation in your process of formation and the ways others allow you to be *in*-Formation with them.

Here are the questions you will journey through in this section of the book:

1. What will I choose to believe?
2. How will I choose to be visible?
3. What will determine my actions?
4. What degree of openness will I generate between people?
5. How will I help others learn?
6. How will I demonstrate regard?
7. In what will I hope?
8. How will I honor others' contributions?
9. How will I hold others to account for their commitments?
10. How will I remain humble?

With that, we encourage you to courageously and generously step into these questions. They will shape and summon a generative future in your life and the lives of those with whom you call your organization home.

Onward.

Question 1:
What will I choose to believe?

Belief is the coalescing force that summons people to action and allows them the freedom to act on the possibility they envision. Numerous forces shape people's beliefs in organizations–the data they do and don't have access to, the spin put on that data, the amount of participation they believe they have to influence the future, and the resources over which they feel they do or don't have control, etc.

Belief is what compels people to action. If there is no belief in a project or new initiative there will be minimal motivation by the people involved to see it through. The terrorist, armed with fear, may be able to motivate people to action, but it is not sustainable action. It's action that is grounded in fear, which is motivating only for a limited time. The liberator, on the other hand, increases others' share of knowledge, share of decision rights, and the freedom to pursue possibility. The terrorist limits others' choices through the use of controlling power. The liberator increases others' choices through increased trust.

Ryan and Oestreich[24] define fear in the workplace–the terrorist's weapon of choice–as "feeling threatened by possible repercussions as a result of speaking up about work-related concerns." Fear is a cumulative commodity, and it need not be felt every single day to nevertheless have a corrosive impact. When people are afraid to speak or act through fear of repercussions, energy is diverted from productive to nonproductive work. Morale plummets, and a destructive cycle of mistrust ensues. Managers and employees begin a downward cycle of observing one another's behavior, interpreting it as aggressive and maliciously motivated, and then justifying fear-based retaliation in response. This cycle is reinforced over time, resulting in fear, gridlock, and other forms of destructive and nonproductive behavior. This is the world in which the terrorist thrives.

The liberator drives fear and mistrust from the workplace. Alaska Wildlife Adventures, winner of the Winning Workplaces 2007 Top Small Workplaces Award, reports that it is a company made up of people who are both good communicators and who possess strong personalities, two traits that often do not mix well. Problems that arise are addressed from a standpoint of how things can be done better and how employees can ensure issues do not happen again. When a miscommunication happens, employees first think of ways to fix the problem, develop a new system, or look for innovative solutions in changing their approach. Staff members are not blamed or embarrassed when a mistake happens; it is simply fixed and then the company moves on.

This speaks to the liberating foundation of the culture, one that is progressive, moves ahead, and looks to the future. As one executive puts it, "We all care too much and work too hard to spend time on the 'ad nauseam' end of business, and all work to support each other and see the company succeed."[25]

One CEO we worked with had an amazing practice of having monthly luncheons with employees two and three levels below the executive team expressly for the purposes of listening to their ideas and the projects they were working on. He would receive brief synopses of each leader's initiative in advance and then connect each one to the strategic plan so he was prepared to engage intelligently and enthusiastically with those leading the projects. When people expressed frustrations about obstacles they were facing, he offered ideas on how to move around them while still maintaining the commitment to confidentiality and safety. He was very honest about what resource constraints the company was facing and what his views were on strategies they were pursuing, and he challenged false assumptions and mythology when people were misinformed, all without judging or dismissing them. As a result, people holding conversations in which they had access to un-spun and reliable information felt more confident in the projects they were working on. One second-order benefit was that it minimized the experience of mixed messages and direction that was potentially lost in translation between the CEO and the rest of the organization. The freedom and value of alignment forced conflicts outside the conversation to be resolved within the senior team, not outside the room after the fact.

In your community, liberation is the experience of being freed from the constraints of fear and oppression that thwart your belief in the ability to effect meaningful change, shackling you to the belief that doing nothing, or minimal action, is simply safest. Terrorists imprison people's beliefs, causing them to relinquish the choice of participation. Liberators release people's beliefs in ways that enable them to embrace many choices to contribute.

Plot yourself and your organization on this continuum at the point you feel honestly reflects your current degree of generative/degenerative posture.

Terrorist   Liberator

Your colleague's experience of a terrorist

So today I had this, like, really big come-to-Jesus meeting with my department head. Wasn't he the clever one to send the Outlook invitation as a "project update" meeting. Stupid me for believing it. So I get in there and I have all my slides ready to give him the update on where things are, and that included sharing with him some of the risks I thought the project was facing. The problem is that I'm having to coordinate too many divisions' input into this new procurement process. No sooner can I get one executive's needs met before I'm immediately ticking off another. For crying out loud! So there's this one department head whose been the biggest royal pain in the you-know-where. He has sabotaged this thing at every turn. He doesn't answer our queries on time. He pulls his people from team meetings at the last minute. And he's out there in public talking about what a waste of time this is. No big surprise there–his department is the one that's always way over their expense budget, and he needs this more than anyone. I've finally gotten so fed up that my core team has said I need to talk to the COO, Denise, and get her to lean on this guy a bit. I don't want to be the tattletale, but I have my commitments too. I don't want to be hung out to dry and have this thing tank just because one jerk can't get it together. Well, how unfortunate for me that my department head and this guy are drinking buddies, or golfing buddies, or whatever. So the meeting starts off okay enough. I start walking through my slides and sharing what's going well, and I'm really excited about what is going well. We actually have made some great progress. And then I start talking about some concerns I have about delivering this new process on time because of insufficient cooperation from all of the divisions. I don't say anyone's name. Suddenly he interrupts me by putting his hand out and in this sickeningly saccharin voice, says, "I think I've got the picture now; you can go ahead and put your slides away." Of course I'm pretty taken aback and off balance. I say, "Uhh, okay. Don't you want to hear about the risks, though?" He says, "No, I know how things work around here. I've seen them before. I'm sure you'll figure them out." I say, "Okay, well, then, are we done?" He says, "Yeah, but just one more thing. You know Denise is a really busy woman and she's up to her neck in big issues right now. However you figure out how to get everyone on the same page in this thing, I'm sure you'll agree that involving her probably doesn't make much sense at the moment. Not everyone is going to cooperate perfectly on every initiative we launch here, and we don't need to be troubling her with issues that, well, would just sound petty, if you get my drift. Wouldn't you agree?" I knew it wasn't really a question. I had a knot in my stomach. I could barely get my head to nod, and then I left. For the grand finale of the ruse, I wasn't at all shocked to see the saboteur department head walking into the office as I walked out. His icy grin confirmed what had just happened, and he was going in to get his trophy. Pretty sick, if you ask me. I honestly don't know why I bother.

You in-Formation

1. When have you experienced a terrorist misuse power this way, instilling fear to manipulate an outcome? What was it like? Are there ongoing experiences of your beliefs being constrained by fear, resulting in your choice not to participate?

2. When would others say they experienced you that way? When are you triggered to behave that way?

Your colleague's experience of a liberator

Ever have one of those days where you really do wonder if you're dreaming? I'm in the middle of trying to put together a whole sales campaign for this funky new product we're launching next year. It's basically a storage device for personal information that is portable. It's actually pretty cool. Anyway, people in marketing have all their ideas about how this thing should be positioned; the developers have their opinions. I've got to develop the material to put in the hands of our sales force to go out and make sure this thing hits the market with a big bang. I get this great idea on how to drive retail placement–which everyone knows gets higher margins–rather than driving for wholesale volume, because I actually believe we can get into the retail channel much faster. We've got some great trade press exposure lined up and some good ads as well. But the thing is, I can't get anyone to listen to my ideas. It's like I'm speaking Greek or something. I'm sitting at my desk pissed because I've hit all these obstacles and I really feel like this is the way we need to go. The last thing I think about doing is going to my boss and asking for help because I don't want to look like I can't get it done. Besides, I don't want to risk his not supporting my idea when he hears I'm struggling to get anyone else to. Pretty crappy bind. Who walks up to my desk? None other than my boss. I guess it was pretty obvious that something was wrong. It's not like I'm all that good at hiding what I'm feeling. He sits down and asks, "What's going on? You look like you're having a bad day." Now I have to decide if I'm going to blow him off and give him some fake answer or just go for it and tell him the truth. I don't know what possessed me, but I told him everything. The ideas, people's responses, my research, and why I feel so passionate about this direction–the whole thing. I tell him, "I really believe in this product, and I believe this is the way to make it succeed." He starts asking me all these questions. At first I didn't get why, but then I realized he was actually trying to help me. After about twenty minutes, he helped me figure out that the way I had pitched the idea to marketing and engineering didn't convey why it was a good idea in a way they understood. He said they probably just didn't get it. He helped me figure out how I could communicate the idea more effectively. I couldn't believe it. Then he says, "I'll be right back." He leaves for about ten minutes, and when he gets back, he says, "I just spoke with Mark and told him about your idea and that I thought he needed to have you pitch his entire team at once. I told him that I would really like his support to make it work, and he said to have you call his assistant and get on the agenda for their next leadership team meeting for an hour." Mark is the head of global marketing for the entire company! I was in shock. As he walked away, I had enough presence of mind to say, "Hey, thanks for your help." He looked back and grinned and said, "And thanks for your great work." Man, what would work be like if I had more days like today?

You in-Formation

1. When have you experienced a liberator this way, someone who set you free to

create and passionately participate? What was it like?

2. When would others say they experienced you that way? How might you provide that experience for others more often?

Your story from the future

With you as the liberator in the story, write about an employee in your organization illustrating how he or she chose to believe and act in the pursuit of a possibility with confidence and without fear. Write it in the first-person voice of that employee.

Question 2:
How will I choose to be visible?

Visibility is the coalescing force that summons a generative future by enabling people to be the distinct and unique individuals that they are. We all want to be seen and acknowledged for our gifts and talents and the contributions we make in our workplace. It helps us feel unique and distinct as well as confident and focused. Often our gifts and talents get overlooked because many organizations confuse recognition with the need to be "fair." Too many recognition systems seek to homogenize people in the pursuit of being equitable. The pursuit of equity as a means to distinguish people ends up homogenizing otherwise unique individuals. The very visibility we seek to bestow ends up eclipsing those we want to see. In short, our recognition systems render people unrecognizable.

The fact that the need to be seen never goes away is a double-edged sword. When people go unseen, they end up working even harder to meet their unmet need for recognition. This situation can be dangerous; as with children, adults may eventually adopt destructive behaviors, in attempts to be seen.

The orchestra conductor has an element of maturity and elegance that the arsonist longs for. Both enjoy being in the front of the room, or at least being recognized as "in front;" however, their attempts to be seen are motivated by completely different objectives. Arsonists have tried to be seen for so long that they actually fear the very acknowledgment they seek. When they are acknowledged for their work, they often brush it off as if they never wanted recognition. Still driven by a need for attention that cannot be positively met, they end up creating disruption and "setting fires" in the organization, and the cycle repeats.

We have seen an example of the arsonist in one of our client systems. We observed a team in a technology company that was tasked with designing a new organizational model, complete with performance metrics to evaluate the benefit of the new way of working. We noticed that one team member was commenting repeatedly outside of meetings to undermine faith in the new model's performance metrics. This behavior was seriously compromising the effort. At one juncture, the CEO complained that there was no way to check on progress. We explored what was happening and discovered that the arsonist on the team had actually written out a comprehensive dashboard of performance metrics three months earlier, but in all the activity in designing the new model, her dashboard had been forgotten and a new approach had been adopted as the team's "first stab." The arsonist was in fact angry and frustrated. She perceived the lack of recognition as deliberate sabotage. We helped her surface her frustration in the team, which had made an honest mistake in misplacing her dashboard. The team incorporated elements of her dashboard into its work, and the arsonist became one of the conductors again, orchestrating the implementation of the new model.

Recognition extends from an acknowledgment of contribution all the way to people's paychecks. While we understand the need for privacy in some issues, we advocate transparency wherever practical. One executive in a financial services firm we worked with was constantly undermining his peers and he was well noted for speculating on individual bonuses with a modicum of bitterness. His attitude was undermining the CEO's willingness to give him more responsibility, yet he was a noted producer in the firm with a proven track record of generating results in his business unit. The great irony, we discovered, was that this executive was actually earning more, both in terms of base and bonus, than his fellow executives. The company had a policy of specific compensation nondisclosure, however, and there wasn't anything we could persuade them to say that would be specific enough to diffuse this particular arsonist's conviction that he was under-recognized. Eventually, the executive left the company.

There are as many permutations of the visibility issue as there are different situations in a company. Many organizations, for example, make their planning and resource allocation processes overly exclusive, inadvertently excluding people who then have to set fires to be heard.

Orchestra conductors act as spotlights, highlighting the unique sound and music of individuals in the community while at the same time blending those gifts into a beautifully integrated symphony. Under the conductor's leadership, everyone gets his or her due opportunity for a "solo" or to play "first chair." They also humbly accept the invitation to sit out on some pieces where their voice isn't necessary and play simple supporting roles when it's others' time to shine. The arsonist burns away the distinction of individuals, and ultimately themselves, through an insatiable need to be watched. The orchestra conductor draws attention to the originality and specialty of others, maximizing the contributions of all the parts into a synthesized whole.

Plot yourself, and your organization, on this continuum at the point you feel honestly reflects your current degree of generative/degenerative posture.

$$\longleftarrow \joinrel\longrightarrow$$

Arsonist   Orchestra
                                                                            Conductor

Your colleague's experience as an Arsonist

It was three o'clock in the afternoon, and I hadn't stopped for lunch, let alone breakfast. I had been running at full speed for the entire day (month, really) on a grande soy latte. I decided I was going to make it to the cafeteria and get a quick bite to eat even if it killed me. I figured at three o'clock it would be pretty quiet and I could get in and out relatively quickly.

As I sat down, I couldn't help privately reveling in all that had happened this past year. I had won the top sales Quota Club Award for two of the last three quarters for our division, had the fourth quarter win pretty much sewn up, and was clearly on a trajectory to get Sales Leader of the Year for our entire company. After all the years I've slaved away to build a great track record, it was finally paying off, and people were watching now. There was only one other possible contender from the West Division who might get it, and I knew I was going to have to work really hard to set myself apart from her. I'd mastered the art of "never taking no for an answer" in my territory, which has grown this year by 28% despite last year's territory splits and upping everyone's quotas, thank you very much! This award feels the same way. The same tenacity that got me this far would be my ultimate "secret weapon" that gets me the big win.

I was finishing my yogurt parfait when it dawned on me. My sales revenues speak for themselves; that's not the problem. What I need is to make it apparent to everyone that between Tiffany and me, I'm just the better salesperson.

She had been neck and neck with me both quarters I won, and in fact, has come in second all three quarters this year and is probably going to come in second in the fourth quarter, but this time I've got her by a wide margin. We've always had this sort of playful rivalry, but what surprised me are the results she's gotten, given how very different we are from each other. She has a background in psychology, and I have an MBA. I think my clients love me because I am a no-nonsense, get-it-done, solve-the-problem type of guy. Sure, I do the relationship thing with them, but in our industry, schmoozing goes only so far. Results are what count.

Tiffany just wears her heart on her sleeve, and it costs her. All year long she has been helping boost Brad and Nigel's sales by giving them some of her referrals. They, of course, were thrilled, and so was I. Their success helped clinch my win! Okay, so I know I must sound like a jerk with how much this "winning" thing means to me, but seriously, can you blame me? What's wrong with wanting to be successful? It's not like I'm trying to sabotage her efforts or plotting some dark scheme to neutralize my arch rival. I just like winning. It feels good, and it keeps me motivated and in the game. C'mon, admit it. You enjoy the thrill of victory too.

Brad and Nigel's boss, Jim, had actually come to me earlier in the year asking if I might be able to introduce them into a few of the networks my top customers were connected to. He thought it might give them some needed confidence to get out and build their networks. Hey, everyone's a rookie at some point, right? I remember the conversation clearly.

He walked into my office with this too-good-to-be-true look on his face. "Hey, tiger! How's it going? You still burning up your territory out there? The other day our department's sales forecasts came across my desk, and I couldn't believe the revenues you're anticipating in the next quarter. How the heck do you plan on doing it?"

I launched into my theory of the hunt speech, and I could tell he was eating it up. Of course I'm throwing in all the stock lines, "Well, without the help of so-in-so I could never do it," or "Hey, luck accounts for a lot of this…" and of course my favorite, "Well, I'm just blessed with the gift of stubbornness, I guess…I just don't like rejection!" That one always gets a good laugh.

"Whatever works," he says. "So I was wondering if you'd be interested in helping me out. Brad and Nigel's team have been struggling this year, and I was hoping you might be able to help them out by introducing them into some of the industry networks you associate with. I think if they just had more confidence in how to work the room, which you are so masterful at, they could replicate it in their own territory. You willing?"

I could feel the lump forming in my throat when he finished. The idea of bringing those two dweebs into my networks made my stomach knot, but I also knew if I said no, I'd look like a jerk, and I didn't want Jim sitting around the sales execs meeting pissing on my possible win by telling everyone I wasn't willing to help. I punted as best as I could. "Gosh, Jim, I'm flattered you'd ask me to help. I'll tell you what. Let me give some thought to how I could best help and get back to you by the end of the week, okay?" I knew I had at least bought some time. Well, tomorrow is the end of the week, and I owe him an answer.

As I emptied my tray into the garbage, it hit me like a bolt of lightning. I could kill two birds with one stone. I stopped by Jim's office, and as luck would have it, he was just coming back from lunch. "Hey, you got a minute, Jim? I wanted to circle back with you on your question from the other day."

"Sure thing. Have a seat. What are you thinking?"

"Well, I haven't thought this entirely through, but I started to think about how I could leverage my networks to help Nigel and Brad's team, and then it dawned on me. How could I leverage what I know to help the rest of the organization? I mean, the goal isn't for them to build better relationships in my networks, but to build better relationships in their own, right? So here's my idea. What if I hosted some kind of series of conversations with all the teams and sort of "open my play book" to them? You know how you guys are always talking about knowledge transfer, right? Well, what if I spent time coaching a bunch of folks that you and the sales exec team thought I could help?"

As I was talking I could see he was lighting up like a Christmas tree. I could just hear in my head the conversation around that sales exec meeting when it came time to choose who gets Salesperson of the Year. I could hear Jim's voice saying about me, "Well, I assume we all think this is a no-brainer, right?" My offer to help would clinch it for sure!

I call my friend to tell them how it all went down, and who overhears my conversation? None other than Tiffany. As I put my cell phone away, I could tell she looked pissed.

"You know, if that stupid award means that much to you, why don't you just buy yourself a trophy and give it to yourself?"

"Oh, you're just jealous because you didn't think of it first, so stop whining m'dear."

"No, I'm not jealous. I value real relationships more than I value using other people to make myself famous."

"Well, Tiffany, whether you like it or not, this is the real world, and in this organization, we value results. Period. And if you want your results noticed, this is what it takes."

"You know, the fact that you have to make others look bad just so you look good is pathetic. You are so busy trying to get watched by everyone for that stupid award that nobody can really see who you are. And if they did see who you are, they probably wouldn't give you that award. And you have to live with that. I may not get an award for it, but at least I know that what people see in me is who I really am. This culture may not value that, but I do. And if that means I spend my career in second place, then I'm fine with that." She stormed away all high and mighty.

I thought about it for a second. "Whatever," I said to myself and went and planned my first "show the rookies how it's done" session.

You in-Formation

1. When have you longed to be seen and recognized in your organization? In your community? In your social circles? Family? How have you exploited your talents or distinctions, even at others' expense, to get noticed? How do you set fires?
2. How have others tried to get you to see them? When have you settled for *watching* others when what they really needed was to be *seen*? What will it cost you to see others? How will you help others stop setting fires by helping them find the courage to be seen for who they are?

Your colleague's experience with an Orchestra Conductor

I don't know about you, but these 360 feedback processes can be pretty anxiety provoking. I don't know which I dread more, giving feedback to my boss and my peers or waiting to find out what they think about me. I mean, we're a pretty close team at the end of the day, and we don't usually pull any punches with each other, so there shouldn't be too many shocks in the data. Usually I expect far worse than it really ever is.

I just finished my one-on-one with my boss, Dan, where he reviewed his results with me and went over my results as well. It's actually a great process, but this year, I was definitely surprised. Every year, the time allows me the opportunity to learn more about what's important to Dan, to share with him what's important to me, and to find out where our priorities are aligned or misaligned. I'm not sure anything we've done in prior years, or this past year, could have prepared me for what I heard in our conversation.

On my feedback report, there was a weird gap in the area of self-confidence. I had rated myself moderately strong in that area, but my team rated me surprisingly low. None of the write-in comments shed much light on the gap, so I thought maybe the computer had miscalculated the data. Overall, though, I didn't think it was that big a deal.

Dan didn't see it that way.

We'd gone over all of Dan's data, and of course, no new surprises there. For the most part we all think the world of him, and while he's gotten better on the "organizational skills" section, it's still his Achilles' heel. We're going through my data, and Dan turned to the back of the report where the write-in comments are, and I could see highlighting throughout his copy of my report, so I knew he had read it thoroughly. He had me turn to page fourteen and asked me, "What do you make of comment number seven?"

I read it, and it said, "He sometimes tries a little too hard, which makes it difficult to partner with him."

To be honest I hadn't given it much thought.

He pointed out several other comments that I'd thought to be otherwise cryptic that all had a similar theme, and again, he asked, "So, what do you think?"

I said, "Darned if I know. What do you think it means?" I knew that wasn't the answer he wanted, but it was as honest as I could be.

He pointed out the self-confidence discrepancy that I thought we'd so nicely danced around until that point in the conversation. Then he floored me. He said, "You know that we all think the world of you, and the data shows that, but sometimes it feels as though you want to impress us, like you are overcompensating for something, or that you're not comfortable in your own skin. It feels like you are trying to 'win us over,' so to speak, and what I want you to hear is that you've already won us over. We respect you. We like you. You don't need to prove yourself to us anymore."

I couldn't speak when he was finished. I'm not sure I would have known what to say if I could have.

He then told me a story of how he struggled with self-confidence when he was my age, and that even today he worries that people will think he's not pulling his weight or not competent to be in his job. "We all have our own version of the imposter syndrome," he said, "but we have to come out from behind those imposters and not be afraid to look foolish sometimes. There's no use hiding." He went on to explain how getting greater alignment across our seven business units was a key objective for him this year, and that the only way to do it was by forming stronger relationships among all the teams. He talked about the competition among us that has eroded some performance and that we all needed to work more closely against our real competitors instead of against one another.

"If you are busy competing against your fellow business units and trying to prove yourself unnecessarily to your colleagues who already know you are good, then you aren't going to be focused on delivering the results we need. Do you believe me when I tell you that you have already won our approval?"

"Well, yeah, kind of. I guess. I'm not really sure." I don't think I've ever felt that vulnerable at work in my life, yet strangely, I felt relieved. On some level, I knew what Dan meant. I know I work hard to keep up a certain image. We work in a driven culture, and it seems like nobody would ever dare to look anything but self-assured.

He finished with, "I want you to think about the relationships you have with some of your counterparts in the other businesses. What would it look like for them to really see you for who you are, not some image you try to concoct to make sure they have confidence in you? The irony is this: the harder you try to look confident, the less confident people envision you to be. The more you are willing to be as unsure as you are sure, the more people will trust you, and the more they trust you, the better your results will be. I need you to be good at the things you are good at and trust that I don't expect you to be good at it all. And just so you know, I'm giving this little talk to the entire division in our one-on-ones!"

When I got back to my office I sat down and thought for a long time about what Dan had said. I wasn't quite sure what to make of it all, but I knew he'd hit on something really important, and that if I chose to, it could be an important turning point for me. It was like he saw past my, as he put it, imposter, and into me, and it felt...well, it felt good. Dan had mentioned one of my counterparts in another division, Faith, who I knew well. He said, "You ought to talk to her. You may be surprised to find that you have a lot to offer each other." From the grin on his face, I got the impression that asking him what he meant wasn't going to get an answer, so I picked up my phone and called Faith. I knew she had her one-on-one with Dan last week, so I figured it would still be fresh on her mind. "Hey, Faith. I just got out of my time with Dan and was thinking about you. Did he give you the 'imposter syndrome' speech?"

She laughed. "He sure did. Funny you ask, actually, because I was thinking about you after our conversation. It was amazing the way he seems to know us so well, huh? He thought I should reach out to you because we might be able to help each other and our businesses. You just beat me to the punch. I was going to call you next week. Do you have any time to connect in the next couple of weeks? Maybe over lunch? You bring your imposter, and I'll bring mine, and we'll see if we can't do some dragon slaying, eh?"

I got off the phone and had to laugh. The very thing Dan wanted to pursue more of was actually happening, and he didn't have to do anything to force it to happen. By simply holding up a mirror to us all, we could come together differently, because we would see each other differently. I wonder if this imposter thing shows up anywhere else in my life?

You in-Formation

1. What experience(s) have you had with someone who is exceptionally gifted at seeing others for who they are and orchestrating them in a way that maximizes their contributions? What effect did that orchestration have on the organization? On those involved?
2. When have you had the opportunity to *conduct*? What do you do when you see someone hiding from being truly visible? How do you invite the person to be seen and to find a personal place in the organization alongside others?

Your story from the future

With you as the orchestra conductor in the story, write about an employee in your organization who for the most part tended to be invisible and unassuming. Write about what happens when you are able to see the person and invite him or her to actively participate more fully in the broader community. Write it in the first-person voice of this employee.

Question 3:
What will determine my actions?

Action is the coalescing force that summons a generative future by creating forward motion toward an intended outcome. Contrary to some popular perceptions of organizational behavior, activity alone doesn't determine results; however, many organizations are full of people moving and changing for the sake of moving and changing. Actions have the power to determine results, but actions apart from reflection offer nothing more than motion.

Organizations that unwittingly promote autopilot as a way to increase productivity end up neutering the imaginations of those performing the tasks. An innocent pursuit of efficiencies and economies of scale ends up creating a colony of activity addicts whose ability to reflect and act with intention slowly disappears. In a crisis, when the organization needs the most creative thinking to solve unprecedented problems, the best they can get is more intense variations on the same rote routines they previously conditioned people to produce.

One of our colleagues suggests that most organizations today have backed themselves into a corner, because so many activities are already stuck on autopilot. He reports that many companies have twenty to forty major initiatives under way, making it difficult for employees to comprehend the key priorities behind those initiatives and draining the organization's time and energy. He emphasizes the need to define three to five things everyone in the organization should be focused on.[26] Why is this essential? Healthy organizations are ones that can respond to changing conditions, and to meet challenges, they need reserves of energy and capacity, which means protecting an organization's time like any other vital asset. Otherwise, a plethora of initiatives will drain away capacity and leave your company unable to respond to change.

Initiative proliferation is one of the deadliest diseases during times of major change. For a variety of reasons–justification of self-importance, opportunism, belief in the efficacy of one's idea, supporting a vision in a vacuum–endless activities are spawned with great fanfare but fail to realize their intended results. The ability and the courage to say "no" is key, and most senior executives struggle with this point. In other cases, senior executives simply forget how many "yes" answers they've doled out, unwittingly outstripping the organization of capacity when the aggregate number of approvals they've given exceeds the available resources and capacity to execute. Once activity addiction sets in, as is the case with any addiction, it is hard to let go of it. The cultural norm necessitating the need to "look intensely busy" and sustain the illusion of exhaustion becomes sanctimoniously ingrained. We knew one client who would deliberately get up in the middle of the night to send emails out, to create the 24/7 look and feel of someone who was ultra productive and committed to his work. It created an unspoken standard of workaholism and activity mania that led to ever-greater eroded performance as people's commitment to the appearance of productivity outpaced their commitment to real results. When this company was eventually acquired, the exposure of poor performance and embellished descriptions of work practices earned most of his department severance checks.

Reflectors make thoughtful choices in the portfolio of initiatives into which they lead their communities. Saying "no," even to great ideas, is a gift they give people that allows them to steward their energy and focus their time toward the collective community's most important priorities. Reflectors invite the greatest levels of performance through their faithful understanding that organizational life is a marathon, not a sprint, and that less often really is more. Activity addicts, by contrast, are mere consumers of capacity and parasites of energy. They leach their communities dry and deplete essential time and resources needed for summoning the future. Consequently, when the future arrives, they are rarely prepared for what it holds, because no future arrives without some element of surprise.

Plot yourself, and your organization, on this continuum at the point you feel honestly reflects your current degree of generative/degenerative posture.

$$\longleftarrow \hspace{8cm} \longrightarrow$$

Activity Addict   Reflector

Your colleague's experience with an activity addict

If she tells us one more time how many hours she spent this weekend working and how exhausted she is, I swear my head will detonate. Does she actually think any of us are buying it? And her cute little speech about the importance of work-life balance didn't fool anyone either, especially her admission that she wasn't good at it. She wears that fact like a badge of honor. If she really cared about balance, she'd have taken all those vacations she canceled, and she would have let the rest of us take ours. She's proud of the fact that her department has the most accrued vacation time, even though HR is in her face about it. Ever since manufacturing jumped off the Six Sigma cliff, on top of new commercialization processes, on top of new performance management and comp systems, on top of SAP implementation, on top of the merger integration that we've never finished, on top of...on top of....on top of–I swear I don't know how she's not committed herself to an asylum. There's no way she can remember everything that's going on around here. I can't even remember what I'm supposed to be working on. Whatever she comes screaming about on any given day, I've decided that's the priority. Until she screams, I'll just make it up as I go. It's gotten to the point where there are so many balls in the air, the question isn't how to keep them all from falling, it's simply which one is going to fall and when. There's just no way we could ever implement all this stuff, so most people I know have stopped taking any of it seriously. That sucks, because some of it is really important work, and we need it. Well, I've finally decided that I've got my own hard decisions to make. My wife told me this morning that our five-year-old son went to sleep this week asking her if we were getting a divorce because he thought I didn't live there anymore. That's pretty scary. On top of that, I've gained twenty pounds in the last year, I can't remember the last time I worked out or did anything fun, for that matter, and I got my labs back from my physical and my cholesterol is way up. Some of that's hereditary, but a big part of it is simply that I'm wolfing down junk food in between meetings and don't even think about what's going into my body. The boss keeps volunteering me for all these corporate initiative teams, saying, "This will be a high-profile development opportunity for you" or "I can't think of anyone else who could do a better job representing us" or "Think about the implications of your voice not being on that team; are you willing to live with what they decide?" She guilts me into these things and there's no room to say "no." I've had enough, and my family and my body are paying a price I never thought I'd pay. I've seen those insane people who forfeit everything to their company, sell their soul just for a few stock options, ruin their marriages and their health, and are absolutely miserable along the way. It scares me to think that I'm a lot more like "that guy" than I've been willing to admit, and I don't like it. If this place is determined to sink itself under the weight of more commitments than anyone could ever keep–even if they are good commitments–then I don't need to go down with them. I'm spending the evening updating my resume. I think it's time. Yeah. Life's just too short.

You in-Formation

1. How much time do you spend feeling overextended in your work commitments? What experiences have you had, gorging on more activity than you could realistically participate in effectively? How did it get that way? Did you consider saying "no" or setting better limits? Why didn't you?
2. When have you made too many commitments that had adverse ramifications for others? How did you see performance erode? Burnout? Did you set stronger priorities, or did you simply let the work proliferate beyond what was reasonable? What did you learn?

Your colleague's experience with a Reflector

How do I feel? Well to be honest, I'm not quite sure how I should feel. Part of me is disappointed. Part of me is relieved. And part of me is actually pretty excited. Why are you looking at me that way? You've been in that room before; you know what happens. How else should I feel? Naively, we all go into that strategy forum thinking we're all going to get funded with priority dollars, and those of us who get turned down are dumbfounded. This year he changed the process, and I think it actually worked great, even if I did get a "no." People used to go in one at a time, present their strategic plans, initiatives, investment requirements, and capital expenditures to the powers sitting on the panel, and then leave. A week later there would be a meeting where the final decisions were unveiled. In some years, it was clear we'd say "yes" to too many things. In other years, we said "yes" to the wrong things. And in some years we just kept putting off the decision on some initiatives. This year he decided to have everyone in the room at the same time to hear each others' presentations, and he told us we could each only have three to five slides and twenty minutes to present with ten minutes for questions. We each had to send in a detailed brief of the strategies and investment recommendations three weeks ago, and they were compiled into one book for us all to read before the meeting. Actually it was a cool process because we could see how other departments and divisions were thinking about the next couple of years. It also exposed where we were out of alignment or had some unfounded assumptions about certain markets. The biggest thing it exposed was that we were collectively looking to invest about 65 million dollars, which is about 25 million more than we actually could afford. He told us last month that he didn't like the fact that we were making such enormous strategic decisions in a one-off manner with almost no time to think about the implications of them. Not only that, none of us have time to consider the implications together. This process forced *everyone* to pause and think about the ramifications of these huge initiatives that, together, were going to consume the energy and attention of the same people. After we each heard all of the pitches, we spent some time evaluating them against criteria we all developed. We were able to combine initiatives and see the collision paths of others, and some leaders reached their own conclusions that their ideas were ill conceived in light of what they'd heard about others. Sure, it was hard to hear "no" at first, but it made sense to me. To see him be so thoughtful and deliberate about the investment portfolio, wanting the choices to really succeed, was powerful. The best part of it is we all walked out confident that we could get it all completed. In past years, we've walked out mumbling under our breath that there was no way in hell we could get half of it done. As for me, the exciting part is that I got assigned to co-lead one of the initiatives that mine got folded into, and I am actually more excited about it than I would have been had only got my own been funded. Sure my ego wanted to spearhead my own major strategic initiative and to be the champion for my own idea, but the questions he asked me and the feedback he had on the idea taught me more than I would have learned had I been given the green light and the funding, and likely I would have either failed or fallen short of the goal. This way I get to see at least part of the idea come to life and get to work with someone new that I can learn from. It's weird that being told "no" could actually feel good. He even admitted that it was hard to resist the impulse to say "yes" to so many good ideas, but I'm glad he found the restraint–and the courage–to do it. Some people left pissing and moaning about its not being fair or only "the favorites" getting the money, but when someone makes hard decisions, there will always be people to complain about it. I'd rather have a focused set of projects to which most of us are committed, even if some are disappointed, than to have a bunch of happy people running out of the room with bags of cash headed off a cliff they can't see. Wouldn't you?

You in-Formation

1. What experience have you had working with others to set clear priorities and boundaries in a thoughtful and reflective way? What was the impact on your work? What was it like to have such clarity, even if it meant your not getting everything you'd wanted?

2. When have you had to set clear priorities and expectations for others? What formative experiences have you had in life that enabled you to show healthy restraint? How did you reflect on the available options to get to the choices you made? How did others receive your decision?

Your story from the future

As the Reflector in the story, write a brief story about an employee in your organization taking action based on a thoughtful, deliberately crafted plan that was intentionally connected to the strategic priorities of the organization.

Question 4:
What degree of openness will I generate between people?

Openness is the coalescing force that summons a generative future by making people aware of where they fit into the larger community. Openness connotes awareness. One's awareness of her contribution and participation in concert with others, not comparatively but synchronously, is the first step toward true openness. Awareness helps organizations increase their collective insight.

The Loan Shark works hard to pit people against each other and increase unnecessary competition. For the Loan Shark, "divide and conquer" takes on a whole new meaning. The Integrator choreographs multiple interactions among numerous moving parts of an organization, making them more aware of one another, and allowing them to work in concert with one another, safely and effectively. The Loan Shark makes unkeepable promises, makes people aware of others only on a comparative basis, and then manipulates them into figuring out how to undermine others for their own gain. The last thing the Loan Shark wants is for others to be aware of anyone else but him, and consequently, their need for him. By contrast, the Integrator thrives when all the pieces of the system over which she presides work interactively with unbridled confidence, enjoyment, and cooperation.

John Ralston Saul in *The Unconscious Civilization*[27] describes the Loan Shark's position, saying that we are succumbing "to the darker side within us and within our society." Saul says this dark side manifests itself in organizations as hidden agendas, collusion, conspiracies of silence, nepotism, victimization, self-interest, and corruption. The motive for the dark side can be largely unconscious and, as Saul suggests, a part of our desire to believe what we hear–that it is all for the collective good, that it needs to be done to avoid threats to our own position or even to feed our own need for recognition.

Sometimes a lack of openness manifests itself as an outright cover-up. For example, Sandia National Laboratories discovered that a sophisticated group of hackers were systematically penetrating hundreds of computer networks at major US defense contractors. One of Sandia's technical staff, Shawn Carpenter, became aware of the hacking, but his superiors instructed him not to report the incidents to the authorities because they cared only about their own systems. Their habits of restricting information blinded them to the needs of anyone other than themselves. When Carpenter nevertheless informed the US Army and the FBI, Sandia fired him. Carpenter eventually sued Sandia successfully for wrongful termination, winning $4.7 million in damages.[28]

There are many reasons people want to avoid openness. Without question, it creates risk, the risk of exposure, of vulnerability, of being wrong. The careful manipulation of our circumstances, conversations, and colleagues perpetuates the illusion that I am less vulnerable to opposition or resistance. Not all Loan Sharks are as scandalous as the Scandia story. Many Loan Sharks believe it is their duty to limit people's access to one another, thus preventing unnecessary conflicts. Acting as the perpetual "intermediary," Loan Sharks believe that it's in everyone's best interest to simply let them broker all of the "difficult" conversations. Though arrogant and pathological, these Loan Sharks derive great degrees of significance from knowing that all roads lead to them, and the rush of heroism that surges from having brokered a "successful" linkage between warring factions is thrilling. One client we worked with used to enjoy a game he called "make them fight." He would deliberately, unbeknown to his team, put competing goals on their performance objectives so that they would be forced into unhealthy competition that led them back to him to play referee. In his mind, he was "toughening them up" as leaders, and it helped him more readily see their development needs. That way he would know which of his team members were ready to take on more complex and difficult responsibilities. Unsurprisingly, turnover in his organization was excessive.

Integrators, on the other hand, open people's eyes to all of the moving pieces of a dynamic organization and draw them into the collective story by helping them see the powerful part they can play in relationship to others. Just as a master jigsaw puzzler knows how to sort and organize all the pieces of an otherwise discombobulated pile of meaningless pieces and then place them carefully into a coherent and beautiful whole, so too is an Integrator able to see and understand the juxtaposing pieces of their organization and stitch them together into a united picture. The Loan Sharks indulge in recreational separation of puzzle pieces, sometimes for sport, but more often to ensure their agenda of only their "puzzle" being the one that ever gets assembled. The Integrator gives everyone access to all the puzzle pieces and ensures everyone is responsible to help complete the collective picture of which they all desire to be a part.

Plot yourself, and your organization, on this continuum at the point you feel honestly reflects your current degree of generative/degenerative posture.

Loan Shark   Integrator

Your colleague's experience of a Loan Shark

Well, the whole project finally came off the tracks today. It's been wobbling along for some time now, but I actually thought we were going to be able to pull it off. I know there is a lot going on in the organization, with earnings down and all the pressure from stockholders to control our costs, but we really need this organization redesign work to be executed, for us to compete down the road. I never should have "volunteered" to be the design team leader. I knew it was suicide from the get-go, but my boss strongly suggested I do it and gave me his word that no matter what was going on in the short term, he was committed to building for the future. I expected that he was telling me everything I needed to know about the situation. That's the last time I'll be caught holding the bag for him. When he came to me in November and talked about the need to change the way we looked at the market and how we structure our sales and marketing organizations to deliver growth, I was skeptical, but we spent a few days behind closed doors really talking about possibilities, and I actually got excited about doing what was right for the company for the first time in a long time. It made sense for me to take on a leadership role because I know the players and have run parts of both organizations. If I am honest about it, there was a part of me that wanted the challenge. I wanted to really believe my leadership could make a difference in an area where I know we are struggling to perform well. I actually went out and used a lot of my own political capital to get people on board; they were as skeptical as I was. But people trust me, and know that if I say something, it does happen. We were making a lot of progress for the first time in a long time. My boss seemed really interested in all the primary data we collected about what was really going on in the market and how we stacked up against competitors. I should have seen the warning signs somewhere along the road, though. In January, when my boss took that trip with the CEO, he came back and spent a lot of time talking with the head of sales in Europe. I had been having a hard time getting this guy on board with our work, although he seemed to be collaborating with me–or so I thought, anyway. I tried to check in with my boss on it, and he said everything was fine and he'd make sure my European counterpart played along. Again, because I wanted to believe him, I did. I also started to hear things in the design team meetings that contradicted what we had been saying about positioning in the field. Every time I asked my boss, though, he said it was the usual change management issues going on and to ignore it. His quote, "You know how the rumor mill heats up when people see change coming. Don't pay any attention to that stuff. If I hear about anything that could impact your work, believe me, you'll be the first to know."

I should have known better. Every time I tried to work on a communication plan with the head of HR, he kept putting me off. I assumed he was busy and would get to it eventually. Well, in today's leadership team meeting my boss dropped the bomb. He announced that we were going to be selling a big portion of the North American business, the business I've just been working on redesigning, and that the new head of our division is none other than my colleague in Europe. And that my boss is moving up to a corporate job to work on acquisitions. It turns out he used all the market and competitive data we collected in the process to make a decision completely counter to what I was being asked to work on. He knew about it at least two months before the announcement. I won't even bother to confront him about it because I can just hear his lame excuse now: "Well, you know how confidential these deals have to be. There was no way I could have told you anything." Sickening, really. The only thing funny about the announcement today was that everyone looked as shell shocked as I must have. It turns out that they each knew only a little bit about what was going on, not the whole picture. Now we each have to go back and, with a straight face, sell it to the organization, which is going to think we are complete idiots (again)! This is absolutely the last time I put myself on the line for him or this organization.

You in-Formation

1. When have you found yourself "left holding the bag" and misinformed by a Loan Shark? What repercussions did not knowing all the information have for you? For the organization?
2. When have you been party to not sharing the full story with colleagues or the organization? How did you rationalize the parceling out of information, and what could you do differently in the interest of creating an open environment?

Your colleague's experience of an Integrator

Today will really go down in the books for me. It started off like any other Monday at the office, responding to a million e-mails. How could so many people e-mail me since I checked last night? Are they programming these things to hit late Sunday? I had to figure out who was yelling the loudest and needed a callback and try to dig out enough to get focused on the work at hand. I had completely forgotten about the talent review until about five minutes before it was scheduled to start. Fortunately, I had the notes I had prepared for my boss and was ready for the usual dog-and-pony show to start. It started about fifteen minutes late, after my peers straggled in and the usual "how was your weekend?" small talk that no one really listens to. Out of the corner of my eye, I saw our boss sitting down and making notes on a pad of paper, not the usual fifty-slide deck he has, and decided something might be up. He started off the meeting by talking about the need for us to really work the talent issue, that we have a huge innovation plan ahead of us and that it is increasingly clear to him that we can't do it without really looking at the capacity and capability we have in place. We've heard this before, so we each started on our independent monologues about why we each had the best talents and how we couldn't do without them. After about twenty minutes of listening to us talk around each other, my boss asked us to stop and take five minutes to write down what we believe to be the most important innovations to implement over the next nine months. It was a strange request because we looked at the list we all compiled last week in a budget meeting. After five minutes, he asked each of us, one by one, to go around the room and share our top two. He cut the first guy off when he got on his usual soapbox and asked him again if those were the most important innovations for the company or just *his* business. After some uncomfortable pauses he actually changed his input. We then each shared and ended up with a list of five, not forty-seven. Once we had the short list, he took the first one and asked me what I thought we needed to make it work and who was most critical to its success. He knew I felt strongly about it, but that I had hit a brick wall trying to get the person I needed, because my colleagues said they just couldn't spare him. I was tempted to respond with a sarcastic remark, but I saw a flash of earnestness in my boss's eye, so I told the truth, rather than insinuating that I had been down the road before. Once I shared my perspective about the talent we needed and who I thought matched the requirements, he turned to that person's boss (my reluctant-to-share colleague) and asked if he agreed about the importance of the innovation ('yes') and the capability needed for the work ('yes'). He then asked about the specific individual, and my colleague shared the reservations he had because the person has actually been struggling to meet his current role expectations and had failed miserably to navigate the political system here, which would be the kiss of death to this project. I was shocked because I thought all along he had been protecting the person for his own benefit, not that there was a performance issue he was struggling with. He had been reluctant to share because he thought it would reflect badly on him and he didn't want the person fired. We then engaged in two really robust conversations. First, who could we use to make sure the innovation got off the ground? The answer we landed on got me a great new resource out of marketing I wouldn't have thought to consider. And second, what do we do about the performer at risk? It turns out that we have actually matched him to the wrong role, and we made the decision to reassign him to business development. It would be a great fit. We repeated this process on the next four innovations and made real progress. I feel like we are finally set up for success and that as a team we actually led the process together. We all walked out with a sense that it was a turning point.

You in-Formation

1. When have you been invited into a conversation where there was a level of honesty that broadened the perspective of those at the table? What did that feel like? What was the result?
2. When have you taken the risk to bring together different views and ideas in the service of a greater outcome than just one person's? What provoked you to do so? What was difficult about it? What was the result?

Your story from the future

Write a brief story about a member of your organization who was able to achieve an important result because his or her perspective was integrated with the diverse views of others. Assume that you were the Integrator in the story. Write it in the first person voice.

Question 5:
How will I help others learn?

Learning is the coalescing force that summons a generative future by increasing collective wisdom, which in turn allows a community the advantage of literally being able to outsmart unforeseen challenges and competitive threats. The concept of the "learning organization" has now proliferated to the point of being more a piece of jargon than a noble aspiration or competitive capacity. There is a laundry list of good gestures companies employ. They may train employees on the tricks of taking minutes in meetings more efficiently, add more experiential activity to training programs, design work spaces with more open access, or allow workers a greater sense of freedom to pursue their own interests. Many organizations now employ all or most of these strategies, but these activities barely scratch the surface of maintaining a generative posture of true perpetual knowledge acquisition.

Corporate propaganda and impassioned sermons from charismatic leaders have become counterfeits for inspiring genuine exploration of new ideas. The surfacing of potentially breakthrough questions has been substituted with enthusiastic sound-bite answers. An authentic facilitator, or "Gold Miner" of generative learning, knows there is always latent brilliance waiting to be tapped within those around them. The Narcissistic Evangelist, by contrast, believes he has the answer already and needs only to make enough converts out of those who have yet to declare their allegiance to his cause. An effective wisdom miner is a perpetual self-directed learner. Someone who already feels he has the answer will inherently avoid surfacing new perspectives that would threaten preconceptions and assumptions. In the world of facilitated learning, ideas are to be surfaced, explored, cultivated, and built upon. In the world of the Narcissistic Evangelist, ideas are commodities to be "sold" and mindlessly ingested (even under the all-too-common ruse of getting employees to think your idea is their own). Evangelists tell and facilitators inquire.

Perhaps the most dangerous aspect of the Narcissistic Evangelist is that he will find plenty of people in the organization to believe him, even if his position is demonstrably false. Gibbert, Krull and Malone[29] describe a study in which a dozen volunteers were assigned to spend a month in a variety of mental health facilities. Each volunteer was mentally healthy, but each was deliberately registered upon intake with a false diagnosis of a mental disability. Despite the fact that the volunteers, who were themselves familiar with the nature of their fictitious illnesses, did not manifest any symptoms, both doctors and other staff members in the institution made numerous entries onto each volunteer's chart that corroborated the initial fake diagnosis. Even perfectly normal behaviors such as yawning upon waking were magnified into examples of illness. By the time the volunteers were retrieved and the study revealed to the institutions, more than a thousand pills had been collectively prescribed for the various "conditions" the volunteers supposedly manifested. A follow-up study was conducted a year later, where the same institutions were advised that another group of volunteers were coming in for another month, but the employees would have no idea which of their recent intakes was genuine. The study was called off after two weeks, because staff members were so sure they had identified who was well, they were urging cancellation of medications to avoid subjecting a well person to pharmacological dangers. The irony was that there were no volunteers at all this time. Every institution had picked at least one person it was sure was a volunteer, yet that person, in every instance, was a genuine patient.

That study is a powerful statement of how difficult it is to disbelieve something you are told by a respected source of authority. It also drives home the point that the Narcissistic Evangelist we describe can be demonstrably wrong in his assumptions and can still lead the entire organization in the wrong direction, with results that can be catastrophic.

It begs the question, as leaders seek to mine the gold of wisdom within their organizations, how do they balance the razor-thin line of not manipulatively imposing an agenda on others, and yet having an agenda for the greater good of the organization's future? In the extreme, too much of an agenda or no agenda renders leaders ineffectual in guiding their communities to a shared future.

The art of facilitating the exhumation of brilliance from her community and blending her voice into that brilliance is the true genius of the Gold Miner. Gold miners consider every circumstance in which they and their communities find themselves an opportunity for learning, thus assuming the presence of undiscovered wisdom. By contrast, Narcissistic Evangelists have no need to assume the presence of undiscovered wisdom because they presume to possess it all themselves. The generative posture of Gold Mining invites organizations to indulge an insatiable appetite to learn and to apply their newfound wisdom toward strengthening their community's collective genius.

Plot yourself, and your organization, on this continuum at the point you feel honestly reflects your current degree of generative/degenerative posture.

←————————————————————————————————————→

Narcissistic   Gold
Evangelist   Miner

Your colleague's experience with a Narcissistic Evangelist

Okay, so I get that I can be naïve sometimes, but can't we all? Excuse me for trying to be positive, but what's so wrong about believing something you're told by someone you ought to be able to trust? I'll tell you what's wrong with it. They could be lying through their shiny-white smiling teeth! I feel like I want to put up a sign outside my office that says, "Beware leaders who tell you they have a vision and that you are a key part of it. If you hear this, RUN!" I should have known better when she came into my office with that book on business intelligence. Things that appear too good to be true usually are. She knew it was a passion of mine, though, and that I'd been spending a lot of my own time learning more and more about how to leverage our technology for greater analytical strength. Every customer defection we've experienced this year, every product-quality disaster, all could have been prevented. We had the data available to make better decisions than we did, and to have predicted the problems before they happened. It makes me crazy. So when she came into my office to "share her vision" for a more business-intelligent culture, I was naturally intrigued. At first we just met for coffee a few times a month to swap perspectives on stuff we'd read. I was amazed at how much knowledge she had on the topic. She knew way more than I did, and I'd become a voracious devourer of anything I could get my hands on. I asked her if she would mentor me, because I really wanted to learn as much as I could, and she said–get this–"Well, I'd be honored to. I'm flattered that you asked." Every time we met, I'd take copious notes and go back to my team and share what I'd learned. I lead a great team of supervisors and technicians who all are starting to see the need to leverage our data better than we do to avoid some of the shortsighted and ridiculous decisions we make as an organization. She and I even went to a conference together on business intelligence and both got really excited by what it could mean for our organization. Then it started to grow into meeting weekly to brainstorm and strategize how to connect our data warehouses to other aspects of our system and create dashboards that could integrate key decision support groups. She even let me bring my team members to a few of our sessions and they were amazed at how far we'd gotten. She kept telling me that her peers on the executive team were starting to buy in to the notion and were charging her with taking the lead for the company to make the necessary investments to ensure we became more analytically astute as a culture. I couldn't have been more excited. Finally I was learning something that mattered to the organization, and it appeared that people around me were starting to embrace it too. At least that's what she made it appear like. She was mesmerizing people with her brilliant insights and ideas. Our small working sessions grew into full-scale town hall gatherings called How Intelligent are You?: Raising Your Sights to See the Future, and people came in droves. They ingested the knowledge almost as feverishly. Pretty soon it became difficult for me to get time on her calendar because she was in such demand. As I listened to how people were regurgitating the message, I became increasingly concerned that they were missing the point. It was becoming less about using our data intelligently to make great decisions, and in very subtle ways, more about becoming imitators of her zeal. Speaking the language of business intelligence became more normative than talking about *being* more intelligent. When I sent her e-mails trying to raise concerns about what was happening, she wrote back a bit terse and said, "We worked hard to get this movement started. The fact that it's not going your way doesn't mean it's not working. These things take time." Movement? You've got to be kidding me. When I saw people using the concepts manipulatively, I got really concerned. I heard one manager say to his direct reports in a meeting, "I appreciate your opinion, but where is the intelligent data to support it? Why don't you go to the next How Intelligent are You session, and then come back and see if your opinion hasn't changed." What was meant to provoke greater curiosity and desire to learn had become a tool to shame others with a sense of exclusivity. It made me sick. Today we got the corporate memo announcing the creation of a new business unit called Strategic Intelligence and Decision Support and she was named the chief intelligence officer. I was outraged to see that several members of my team were named as part of the new unit, which totaled nearly twenty people. They never even told me they were applying. Part of me felt really angry and disappointed that she never even asked me to join the new initiative, but an even greater part of me feels very relieved, because once she makes a name for herself, she'll probably leave and go somewhere else for more money and leave everyone hung out to dry. No thanks. I've drunk all the Kool-Aid I care to drink for now.

You in-Formation

1. Have you ever felt the allure of a Narcissistic Evangelist before? What was it like? How did it effect your desire to learn more or to let others influence your thinking?
2. When have you let your passion and zeal for something influence people in a way that closed off your receptivity to the thinking of others? What happened?

Your colleague's experience with a Gold Miner

This is where it happened. Yes, you should look perplexed. It's a parking garage. Believe me, I didn't see it coming either. I mean, we all know she's the smartest kid on the block by a long shot, so I never thought she'd ever be interested in anything I was doing, much less want to help. I don't know about you, but anytime I'm around her I regress into "idiot" mode and become the incompetent jerk I feel like in her presence. I don't know that she actually tries to make people feel like that, but when you're as brilliant as she is, that's just one of the things that happens to those around you. So there we were walking out to the garage late one evening. She got into the elevator, and I was the only one there. I could already feel my mouth drying up before she asked me to hit the button for her parking floor. Realizing that it was already lit up, she said, "Oh, you're going to P-5 too? Great. You must have gotten here pretty early then too. That floor usually is full by 7:30." I'm thinking, "Wow, she's actually being nice to me. Don't say anything stupid!" I manage to eek out, "Yeah, well, big deliverable this week, so getting here before the crowds gives me lots of uninterrupted time." I hoped that managed to quell the conversation so I could get out unscathed. No such luck. She pressed the point. "Oh, really, what are you working on?" I was not fast enough on my feet to make up impressive sounding BS, so the self-deprecating play-down approach was my only option. "Oh, it's nothing, really. Nothing compared to the stuff you get to work on. It's just a research project to look at the feasibility of our manufacturing plants in Malaysia and how to make them more sustainable there before we try to scale our Pacific Rim operations. My boss has to present it to the board in a couple of weeks." She got a odd look on her face, and I didn't know what to make of it. She lowered her head, and I felt like a real jerk, because I obviously said something stupid and I didn't even know what. I asked her, "What's wrong?" She said, "Stuff *you* get to work on?" I gave her a look that I hoped conveyed that I don't know what she's talking about, and she got the hint. "You said 'nothing compared to the stuff I get to work on.' I wish people didn't always put me in that box of comparison. It sounds like an amazing project you are working on, and sometimes I get really frustrated with how disconnected people make me out to be, just because I happen to be good at what I do. People diminish their own work to me and put me on this pedestal, and I never get to have real conversations with anyone. What's that about?" It wasn't a rhetorical question. She really wanted an answer. "Well, look, everyone knows you're a genius, so we all just feel intimidated by you. I don't think you lord it over people at all; you're nice enough to us. Sorry if I made you feel bad. I didn't mean to." She got a little smirk on her face, and without skipping a beat, continued, "So tell me about your project." I started telling her about the research and what I was looking to prove, and I realized I was going to have to tell her where I was stuck. "I haven't been able to correlate the economics and the environmental issues to the expansion strategy because the regulations in the Pacific Rim are constantly changing. I feel like everything I'm writing is just pure conjecture and isn't going to help anyone make the decisions they have to make. That's why I've been staying so late, so I can make calls to Malaysia while it's still during their workday. So far I haven't come up with anything, though, and this thing is due at the end of the week. Now I feel like a complete jerk for telling you that. You probably think I'm dumb and that I'm missing the obvious." She gave me a really strong you're-doing-it-again look, and I put my hand up in a peace-making apologetic wave. She started asking me questions, not like she was interrogating me, but genuine questions about my research approach and my hypotheses. I don't know how much time passed, but it felt like a week before we actually got to our cars. We stood for another thirty minutes or so, and all of the sudden, she asked me a question about one of our competitors' facilities in South America and the light bulb went on like the floodlights at a ballpark. I thought about all of the questions she'd been asking me, and I realized I had been both proving and disproving my hypotheses the entire time. I knew what I needed to say, but I was afraid, because I suspected it wasn't what my boss wanted to hear. She could tell the epiphany had hit. I thanked her profusely, and she smiled a very knowing smile and said, "Good luck with the research." I realized what she'd done. I started to ask her, "Did you know from the very first question you asked where you thought I...." but she interrupted and gently and politely said, "Goodnight. Get home safely." She got into her car and drove off. Here was one of the smartest women in the organization–probably on the planet–and she could have been condescending and mean, or at best, just "told" me the answer, but she knew that what I needed to know I already knew, and she helped me figure it out for myself. She was also genuinely curious about my work the whole way through. I never figured a parking lot for a classroom until now.

You in-Formation

1. When has someone drawn out unearthed knowledge from you in a way that was both honoring and enlightening? What was it like? Was it harder than just having the person give you the answer?
2. When have you resisted the allure of just giving someone an answer either for efficiency or for the chance to appear smart–and drawn out of the person his or her own knowledge and insight with curiosity and intrigue? What was it like? Did it come naturally, or did it feel counterintuitive?

Your story from the future

Write a brief story about a member of your organization who makes an important discovery of an insight or perspective that had been eluding her, but through your inquiry and curiosity is able to garner an entirely new perspective on a previously frustrating problem. Assume that you are the Gold Miner in the story.

Question 6:
How will I demonstrate regard?

Regard is the coalescing force that summons a generative future through an act of consideration of others. Every organization and community faces unexpected crises. In times of extreme distress and fear, people are naturally inclined to self-protect and "hunker down." The question becomes one of degree. When the stakes are high, when the pain is acute, when the potential consequences dire, to what degree does making sure you come out unscathed totally eclipse any sense of considering others' needs? Whether we like it or not, situations of urgency bring out our true colors with respect to selflessness or selfishness. It's not a question of *if* we think about others during times of misfortune; it's *how* we think about them–as those we could help or those who may prevent us from getting what we need. Even the most self-absorbed person thinks of other people, though that person may manifest unproductive behaviors, such as seeking a way to sabotage an organizational nemesis. *How* people think of others defines their posture of regard. If a person is constantly trying to outmaneuver others in a passive-aggressive contest for limited resources, advancement opportunities, or corporate notoriety, his posture of regard toward others is one of hostility and a desire to protect himself against perceived hostility. This desire leads to active pursuit of opportunities to undermine others' agenda if it is seen as threatening. In contrast, a person who puts others' agendas ahead of her own, or at least on equal footing, has a regard posture of "ally," someone for whom she will actively pursue success, regardless of whether or not she benefits directly. The generative notion that one is contributing, even silently, toward another's good is reward enough.

The creation of open-source software is a good example of generativity, in that it benefits others as well as the software author. This fact might seem counterintuitive. Organizations like Microsoft make their living with software and vigorously uphold their rights. A vibrant subculture of open-source software writers has flourished for almost twenty years, however, arguing that giving software away is a sound business strategy. Dirk Riehle, leader of the Open Software Research Group at SAP, points out that "before the advent of open-source software, entering an established and well-defended market was a risky proposition. With increasingly well-understood open-source processes, setting up an open-source project that competes with an established closed-source market leader's product is much less risky and carries a significantly higher chance of success than before. It's not just a specific system integrator that will want to do that, though. It's pretty much everyone who isn't the closed-source market leader.[30]"

We have seen a significant number of selfless actions within organizations that parallel the open-source approach. This is especially true around nurturing potential new businesses, where applying uniform standards of return on investment would kill new projects that seldom generate returns at first, no matter how lucrative they will be in a few years.

Like most management fads, innovation comes in and out of vogue every five to seven years. Given how US markets have failed to produce any game-changing fundamental breakthroughs in our key service, scientific, or technology sectors in quite a long time, pressure is mounting globally for someone to produce the next "big win." Innovation must move from being a fad to a mainstay in organizations if we want to stay globally competitive. In one consumer-product goods client whose stable of brands was typically outperformed by lesser competitors simply because they'd never learned to commercialize their brands at retailers effectively, a newly appointed head of research was met with great surprise when she walked into an organization entrenched in paranoia, suspicion, and the expectation that she was there to fire them all. When she finally established enough trust to ask someone what the paranoia was about, a young scientist courageously confessed, "Well, we all know we're just stupid, and we're sure that after you find out, we're all history."

She was dumbfounded. She asked him, "What makes you think you're all stupid?" She found his next response more disturbing.

"Well, that's all anyone's ever told us. Anytime we've brought ideas for change to your predecessor, he'd roll his eyes and mumble under his breath something like, 'How did I get stuck with such stupid people?' Then the next day, whoever brought the idea usually didn't come to work and their work station was vacant."

She said to him, "Well, one important thing I'd like to point out is this: you are still here, and he's not. That's not how we're doing business anymore. I'm not here to pick people off one by one. I'm here to make this thing *work*." She spent the next eighteen months rebuilding the confidence and commitment of the organization by rolling up her sleeves and getting down to the development benches with her scientists, helping them with their crisis of confidence, and spurring on their ideas. True, some of them were not impressive, but the organization's ability to ideate had been handicapped by a leader who found more gratification in taking out anyone who threatened him than he did in actually producing new products. When the Sniper comes in the form of a leader, the aftermath can be especially devastating.

Acting like a Sniper and taking shots at a new business or process is easy to do, especially when the chips are down, but you risk compromising your organization's ability to ever do anything new. Far better to be a First-Responder aiding where you can, regardless of whether the benefit to you is immediate or if your agenda gets a boost. This is a vital part of manifesting consideration toward others and generating a bright future for your organization.

Plot yourself, and your organization, on this continuum at the point you feel honestly reflects your current degree of generative/degenerative posture.

←   →

Sniper   First-Responder

Your colleague's experience with a Sniper

All of us scurried into the conference room for the impromptu all-staff meeting Derrick, our VP of R&D, had called. Everyone knows that consumer electronics, like any commodity business, is a bear to try to innovate within. Cheesy brand extensions and adding new "deluxe" product features is about the best anyone's done since the iPod. It had been nearly eighteen months since we were able to get a new product onto a shelf, and even that was just a gadget flash in the pan whose sales rose sharply and then flattened the minute the market figured out that the novelty wore off fast. Derrick was getting some pretty intense heat from the other cooks in the kitchen, namely the CEO, whose product genius got the company started. He had called us all together because, as he put it, we needed "a new idea." He had asked our skunkworks team to come prepared to lead a discussion and wanted us to offer some of our newest ideas as a starter for our time together.

For him to have put it that way, I knew he was feeling desperate. I had been working my butt off sending him all kinds of ideas from my team for months, so it's not like he hadn't seen any. In fact, our entire team had proposed nearly seven new products, both new and product extensions, within the last year. Derrick even lit up at several of them, but they all were single-handedly shot down by our CFO because we, "don't have the money or the resources to actually make them a reality," as he so unkindly put it. Doesn't he understand that we can't afford *not* to afford to bet on some new idea? Well, I sure wasn't about to throw my hat in the ring and get shot down in front of everyone yet again; however, I also knew that we had no choice. Derrick asked us to come with ideas, so we had to show up with ideas. I just figured I would have two of the developers talk about what they were working on so that I didn't have to be directly responsible for another un-fundable idea. It may be wrong to put others into the line of fire, but hey, I have to survive too, right?

Everyone eventually settled into seats for what was going to be another long meeting. Derrick, and Dick, our CFO, were the last two to walk in. They came in together and assumed their seats at the head of the conference table. Derrick started us off with his usual leadership spiel, and then passed the baton.

"Thank you all for being here today. I'm really hoping our time together pushes us to prioritize some bets and focuses us on some ideas we all are going to get behind. I've asked Gail from the skunkworks team to share a bit of what they've been thinking about lately and help guide the bulk of our time today. Gail?" Derrick, too, had learned too well (and taught us) the art of putting others on the front lines.

Gail charged in with all of her usual enthusiasm. "Thanks, Derrick. As we all know, we've had an extremely difficult time commercializing any new products in the last eighteen months. That isn't to say that we haven't had any good ideas, though, because we have had quite a few. We've just had a difficult time translating those ideas into realities. We all know, too, that our best ideas come when we have some friction, when we can spark one another's thinking." Gail was notorious for her innovation-business-book addiction, so she had to read us quotes from several of her latest "fixes." "Today we want to engage some of the ideas we put out and work with them in a way that allows for possibility instead of dismissal. We'd like to have two project leads give an overview of what they've been working on and then invite each of your areas of expertise to help refine and evolve those ideas. Any questions before we get started? Yes, Dick?"

I knew we were all thinking the same thing to ourselves. "Boy, that was fast. He usually doesn't take out his guns that soon into the meeting." We all knew Dick was good at his job–counting the money–even though he had no clue what we really did as a company. He'd known the CEO for years and clearly knew how to manage up well, but he was all about the numbers, and it was clearly his job to teach us a lesson when he felt we were going to lead the company into financial ruins. Problem was he knew nothing of innovation and not much more about the consumer electronics markets. He saw us as nothing but a cost center to be controlled and financially irresponsible prima donnas who needed to have our wings clipped. That's exactly what he'd come to do.

"Yeah, thanks for that setup Gail. This should be a discussion, and I hope we make some good headway. I know you and I haven't had the chance to sync up prior to this meeting, Gail, which shouldn't be a big deal, but I just wanted to double check to make sure you had a chance to look over the budget I sent you earlier today. We had to make some last-minute changes, and I thought it might be helpful for you to see where some of it was allocated. If not, we can talk about it afterwards."

Clever opening move by Dick. His famous stealth shot over the bow. All heads turned to Gail to see if she had something up her sleeve. No such luck. She looked a bit off balance.

"Wow. No, Dick, I hadn't had the chance to look at that e-mail yet. Our team was in meetings all morning. I can't imagine those adjustments having a huge impact on what we'll present this morning. I mean, if they were that critical, I'm sure you would have sent them much earlier than a few hours before the meeting. You and I can talk about that offline. So why don't we have Jim tell us a bit about what he's been working on. Jim?"

Touché, Gail, I thought. At least she got a bit of a jab back before the games began, although of all people to ask to speak, Jim was probably the worst choice. He led the team that had overspent its development budget last quarter by 20%. It wasn't really a big deal, because it had probably allocated too little, and he'll likely make it up before the year is out, but that explanation never worked for Dick. Overspending your budget was a mortal sin, because it risked making Dick look bad to the board. We all suspected Jim was about to receive his penance. You'd think Jim would have known better than to say yes to such a kamikaze mission, given Dick's track record, but then again, given what a jerk he can be, you'd think Dick would be smart enough to go by "Richard."

Jim went on to tell us about a new wireless concept for interfacing between cellular technology and PC, an easier way to transfer information between them besides USB. It was pretty interesting and surprisingly inexpensive to produce. At least that's what *we* thought. He opened the floor up for thoughts and questions, and of course Dick was the first to chime in.

"Yes, Dick," Jim pointed pretty sheepishly at him. I could feel him bracing.

"I think it's a very interesting idea for us. I am just wondering if we've run the numbers to see how fast we can recoup the investment dollars. What's the uptake in the market expected to be? Have we talked to any wireless providers to test their interest for distribution?" Dick knew perfectly well that Jim and his team hadn't yet gone to that level of detail but had only projections, and yet he asked anyway.

Jim began to crumble under Dick's interrogation, and within twenty minutes could barely finish a sentence. I wanted to pass out Kevlar jackets. Then everyone started piling on, almost hiding behind Dick and firing shots with him. We hadn't explored the idea one bit before the room was completely dismantling it, rendering it totally implausible. Dick has the uncanny ability to, in the nicest of tones and looks, shoot you down along with any idea you have and rally the entire room behind him. Joan and Paul, who'd previously *encouraged* this project, were even climbing on Dick's *"I really don't see how this can work"* bandwagon. Derrick, of course, sat there silently and watched as the room went up in flames.

What did I do? Oh, I completely checked out and worked on e-mail. Frankly, I never really thought the process would work. The very thing we had agreed not to do was happening right in front of our faces, and none of us, including me, had the guts to say anything, because we've all felt Dick's bullets before. In my e-mail, I'd gotten a LinkedIn invitation from an old colleague to join his network. It was fascinating to see what he was up to in his career. We'd been to engineering school together in the same technology specialization. He said his company was hiring. I think I'll send him my résumé for the heck of it. This place sure doesn't have a chance in hell of innovating anything. We'd be lucky if we could approve changing the color of our packaging without a bloodbath.

You in-Formation

1. When have you experienced a Sniper who disregards your thoughts, solutions, and ultimately your work for no apparent logical reason? What was it like? How

did it effect your ability to participate and be engaged in the work you were involved in?

2. When have you, even inadvertently, shot down someone's ideas or thinking? How thorough are you in showing regard for others and their views? How inclined are you to dismiss others' input? How do you treat the participation of those you tend not to like or agree with?

Your colleague's experience with a First-Responder

"I can't believe it! How is it possible? I made it perfectly clear that it was going to be difficult for us to land a location in light of everything that's happening in town during the week of our conference, and now you're trying to tell me that we still haven't secured a location for our event? I thought we had worked through all this and signed a contract. I thought Wes knew how crucial this was from the start." I hung up the phone and was instantly flooded with all sorts of questions, questions that I shouldn't have to be asking again, and certainly not *now*.

We had almost a year to select and secure a location for the event. We have people flying in from all over the world, and somehow, with only ten weeks left before we were scheduled to launch the conference, we somehow managed to miss the little detail of a venue. Surely you can understand my outrage! I had been hounding Phoebe and Wes from the start to make sure to line up our venue location. I knew it was going to be difficult for us to find the right space because of how we wanted to set it up, the number of people we had coming into town, and the fact that there were two other large conferences happening the same week in the city. Wes had told me that three *perfect* venues were on deck and that we just needed to confirm one and go with it.

His supervisor, Phoebe, had just informed me that while Wes was on vacation, all three conference centers had been approached by other groups wanting to book large portions of their conference space. Apparently each one had left Wes numerous messages informing him of the other requests, and that they needed his commitment or they would have to release the space, but he never got the messages while he was away. Naturally each venue assumed he had signed a deal somewhere else, so all decided that, because they had no signed contract and he didn't return their calls, they were free to book the space for other events. It was like a REALLY bad dream.

There I was, responsible for the entire conference with no place to host our 500-plus registrants. How was I going to explain that one? I was more than a little stressed, and then my phone rang. Phoebe's name showed up on the internal caller ID. Just seeing her name made me outraged again. "Phoebe, how could you let something so simple as the venue slide through the cracks? You're responsible for your team, including Wes. Why weren't you on top of this? How can we have a conference without a location?"

I was more than surprised by her response. "I totally own it. It's my fault. I should have made sure Wes had it secured months ago. I was calling because I wanted you to know that I—"

Not listening at first, I plowed ahead. "This is totally unacceptable, Phoebe! You're not giving me a lot of confidence in your ability to make the conference a success. I gave this project to you because you had wanted to take on more responsibility and because you thought it would be a lot of fun—"

"The reason I called is that I wanted to let you know I put together an emergency search committee the other day, and we have already talked with two conference facilities. We are getting bids back from them tonight. Since we've already put deposits on rooms at the Hyatt, I've checked with the Hyatt, and we can arrange bus transportation to and from the conference events which, in either case, will be only about ten minutes away. The Hyatt can still handle both dinners, so we can keep the evening events where they are. I immediately reached out to Alexa in marketing communications; she runs all our trade shows. I figured she'd be able to help, and she's been an angel. She got me hooked up with the folks at the conference centers where we've given our trade shows before, and when I told them the jam we were in, they were right on top of it, helping. They're even going to give us the negotiated corporate rate that we've had in the past. Alexa has great connections, and because she's had this kind of thing happen to her before, she's jumped in to help very graciously. I expect that we'll have a deal signed by the end of tomorrow, pending your approval. I was hoping you and I could drive out to see the Arrowhead Conference Center together. I think they will offer us the best deal and the nicer facility, and Alexa recommended them the highest. Once we sign, we'll still have about a month to inform all our registrants of the new meeting location and the logistics of transport between the Hyatt and the facility. I know this isn't ideal and that you wanted everything in one place, but I've asked a few folks if they think a ten-minute bus ride in the morning is a big deal, and no one seems to think folks will be all that put out. Wes has already contacted a bus company and booked four luxury coaches for the event. Alexa has taken on working the job of with marketing communications and is working out a plan with them to creatively communicate the change and print and distribute a logistics update. Our folks in IT are ready to change our Web site and other important onsite conference tech pieces when we have the available information. And you should know that Wes is feeling pretty bad about all this. He's been here very late for the last few days working on the triage team. Again, I'm just really sorry this happened. Is there anything else you can think of that we need to be taking care of?"

I really didn't know what to say. "Well Phoebe, I must say that I am a little surprised. And I think, before anything else, I need to apologize. You just got the brunt of a lot of what I've been feeling about this whole mess, and that's not fair to you. I'm sorry. Okay?"

"I totally understand your frustration and wish we weren't in this position either. This is the last thing you needed to happen. No worries–apology accepted. And I hope you'll accept our apology as well, and that we can just move forward from here and make this an amazing event."

"Absolutely, Phoebe, it's time to move forward. We're still only nine weeks out, so there's a ton to do, but you've taken the reigns toward landing a solution and, at this point, I can't ask for a whole lot more. Let's plan to touch base weekly between now and kickoff, at least half an hour a week. Work with my admin to schedule a weekly update, okay? On another note, I really want you to know how much I appreciate your willingness to step in and make things happen. You could have come in with all sorts of excuses and explanations, or worse, blaming everyone else for dropping the ball. Instead you picked up the hand we got dealt and started playing to win. I understand that things go wrong in life, even though I still have some deluded sense they shouldn't go wrong for me. I wish more people could show the kind of leadership you've shown by putting aside their own needs and agendas and jumping in to help. I'll be sure and send an e-mail to Alexa as well. Sounds like she's been amazing."

"Well, you're welcome, thanks for saying so. And yes, please do thank Alexa. She'll appreciate the recognition from you. Without her I don't know what I would have done. I'll make sure to get a weekly time on your calendar to update you on our progress. We'll make it happen. I know it."

After we hung up, I was stunned by what it felt like to have real help. Usually when the ball gets dropped, I feel I've been left holding the bag and have to fend for myself. Sure, I wished the situation hadn't happened, but hey, things happen for a reason, right?

You in-Formation

1. When have you experienced a First-Responder in the midst of a difficult conflict or unforeseen crisis? What effect did their willingness to respond have on you and your engagement of the situation? How did it feel to have your needs put before another's? What effect did it have on the performance of the project?

2. When have you had the opportunity to First-Respond to help out in a crisis? Did you step up, or just hunker down? What effect did that have on the situation? How can you shift your regard for others to more of their needs than your own?

Your story from the future

Write a brief story about a member of your organization who finds himself or herself facing an unexpected major obstacle in a critical project and needs important help from others to avert disaster and realize the desired results. Assume that you are the First Responder in the story.

Question 7:
In what will I hope?

Hope is the coalescing force that summons a generative future through an act of faith that is certain of a different way forward and sure of that possibility even if it can't be seen at the present time. Hope is the posture that has the power to propel an organization into a sustainable future. It doesn't wait for the conditions to be right. It's a posture that is grounded on conviction in the absence of factual proof.

There is a well-known cliché that says people either see a glass as half empty or half full. One might think that an optimist sees the half-full glass and the pessimist sees the half-empty glass. The reality is a bit different. The Prophets of Doom see the proverbial glass as full of poison–a posture that conforms to their view of the organization as adversarial, difficult, and threatening. They exploit any piece of bad news available, and with the artful use of hyperbole and broad generalization, can paint a picture of corporate Armageddon that makes even the most resilient people feel dejected. True hope sees the glass and simply fills it. This is done without questions or arguments. Hope is a posture that is compelled to act because of a deep-seated belief that *things can and should be different*. This is the notion that has driven every great innovation in every sphere of human endeavor. It doesn't matter if you're talking about digital value creators like Google; hugely successful manufacturers like Toyota; successful entertainers like the Beatles; successful explorers like Sir Edmund Hillary and Tenzing Norgay, who were the first to ascend Mt. Everest; or great scientists pursuing treatments for devastating diseases. The unifying thread for all is that things can and should be different. These people act upon hope and bring change into the world.

Peterson and Byron[31] point out that high-hope individuals are more goal-oriented and more motivated to achieve their goals than those with low hope. It doesn't matter where in the organization people are. Peterson and Byron found that regardless of whether they were talking about sales employees, mortgage brokers, or management executives, high-hope individuals had higher overall job performance. They also found that higher hope executives produced more and better quality solutions to work-related problems, suggesting that hopefulness may help employees when they are confronted with problems and encounter obstacles at work.

Once the degenerative spiral toward hopelessness has begun, it can be difficult to reverse. "What's the use" becomes the underlying mantra of those in environments bereft of the needed hope to transcend the challenges, but genuine, sustaining hope rarely comes in mass quantities all at once. Instead, lasting hope comes in accumulating doses. It multiplies into more and more hope as momentum gathers and evidence of change peeks its head out from behind the wall of black despondence.

Hope, then, is also a fundamental choice. Hope would not be the powerful force that it is if it were chosen only when a reason to do so was obvious. The true power of hope lies in choosing to have it when the presenting data would suggest doing otherwise. Unlike belief, a posture that invites a turn from fear and an investment of conviction into something liberating and tangible, hope invites the leap of faith to place one's confidence behind an initiative, an endeavor, a dream, *without* necessarily having the tangible evidence to back it up.

Barack Obama, in his manifesto on the subject, suggests choosing hope is an audacious prospect. Against the powerful trends of cynicism and erosion of trust in our public leaders, he compels us to consider the many reasons to put hope behind the possibility of fundamental change when every candidate that ever came before him has made and broken promises for the very same change. Despite the odds, he still suggests the force of goodness over time, even in the face of the gloomiest track records, can convert cynicism into hope. He says, "I remember seeing the news reports of the tsunami that hit East Asia in 2004, the towns of Indonesia's western coast flattened, the thousands of people washed out to sea. And then, in the weeks that followed, I watched with pride as Americans sent more than a billion dollars in private relief aid and as US warships delivered thousands of troops to assist in relief and reconstruction. According to newspaper reports, sixty-five percent of Indonesians surveyed said that this assistance had given them a more favorable view of the United States. I am not naïve enough to believe that one episode in the wake of catastrophe can erase decades of mistrust. But it's a start." [32]

My (Ron's) daughter is learning algebra. Like most teenagers, she becomes easily despaired at the notion of trying to grasp abstract mathematical concepts she believes will be of no use to her after junior high school. Her teacher's proclamation that, "You will use this in your everyday life" only fuels her pessimism and discouragement. One night while I was studying with her for a test, going over coefficients and complex equations, I learned an important lesson about hope. Her frustration level reached its limit and she broke into tears, feeling incompetent and hopeless in what felt like a futile attempt to learn something she couldn't. It surprised me, because she is normally one of the most joyful and optimistic young women I've ever met, able to persevere through most things that aggravate her. I was sad to see her spirit break, and I didn't want her to head into her test believing she would inevitably fail. We kept working at the concepts and I tried several ways to help her remember the steps to solving the equations. I also kept expressing my firm belief in her ability to learn them, assuring her that despite her inability to see how, these skills would be important for her later. Eventually she began to get it and was able to work through the equations without my guidance. Later that evening when she came to kiss me goodnight, restored to her usual joyful spirit, I asked her how she was feeling about algebra. Gleefully she said, "I still think it's a waste of time."

I asked, "How are you feeling about the test tomorrow?"

She said, "I hope I get at least a B plus."

Hope – without seeing a reason for it.

Both examples point out the important relationship between hope and perseverance. Hope isn't something that just appears once beckoned. It must be relentlessly pursued. Its most powerful expression often comes in the face of staunch opposition. In his landmark letter to the Roman community, a community facing tumultuous change and conflicts at the time, St. Paul inspired his friends to believe that hope is the result of embracing struggles and the character that ensues. He said, "We can be glad for the struggles and suffering we face, because we know that they teach us to persevere, and that perseverance produces proven character, and that proven character produces hope. And hope does not disappoint..." [33]

The Optimist builds bridges of hope between the impossible and the possible, freeing the paraplegic to walk, the once unsolvable dilemma to resolve, the chronically failing prototype to reach the market successfully, the broken relationship to mend. Optimists give us faith in what we can't see and hope on our behalf until we can hope on our own. Prophets of Doom parasitically suck the life out of a room and turn everything into a funeral, stealing energy and vitality to draft others into their army of hopelessness. For the Optimist, there is no need to give up, even in the face of what appears impossible. Giving up is never an option. To the Optimist there is always hope.

Plot yourself, and your organization, on this continuum at the point you feel honestly reflects your current degree of generative/degenerative posture.

←——→

Prophet of   Optimist
Doom

Your colleague's experience with a Prophet of Doom

Good Lord, that guy can suck the life right out of a room! Look, I know things may not look as good as we might want them to, but for cryin' out loud, do we have to start planning the funeral already? The way this guy is talking, we might as well file for chapter 11 tomorrow. All he does is make people want to lie when they get in the room just to avoid having to hear the death-march speech. Poor Jennifer left the room in tears after her presentation, but of course he was too stupid and obtuse to even notice. Here's this young woman, fairly new to the organization, presenting the risk assessment on the Northeast region's retail operations' prospect of making its plans for the next two quarters. I mean, this woman has done her homework and she's come to play. She's done a district-by-district assessment of all the retail channels and the trends in their local markets, and even has some ideas for how the lower performing districts might boost their sales. We're all pretty impressed. No, it wasn't perfect and there were a couple of places where she didn't have a few facts as buttoned up as possible, but heck, she's new. And her hypotheses were certainly well grounded. For a new person, she was doing amazingly well. She also didn't pull any punches. She made it very clear what we at headquarters are going to have to do to support the region's execution of the sales plans. All through the presentation, he sat, not saying a word, but huffing out big, windy sighs, shaking his head as though he'd just heard the worst news of his life, and drawing big sweeping red lines all over the slide handouts. We were all trying to stay focused on Jen, ask her questions, and stay engaged with her, because it was pretty clear the wind was coming out of her sails as she was watching him have his little dramatic spasm. Finally, right in the middle of one of her sentences, he put up his hand and said, "Excuse me." He squeezed the bridge of his nose as though he had a bad headache and mumbled something like, "I don't know why we bother." Then he looked up and said, "Jennifer, thank you for all the obvious hard work you put into this. It's clear you came quite prepared. Let me ask the rest of you a question. Do you actually like having jobs? Do you get that the Northwest region is about to implode? Putting Band-Aids on things isn't what's needed here, folks." Well, first of all, it's hardly about to implode. And second of all, does he really think the way to motivate us is to remind us we could all lose our jobs? Jennifer tried to politely push back on some of his depressing diatribe but he wouldn't have it. He said to her, very condescendingly, "Look, Jennifer, it's nice that you are trying to paint a rosy picture for us, and as the new kid on the block it's not fair of us to expect you to tell it like it is. But I've been talking directly to the district managers and hearing straight from them just how grim things are." Jennifer took a huge risk by saying to him, "Gosh, that's so weird that they would tell you such a different story than they told me. There's no question things are tough right now, but I didn't hear the kind of gloom you're talking about." So he said, "Well, I wouldn't expect them to tell you the truth. You're too new, and they don't know you that well. We all go way back, so they know they can tell me anything." At that point everyone was fighting back one big room-wide eye roll. Nobody in the field can stand him, and when he visits or talks to them, the rest of us get e-mails asking for help cleaning up the mess he makes. Jennifer tried one last time to use the Boston district as an example of where a strong turnaround was possible, but he cut her off. His grand finale was, "Look, people, it's clear you don't understand how serious this really is. Let's not waste any more time today. I'll send you an e-mail by the end of tomorrow outlining some ideas I think will really work to turn this mess around. Please be prepared to stay late tomorrow night." That was that. He got up and left, and the rest of us just yawned and went back to our desks. We've been through this drill many times before. He'll whip up a bunch of plans that nobody will adopt or even listen to, and then we'll quietly go about implementing Jennifer's ideas, and he'll keep screaming that the sky is falling. How ridiculous can you get, right?

You in-Formation

1. Have you ever worked with very negative people before? What impact did they have on you and on those you worked with? As a leader, what hidden costs did they impose on their teams? How did you feel after being with them?
2. Have you ever caught yourself "letting the proverbial air out of others' tires"? What was behind your deep pessimism? Do you struggle to sustain hope in difficult circumstances? How do you regain it when it has flagged?

Your colleague's experience with an Optimist

I gotta tell you, I am so glad I work for him. There's nobody I'd rather hear bad news from than him. If I had my way, of course I'd never want bad news, but when it has to come, he's the guy to hear it from. Last month when management announced that we lost our contract as an exclusive supplier to the state university system and were now going to have to bid on it, we all wanted to cut and run, because none of us thought we could compete and win. I could see the handwriting on the wall–a tighter bid, lower pricing, cutting heads, and everybody doing way more with way less–and that's if we actually got the bid. If we ended up losing, it would get even more gruesome. He came to our entire department right after the announcement and asked us to "please hang in there with us." He said, "We can get through this together, and we can figure out how to make it work. We've done it before, and we can do it again." There are some people who try that cheerleader crap and it sounds as phony as a three dollar bill, but we all knew he meant it. Two folks still bailed, but a lot more could have and didn't. The place was like a madhouse for the next week, trying to pull together a bid that made sense, that we could actually deliver without cutting way into the bones, if you get my drift. The package got couriered over about a week ago, and this morning he called us all together to give us an update. The look on his face was pretty telling. Things weren't looking good. I got a copy of his notes, and here's what he said to us: "Look, I'm not going to lie to you or try to twist this into something it's not. The director of Facility Services over at the university called us this morning to let us know she was leaning toward splitting the bids, with the greater share of the work going to Thodexo and the rest to us. She said that the university was trying to broaden its supplier base, and while it valued the longstanding relationship it had with us, a shot of fresh approaches and new blood could do it good. The university decision makers also realized the hardship the change could put on us, and subsequently the local community, if they took the entire thing away from us. They wanted to be responsible members of the community and not induce needless adversity on a local and upstanding employer. Right now, it's not clear what they mean, and they haven't made a final decision. We asked if we could come and meet with them first thing tomorrow morning, and they've agreed. Personally, I think the cost of coordination between two suppliers for them would be a nightmare. But more importantly, I honestly think we can do a better job than Thodexo. They've obviously lost confidence in us, and it will be our job to try to restore it tomorrow. That will require us to make some commitments, and likely some sacrifices, to persuade them. We know the kind of service we can provide when we're at our best, and if we're honest with ourselves, we've gotten pretty comfortable in this relationship over the years and probably haven't delivered our best. That doesn't mean we can't deliver our best going forward, if they'll give us a shot. I believe in you. And I need each of you to give some hard thought to what it will mean for us to not just win their confidence back tomorrow, but to win it back with our own version of "shock and awe" in how we actually deliver our service. Think hard about each of your areas and where you could ratchet up going the extra mile wherever possible. Think about the people you interact with directly over at the university and how you can strengthen those relationships. Whatever happens, we know how good we can be. If we are fortunate enough to get a second chance with them, we'll need every effort redoubled. If we're not fortunate enough to get a second chance, we'll still need every effort redoubled and then some, because we're going to have to get out there and win the confidence of some new customers. Either way, we know what we're made of. You know I'm not much for pep talks; that's not my thing. I'm about getting the job done, and we need to have the hope that no matter what happens tomorrow, our company is going to be okay."

Isn't that cool? I mean, I felt like I was watching an amazing motivational speaker or something. It was coming right out of his gut, and I could tell he meant it, and we all believed him. After the meeting ended, people were scrambling into huddles, generating all kinds of ideas to completely wow everyone we work with over at the university. We could have walked out with our tail between our legs, but instead we all rose to the occasion and wanted to knock the ball out of the park. Sure, I definitely hope we get the contract tomorrow, but if we don't, for some reason I'm not so worried anymore. Last week I was scared spitless–I'm not in the mood to be unemployed right now. After what I just saw in that room, we all have the faith that we could pull this off. That says a heck of a lot about us.

You in-Formation

1. When have you been inspired to hope by someone else in the face of a great challenge? What made the person's words/actions credible to you? Were you aware of choosing hope as a result of the person's influence?
2. When have you inspired someone to hope in the face of a challenging circumstance? From where did you draw the hope to do so? Are you more naturally inclined toward hope or pessimism? How can you increase your quotient of hope?

Your story from the future

Write a brief story about a member of your organization who is able to persevere through a difficult challenge because he or she uncovers untapped reserves of hope. Assume that you are the Optimist in the story.

Question 8:
How will I honor others' contributions?

Honor is the coalescing force that summons a generative future through gratefully acknowledging the sustainable contributions of others. It is a posture that implies you can't do it alone. It is motivated out of the belief that others are valuable and vital to your organization. This is different than visibility. Visibility is the ability to see others for all they are and bring. Honoring contributions is the tangible way in which we respect the value others create through their work. Both are postures that distinguish one individual's presence from another's.

Every CEO we've encountered has said that people are invaluable to their organization. However, we have come across numerous organizations where the people had no idea of the value they offered the company because no one had ever told them. In many cases those people are left to their own devices to deduce the value they offer through elusive clues and feedback-fishing expeditions. In the end, this approach to honoring people's contributions usually proves quite unproductive.

In our book *Leadership Divided*[34], we point out how peculiar it is that valuable employees are appreciated the most after they submit their resignation. These errant employees frequently find themselves showered with appreciation, and contributions that went unnoticed before are lauded as their employers attempt to win them back. Ironically, dissatisfaction with the way things are at work is one of the biggest catalysts for early departures. What if these same employees had experienced this level of gratitude before they decided to leave?

It is no surprise that companies able to retain top talent perform better than their counterparts who cannot. Michaels, Handfield-Jones, and Beth Axelrod[35] conducted surveys of 13,000 executives at more than 120 companies and discovered compelling evidence that better talent management leads to better performance. On average, companies that did a better job of attracting, developing, and retaining highly talented managers delivered 22% higher return to shareholders. The researchers concluded that "once a manager believes that talent is his or her responsibility, the other imperatives seem the logical and natural thing to do."

Gratitude is a timeless value that all reasonable people would hold as an important virtue, much like most of Emily Post's common etiquette. What most people fall short of understanding is the powerful force for change that gratitude is. Feeling thankful for opportunities we are afforded, privileges we enjoy, colleagues with whom to share workloads and learn with, resources with which to get our jobs done, and families that love us allows us to keep perspective on life when setbacks befall or unforeseen misfortune visits. Rather than feeling entitled to our better due, we can remain unencumbered by the shackles of resentment, bitterness, comparison, envy, and presumptuous prerogative that not only put others off, but also tends to spread like fungus through a community. Once people start keeping score of what they do and don't have relative to what they believe they deserve, you can bet others will follow suit. By contrast, once one person offers a sense of gratitude for the experience he or she is enjoying–even if that experience is far from perfect–you can also bet that others will rethink their positions of entitlement and resentment, more inclined to inventory the blessings for which they ought to be thankful. Once we are grateful, we are naturally provoked to be generous. Out of our deep appreciation for what we have been given, we unsurprisingly desire to give. The generative nature of gratitude becomes far reaching, as gratitude begets generosity, generosity begets gratitude, and the crescendo of giving and thanking proliferates throughout an organization.

A Grateful Host is one who intimately knows the gifted contributions of those they invite to participate in the work of advancing the community. Those who are invited to participate are aware of the ways in which their host is grateful for their contribution. Just as any gracious host makes every one of their dinner guests feel honored with hospitality that expresses a deep understanding of their uniqueness, so too does the grateful host within an organization welcome with delight and wonder the "guests" who participate in the hard work of the organization. Ingrates don't have the capacity to know the breadth of those with whom they work because they're too busy expecting everyone to thank them for the amazing and heroic contributions they've made. Ingrates dishonor the work of others through the obtuse and self-centered way they move about life. Unable to believe that anything good in the community could happen apart from them, they see the contributions of others only as a tool to bolster their own agenda. Ingratitude begets ingratitude as the inability to genuinely receive the contributions of others de-escalates into a tit-for-tat exchange of contempt. A Grateful Host honors the sacrificial and important contributions of others by constantly letting them know through words and actions how much they matter.

Plot yourself, and your organization, on this continuum at the point you feel honestly reflects your current degree of generative/degenerative posture.

Ingrate   Grateful Host

Your colleague's experience with an Ingrate

Fine. So I'm a cry baby. Do you feel better now? I admitted it. But how would you feel if he'd done it to you? I doubt you'd feel much different. To be honest, nobody should be treated that way. I wouldn't want my worst enemy to feel the way he made me feel. "Don't take it so personally," he says. "What are you crying about?" My work *is* personal to me. And he should be glad it is. I'm not like one of his other pawns that just salutes and does what he's told. I actually *think* for myself. And he ought to be damn glad I do. I've saved his butt more times than I care to count. This time he's crossed the line with me. I've spent six months building the curriculum for the marketing certification process, his pipedream that we meet world-class manufacturing benchmarked standards. He knows I've done this work on top of everything else I'm doing. It's not like I got excused from the rest of my job. It was just additive. So today I present the final design and rollout strategy to his senior team to get the final nod to move forward. This thing is buttoned up as tight as can be. Completely turnkey. I was up until two this morning getting ready for this. I wanted to make sure he knew how seriously I took the project. I'd given him updates along the way, but he had not seen any of the content. Just for the heck of it, to get his organization some props, I submitted a write-up to *Chief Marketing Officer* magazine, and a reporter came and wrote a featured Best Practice article on it. I had preview copies of the article that will be out in next month's edition attached to the packages today. I was really proud of that. What does he do? Throughout the entire presentation this morning, he was going through his mail! He didn't look up once. Everyone else was engaged, asking questions, and clearly impressed with the work. He was totally checked out. I think okay, maybe he had some really bad thing happen, so he was just distracted. I mean, he can be a jerk sometimes, but even this seemed unusually obtuse for him. At the end of the meeting, he glanced up and had the nerve to say, "Yeah, nice work. I'm wondering. Is there some reason you're a month behind the original date you committed to?" I was flabbergasted. When the room cleared out, he lingered, so I thought, okay, now he's going to thank me privately. Wrong again! He said, "You know, when I give people high-visibility development assignments, I expect them to hit their deadlines. I'm disappointed that we're a month off the mark. I'll let you know what the exec team says after I present it to them." As if it couldn't get worse, I heard this morning that he presented the entire package to the senior team and not *once* did he mention my name! Can you friggin' believe that? He acted as though it was all his work, his ideas, his design. And the team response? I heard the CEO said it was one of the most brilliant pieces of work the marketing group had ever produced. He got lots of handshakes, high-fives, and congratulations from them all. And I got crapped on. The first thing I did this morning after I heard what happened was call a headhunter. I am so done with him and this lousy job.

You in-Formation

1. When have you experienced the ingratitude of a leader whose appreciation and respect was very important to you? How did it make you feel? What impact did it have on your relationship? Your commitment? The longer term results you were pursuing?
2. When have you demonstrated a lack of appropriate gratitude to someone you lead or work with? What caused you to miss the opportunity to be grateful? How did it make you feel when you realized it? How do you imagine it made the other person feel? In hindsight, what impact do you see your absence of gratitude having on that person and the person's work?

Your colleague's experience with a Grateful Host

I'm sorry, did you say something? Didn't hear you. My bad. I guess I was zoned out. Why am I smiling? Oh, well I was just thinking about a conversation I had last night and remembering how good it made me feel. I guess that's where my mind had drifted when you walked in. Did you ever work with someone who had an uncanny way of making you feel like a million bucks? Like you could do no wrong? Like what you did really mattered? I know there doesn't seem to be too many of those types, but whenever you come across one, it's sure not something you forget anytime soon. I gotta tell you, I could go a long way on the steam of a conversation like that one, believe me. You know how hard my team has been working on this corporate social responsibility effort in the wake of shutting down the two plant facilities in the Midwest so we could consolidate those operations, right? At first no one wanted to take it on because it just felt like corporate dirty work that no one else wanted to do, so we got asked as the "team of last resort." We've gotten dinged on some of our labor practices in those congressional districts, and it's caused some political heat in DC with some lobbyists. In addition, we're trying to figure out how to create some good will in those communities and make sure that we've done all we can in terms of transition support for those displaced as well as for the local economies. Why the heck HR couldn't do all of this is beyond me. I thought that was its job. Anyway, the more we got engaged in the process, the more we visited those towns and got to know the employees and their families, the more it got under our skin. It became personal to us. We just couldn't help it. We really got invested in doing as much as we could for those communities. Some of those folks had worked for us for more than thirty years. That's a lot of loyalty. The amazing thing is that for as angry as they could have been, most of them seemed to understand why we were having to do it. We'd done a lot of work on the front end with long communication lead times so that no one was caught off guard, but now, in the wake of preparing to shut down, my team took this on as our personal cause to make sure every one of those employees had a personal transition plan. We've worked nights and weekends for months, not because we ever wanted any kind of special recognition or applause. We just cared about them. We wrapped up the work last week and said good-bye to all the folks we'd worked with. One of the plants threw a huge barbeque to thank us for our dedication and time. You know, we never felt like we were just doing something for them. For all of my team, it really became a privilege. This morning I got an e-mail from the CEO's assistant that says he wanted to see me whenever I have the time. Well, of course I had the time. I was nervous at first, thinking "Oh crap, what went wrong out there?" I walked into his office and we shook hands. We'd met once, and I was surprised he remembered the conversation. We sat over in the little sitting area, and he had a file with him. He told me that while he knew that my team was working with the two communities on transition support, he had absolutely no idea the extent to which we were doing it. He said, "I got this stack of letters earlier in the week, and normally this stuff wouldn't reach my desk, but I'm glad these did." He handed me a second file and told me that in it were copies of the letters. "These are letters from the two communities to me about what your team's support meant to them." He pulled one out and said, "You need to read them all and read them slowly. They will unquestionably change your life. But I want to read this one out loud to you. It changed mine."

He read the letter out loud. In the middle of it, he got kind of choked up. I couldn't believe it. I didn't know what to be more awed by, his reaction to the letter or the words in it. They both undid me. The level of gratitude expressed in the letter–and all of the letters–was something I'd never experienced before. After he composed himself, he looked up and said, "I'm not a grateful enough man. From where I sit, most of our employees are nameless and faceless except for those I occasionally get to chat with in the halls or when I visit our sites. Their letters made these people real to me, and I realized that my gratitude for them was deeper than I ever thought, and more unexpressed than I can excuse. I'm flying out Monday to visit both of these communities personally to let them know how thankful I am for all they gave to our organization. I wanted you to know directly from me that because of your sacrifice and devotion to our organization, to our reputation in these communities, and most importantly, to the well-being of these people and their families' future, I know I will be a more thankful man. I know my just saying it doesn't even come close to the level of gratitude you and your team deserve for all you did, and frankly, most of us will never know. Just the same, your story needs to be told and honored. Next month is our annual shareholder's gala after the annual meeting. We had some guru author coming to speak. I've canceled him. If you'd be willing, I'd like you and your team to come and tell your story to our entire community of shareholders and leaders. I'd like to honor your team in their presence for what you did. It's truly exemplary, and if more of us were as dedicated as you and your team, and I hope more become as grateful as I feel, then it will make an impact far greater than anything else I can think of." He reached over, shook my hand, and gave me a big bear hug. He looked at me–almost through me–and said, "Thanks. Will you join us next month?" No one has ever thanked me like that before. I mean, in a way that I understood what I did mattered a lot to them. I never knew that being thanked for something I thought was no big deal could be such a big deal. Now I'm glad I know. I realized that throughout the entire process, I never said thank you to my team for the sacrifices they were making to do the work. Because it didn't seem like a big deal to me, I made the unfortunate assumption that it wasn't to them. Before we can tell our story in public, I need to make that right and let them know that I am thankful. Gotta go. I have some phone calls to make.

You in-Formation

1. When have you had an experience of another's gratitude that was expressed in a special way? How did it make you feel? What was the lasting impact?
2. When have you expressed your gratitude to someone in a way you knew left a lasting impression on the person? How did it make you feel? What difference did you see it make for the person? What indicated that your gratitude made a difference?

Your story from the future

Write a brief story about a member of your organization who experiences gratitude in a way that alters the person's understanding of the importance of his or her contribution and participation in the organization. Assume that you are the Grateful Host in the story.

Question 9:
How will I hold others to account for their commitments?

Accountability is the coalescing force that summons a generative future by *calling people to account* in a way that allows them to take deeper responsibility and ownership for the choices and commitments they make. Accountability is generative when it is mutual and collaborative, and the devices in which it manifests itself–like HR systems–are adjudicated with reciprocal participation.

Accountability can become a generative process by assuming the posture of a Sage. A Sage knows the way forward but doesn't necessarily tell companions where to walk or how to get there. Rather, a Sage watches and learns how those they are leading learn and develop. A Sage holds those they lead accountable by creating an accountability structure that is intimately connected with the person being held accountable. It may be that the people they are journeying with need decisive direction and a Sage knows both how and when to deliver a decisive message; however, a Sage is also aware of the people on the journey who learn better when they are given the freedom to try new things and learn from their mistakes. When tried-and-true ways of learning cease to be effective, the Sage knows how to invite others to new ways of development. A Sage is always concerned with the growth and development of people and is careful not to impose structures that replicate only what has worked for the Sage. As such, the Sage invites a natural trustworthiness that makes it easier for them to confront performance shortfalls and name skill deficits. Further this natural trust creates more receptivity on the part of the receiver to hear the Sage's insight. For the Auditor, the fear of confrontation or desire to correct make such interventions either too difficult or indulgently enjoyable.

For a Sage, accountability is less about fixing what is wrong and more a means of unleashing the characteristics and qualities that lay dormant in that individual or group. A Sage uses accountability not as a device to clone or correct, but rather as a device to help shape that person in his or her own right.

What does it mean to shape people in their own right? We typically don't think of people needing to be developed or held accountable as having *their own right*. Why is that? Because the underlying assumption is that if they knew what was right for them, they wouldn't be in the place of needing to be developed or held accountable. More often than not, people–even inexperienced employees–do in fact know what they need to change and how they need to grow, and they desperately want to.

Developing people *in their own right* means starting with the assumption that the one being held to account knows what they need. This may sound a bit counterintuitive, and it is. For many years, developing others, holding them to account through correction, has meant replicating oneself in another. It has meant taking all I have known and learned and replanting it in the one "less experienced," who, if more like me, would obviously perform better. While well intended, it is arrogant and harmful. And here's what allows it to happen: inexperienced employees "being developed" or "mentored" can often have a very limited understanding of who they are, and because of their limited sense of themselves, they are more naturally willing to soak up anything offered to them. In essence, they are willing to become anything at the expense of finding themselves. Understandable, but dangerous. The leader "developing" and "holding to account" misguidedly sees this eagerness as a good thing, thinking, "Oh, I have so much to offer them, and they are eager to learn what I am offering." The ego surge that results perpetuates the "accountability as correction and cloning" mentality so rife in today's organizations and increasingly resisted and resented by emerging leaders.

Here's the problem: cloning depletes our organizations of the very uniqueness that sustains and develops them. Most leaders tout a belief in the importance of diversity and celebrating differences. No one would dare admit he or she wants an organization of "people like me" despite so many hiring and promotion practices clearly showing that leaders are inclined to hire and promote "in their own image." To avoid the danger of this, people must be developed in their own right. Doing so will unleash the uniqueness of everyone you work with and not replicate your own uniqueness in them. Why? Because once replicated, it's no longer unique. You just manufacture cheap knockoffs of yourself, then spend your days auditing them for "compliance" with you. Accountability is no longer about helping others rise to greater levels of their own performance, but rather policing their ability to "do it the way you would." Accountability will stop being a dirty word once it stops being about compliance inspection and starts being about helping others stretch to the limits of their own capability. Your work is to learn how others desire to be shaped and stretched and meet them there.

Unfortunately, the moment you say "accountability," you suggest audit, consequence, and control. The Auditor digs down into everything people have done and seeks to reconcile every action with an outcome. An Auditor digs into every transaction and reminds others he has the power to levy penalties. The irony is that auditing seldom promotes accountability. It becomes micromanagement, retarding growth in the organization and promoting low morale, high turnover, instability, and inefficiency. Chambers[36] observes that whole organizations may develop a culture of micromanagement, typically establishing it at the top of the organization and hiring managers in a manner that perpetuates the problem. A pervasive environment of inspection permeates the community, contributing to significant direct, indirect, and hidden costs. Despite these costs, people throughout the organizational food chain eagerly try to outdo each other in mimicking the top leadership's audit and micromanagement behaviors. As Chambers says, "Everybody wants to be like the boss, and they quickly learn to develop the behaviors they need to get ahead."

Curiously, the Auditor and the Sage both seek to hold people accountable for their commitments, but the Auditor is spectacularly unsuccessful, while the Sage is quietly effective. It comes down to *how* you call people to account and whether you have the wisdom to deliver the right messages as opposed to merely inspecting and correcting.

The Sage invites others to learn to enjoy continuous improvement and the experience of pursuing greater levels of performance without the fear of blaming correction or of punishing scorn when a mistake is made. The intimidation inflicted by the Auditor paradoxically leads to more mistakes and eroded performance. The invitation of the Sage to courageously face shortfalls ends up leading entire communities to higher levels of performance because they can do so free of the anxiety that comes from simply avoiding failure. Auditors inspect people right down to their lowest possible levels of capability. Sages challenge others to reach their highest levels of capability by unleashing them to take responsibility *in their own right* for the commitments they make and then decide how best to keep them. The Auditor's process of inspection suffocates performance by homogenizing people. The Sage's process of invitation fashions performance by allowing people to distinguish themselves.

Plot yourself, and your organization, on this continuum at the point you feel honestly reflects your current degree of generative/degenerative posture.

← ——→

Auditor   Sage

Your colleague's experience with an Auditor

I'm sure you've been where I am right now: Deep regret. You've felt the frustration and anger and have beaten yourself up when, at some point in your life, you bought something that you instinctively knew wasn't right. In fact, they call it, Buyer's Remorse. It might have been a car, a house, or some other big purchase. In my case, it was this cruddy job! Wasn't I told what the job was? Oh, sure, the job as it was laid out to me four months ago is still mostly accurate—well, on paper, anyway. Actually, the big regret turns out to be my new boss, VP Organization Development Larry. After all the questions posed through the interview process, I thought the opportunity to contribute and grow seemed terrific, but there was still a nagging feeling in my gut that said, "Run!" But with the appeal of building and leading a new development group and also moving closer to family, I didn't listen.

I am supposed to be responsible for heading up the management and leadership development effort for a much larger, more complex and growing packaged goods business that recently changed its competitive position in the market. That's what I was told, at least. "With your track record and accomplishments, you'll be great here," they touted, making me feel as though they thought I was a real catch. Sure, my ego felt stroked. We all want to be wanted, right? I really felt my experience was solid and had prepared me well for this next step in my career. I was eager to learn, grow, and contribute.

My first clue should have been the endless hours my boss spent in my office during the first few months—late evenings and even a few weekends. Always one to assume positive intent, I believed it was his way for us to get to know each other and jointly develop our approach. Now I recognize that his hovering is really the norm rather than him trusting me to do the job and tap into my well of experience. He called it "collaboration." What initially seemed like an opportunity to test and develop my own skills has turned out to a stifling life under a microscope. Looking back I can see that even when he asks for my opinion, he isn't really interested. He only looks for validation of what he's already thinking. I'm value added only to the degree I support his approach. When I offer contradictory input, I'm usually dismissed by telling me that I don't yet "understand the way things work around here" and that "the idea would never fly with these executives," even though Larry's been here only six months longer than me. Whenever I give him my work to "look over," it comes back all marked up in red, or with extensive use of the Track Changes feature. I used to look forward to the input of colleagues on my work to make it even better. Now I just flinch. I can't recall one time where he's actually complimented a piece of my work or even indicated that something I'd done was good I remember feeling this insecure when I was a beginner, but I never imagined feeling this way at this point in my career. I now fight a constant internal battle to remind myself that I do know what I'm doing despite how incompetent he makes me feel.

Last week was the final blow. I spent another late Friday night and early Saturday redoing the Power Point presentation for the executive committee with my boss literally looking over my shoulder and scrutinizing every key stroke—art directing *and* editing content. With every comment, my blood boiled. "Make that line fly in." "Use a better photo for that graphic." "We need more detail." "They wouldn't buy that." "Well, in our culture, spelling things out is critical." It was insufferable, I'm telling you. I had deep reservations about the end result and felt helpless to influence the outcome. On Tuesday afternoon my boss presented it to the executive committee. I originally assumed that I would present but was informed that the SVP of Human Resources preferred to minimize the number of "underlings" in the room, especially for projects where significant capital allocation discussions were on the table. After all, we wouldn't want peons like me with nearly twenty years experience to hear about any of the really important projects. That's only for the *smart* people in the company, right? And we know how uncomfortable we commoners can make the royalty feel. So late Tuesday night, I got an urgent voice mail message– well, actually two messages, because the first one used up all the record time—from Larry telling me that we had plenty of work to do on the proposal following the meeting and he wanted to see me early Wednesday morning. He rattled off a really long list of issues the exec team had with the proposal, some of which I actually concurred with but never had the opportunity to voice. On my way in I stopped for coffee and ran into the SVP of HR in the cafeteria. He confirmed that the presentation and discussion didn't go as he had envisioned and that there was still a lot of work left to do to design an approach the executive team would invest in. "I understand you've been here only a short time, but I would have expected to see more thorough work based on the experience you shared with me during our interview. Larry did a good job covering for you, and he personally committed to working with you more closely to get this into shape so I can look at it next week. There is a lot to learn about working here, so don't hesitate to ask Larry for insight." Then the real kicker: "And don't get too caught up in the Power Point slides; we're trying to simplify around here…less about form and more about content next time!"

No big mystery why turnover on this team has been so high.

You in-Formation

1. What experience have you had being audited? How did a perpetual feeling of "inspection" impact your work and confidence level?" What happened to your relationship with the Auditor?
2. When have you struggled to trust the work of others? How have you managed your needs to have things be a certain way? When have you caused someone to feel "audited?" What would you do differently in hindsight?

Your colleague's experience with a Sage

Stranger things have happened, I'm sure, but not in my career. Today I was offered a job and promotion by someone who just three short years ago asked for my head on a platter and then asked to have me fired!

I had been in the organization only a few years when I made a terrible mistake. Business was tough, the executives were nervous, and the marketing group was feeling a lot of pressure to perform. It isn't an excuse, but the reality was that key dates were missed early in the project by others, which put the whole project behind. I had been working long hours for several weeks to get all of the promotional materials finalized for the critical Back-to-School season. When one of the final proofs came back with a slight error that fell outside brand guidelines, I felt panicked, and in that rush to hit a ship deadline I approved it for final runs, not realizing that the error also violated a branded licensing agreement with our partner. You can imagine how sick I felt several days later when the error was discovered. I walked to my cubical early that morning and could hear raised voices in my boss's office. I could see only the back of the head of my boss's superior through the doorway, but his raised voice was clear: "A one-hundred-twenty-thousand-dollar mistake, and you want me to just let it go? She should be fired!" Instinctively I knew they were talking about me. I felt sick and looked around for the closest escape, but my legs felt shaky and all I could do was sink into my chair.

The next thing I remember was hearing my boss's voice over the top of the cubicle. In a firm voice he invited me to join him in his office. I followed and closed the door. He sat down in a chair next to me and began. He didn't have to say anything; I knew what I had done, and I knew it would have an impact on our financial results. I wanted the meeting to be over. I'd have gladly put my head on a platter to speed things up so I could quickly go to my desk, pack up my things, and leave.

He started in a calm voice by explaining some of what I already knew. I had never known my boss to be a screamer, and he didn't disappoint me. He was deliberate and measured, and when I finally had enough courage to look him in the eye, he assured me that the 120-thousand-dollar education I had just received was not going to benefit a competitor's organization. "No," he said, "You'll be here with us for as long as I have any influence over it."

My emotional tension suddenly made a U-turn. I was confused.

"Your lapse in judgment was clear and it has cost us in time, money, and maybe reputation." He didn't dismiss the impact of my mistake, and I felt its weight on my shoulders. I asked him why he didn't fire me. He certainly had every good reason. "If this were only about the immediate cost of the mistake, I should have, but this is far more about developing employees who can run this company profitably long after I'm gone. Sure, Jack told me I should fire you, but he knows how I feel, and I also know he will respect my decision. And I think, inside, he knows he's just angry right now and likely just wrong. Anyone can coach an employee when things are going well. But we all know some of our greatest learning comes when we fail. The worst failure is not to learn from it. My role isn't to make you feel more shame than you've made yourself feel. My role is to make sure the experience contributes to your becoming a stronger and more capable leader. And if you aren't here, I can't do that.

Let me tell you a story," he began.

I listened as he told me about how, when he was younger, he had earned money by mowing lawns in his neighborhood. Early in his experience his father would go with him and watch to make sure that things were done right and that the customers were getting their money's worth. He mowed the lawn of a particularly fastidious and stern widow who was also a prize-winning gardener whose yard was decorated with beautiful shrubs and flowers. One evening while mowing he was distracted and let the mower get away from him. In his attempt to get the mower back under control he cut into two of her shrubs at the front of the lawn. Immediately the widow came out the front door, scolding him as she hurried to survey the damage. He said he felt something like he imagined I was feeling. His father was close by and came over to intervene.

Turning her attention away from him, the widow began telling his father what a bad son he had and how severely he should be punished. His father calmly expressed regret for what had happened. Then, to address her suggestions for punishment, he said something my boss had never forgotten, "Madam, if this were only about mowing your lawn, I might act on your suggestions, but my goal is to raise this boy into a responsible man." He was fired from the job, and he did spend the next several weeks earning money to replace the shrubs.

That experience shaped my boss's philosophy and, in turn, he has had a profound impact on mine. Just like he replaced the shrubs, there were also commensurate consequences for my lapse in judgment. My year-end review certainly reflected some of that experience. However, I was grateful that over these past few years I've also benefited from a clearly targeted development plan and direct coaching from this man I've come to more deeply respect and admire. I appreciate that he sees within me something more than I often see in myself. He never backed off on the amount of responsibility or authority he gave me, but he has been vigilant to follow up and support me through the questions he asks and the guidance he provides. Honestly, if not for that experience, I'm not sure if this new opportunity would have happened. So imagine my shock when my boss told me Jack wanted to see me in his office right away. I could feel the knot in my stomach forming, remembering the sound of his shrill voice just three years ago. To my shock, he made me the offer for this new role. While he didn't come right out and admit it, he certainly hinted about that experience being a turning point, and as much as his pride would let him, he was glad that I was still here and that his impulse to fire me didn't prevail. So, here I sit, promoted by and soon to report to the man who asked for my head on a platter. Strange!

You in-Formation

1. What experience do you have with being held to account for results that didn't go as you'd hoped or expected, in which your leader focused more on your learning than on blame? What was that like? What were the lasting effects? What experience do you have with being held to account for results that exceeded expectations? What were the lasting effects?
2. When have you held people to account for their commitments where the results fell short of what you'd hoped for? How did you prepare for that conversation? In hindsight, would you have done anything differently?

Your story from the future

Write a brief story about a member or members of your organization who experience being held to account for a commitment in a way that bolsters their capability and confidence and disconfirms their cynical beliefs about what accountability is really meant to accomplish organizationally and relationally. Assume that you are the Sage in the story.

Question 10:
How will I remain humble?

Humility is the force that summons a generative future by inviting and allowing space for *other* people in the specified process and/or work to be accomplished. That means that people with fewer credentials or less experience are invited to the table to express a point of view because the more in-formation we can get it the room, the better information we'll have to make decisions on our desired way forward. It means that those involved are open to being swayed and converted to a point of view that differs from the one they hold. Humility, in this context, is about shaping relationships in which people are eager to have others mark their thoughts and behavior with input they would otherwise not consider on their own.

Often the hardest and most painful experiences are what move us to a posture of humility. "We had no idea how hard the analysts were going to come down on us." "We thought we were launching the product of all products...until our competitor launched one that was better." In most cases it is the arrogance of acting in a vacuum that sends individuals and organizations into a freefall off of perches of success. One of the ways to safeguard against such a fall is to take the posture of a continual learner. Apprentices know they don't know it all, and they don't believe they have to know it all, but they are motivated to learn no matter how intelligent they are. They are willing to pursue the expertise and wisdom of others from all sorts of places and have a hand-picked and well cultivated set of relationships from which to solicit help.

Collins[37] cites the example of Ken Iverson of US steel producer Nucor. When Japanese steelmakers penetrated the US steel market in the 1960s, American producers suffered severe losses. The CEO of Bethlehem Steel blamed the Japanese, but Iverson believed that the reason US steel producers were losing so much ground had to do with their own management practices. Iverson vigorously advocated a lean management staff, decentralized decision-making structure, and egalitarian work environment. At Nucor, he brought the number of levels of management down to four. A janitor was literally four promotions away from the CEO's job. Iverson was definitely humble. He answered his own phone whenever he was in the corporate office, and he reduced his own staff to a mere twenty-two, despite the fact that he was running a multibillion-dollar business. Iverson was credited with turning Nucor around from near bankruptcy into the largest and most profitable US steelmaker. His management philosophy has been used with profit by companies all over the world. A key to Iverson's success was the humility to admit things were wrong and then do something about it. This is a rare admission in

108

today's business environment, but it is also a potent one.

Apprentices remain curious and malleable to learning. No different than medieval guilds where young people sought relationships with master craftsmen to develop their skills, Apprentices today, regardless of age and experience, seek out others from whom they can gain new ideas and expertise. Know-it-alls find no reason to be curious, because for them, nothing is new. One of the saddest consequences of corporate America's career ladder is that we've reinforced the notion that conferring upon people a new place on the hierarchy also confers upon them greater wisdom. So leaders climbing that ladder feel compelled to make it look like they have greater wisdom, whether they do or not. Know-it-alls use relationship in a utilitarian way, to get others to ratify and endorse their preexisting ideas. Humble leaders know that the higher up they rise in an organization, the *less* they know. And they aren't ashamed to let their ignorance show. They are free to be confident in what they do know and curious about learning what they don't. Apprentices build relationships for the sheer delight of mutual learning and invite that same posture from others, generating humility beyond themselves by allowing room for others to learn with them.

$$\longleftarrow \qquad\qquad\qquad\qquad\qquad\qquad\qquad\qquad\qquad\qquad \longrightarrow$$

Know-it-all   Apprentice

Your colleague's experience with a Know-it-all

Have you ever been in one of those meetings where your input is requested but not really wanted? I was in one the other day. Actually, it happens all the time! Our SVP, Bill, has been around for ages. Literally ages. He started in the storeroom and has gradually worked his way up over the past four decades. He's bright and very gifted at what he does, but sometimes I get the feeling that it wouldn't really matter if I were in the room or not. He's not overtly impolite; he just doesn't seem to be aware that other minds and hearts are engaged besides his own, so sometimes I just check out, give the appropriate head nods at the right time, and go about my business.

Six months ago Bill asked me to lead a transition team chartered to determine the best place for us to open up a new plant. He said, "I think you're perfect for this! You know how to get the information we need to make the best decision. And, on top of that, you have great relationships with our best up and comers. I think this would give you some of the visibility you've been looking for." He went on to tell me I could pick my own team and that he would support my decisions along the way. He said he was, "Giving me free reign to run this team the way I saw fit." The follow-up caveat should have clued me in to what lay ahead, but to be honest, the assignment sounded like a dream come true, so I didn't think much of it. "You'll want to be checking in with me along the way, of course. The more informed I am, the more supportive I can be."

I had been waiting for an opportunity to take on a bit more responsibility and was excited for a chance to shine, so I heard the "more supportive I can be" part more than the "checking in with me along the way" part. What I hadn't bargained for was exactly what that meant. It became the excruciatingly painful task of learning how to *strategically communicate* our learning back to Bill in a way that confirmed what he already knew.

As the process began, Bill and I met regularly, and I was glad to have his input. I'd never done something like this before, so I found his guidance helpful. He had ideas about everything from meeting agenda formats, research methodologies, team startup, and legal and federal complexities, all the way to how to organize my slide presentations, what size and color fonts to use, and what to serve the team for lunch. "Order individually wrapped sandwiches. You'll find those easier for a working lunch than salads." At first his vast knowledge was impressive and he seemed generous in how liberally he shared it., but the more confident I became, the less I needed to rely on him. And that's where things started to get uncomfortable. He would mysteriously show up in meetings to "just check in and say hi" to the team, and casually drop comments to me in front of the team like, "Oh, I see you are using McWrath's online research tool. Hmm. That's surprising. I would have thought you'd have used Hoover's. It has so much more depth when it comes to the Pacific Rim. Oh well. I'm sure you know what you're doing." He'd leave with a perplexed look on his face and a lingering awkwardness hovering in the room behind him. One time he came in and we were eating pizza for lunch and taking a break. He slipped an envelope to me that I didn't read until after the meeting. Inside it were coupons for the local Quiznos sandwich shop, a Post-It note with the phone number, and a note that said, "For your next meeting in case you want to serve sandwiches so you can work through lunch." While the event felt a bit irritating, I still wasn't getting the hints.

I really started to catch on four months into the process when Bill started pulling me into some of the executive team meetings that addressed potential new plant sites. Apparently they had been talking about the subject for the past couple of years. Turned out it was not as new a conversation as I thought it was. They talked a lot about opening a plant in China and were excited about the possibilities of starting a joint venture with another company there. They seemed to be more excited about the joint venture than they did about finding a sustainable location for a plant. I remember feeling a bit deflated leaving that meeting. I began to sense our transition team's work really mattered less than I originally believed it did. Each time I tried to advocate for the great work the team was doing, I was met with dismissal and disregard. Up until that point, our team had been focusing much of its efforts on looking into the area just south across the border of McAllen, Texas.

Later that week, Bill shot me an e-mail and said he wanted to meet and talk specifically about some of the work the transition team was working on. I was excited to get some feedback from him, and I knew that earlier in the week he had met with Andrea and Michael from the team, who had played key roles in the research that discovered key benefits of opening a plant in Monterey, Mexico. I thought maybe they had talked to him about it and that Bill was excited to follow up with me. Again, my naiveté got the better of me. Despite feeling a tad suspicious, I still thought maybe he would be eager to hear our ideas. What he told me quite clearly was that the new plant needed to be in China and that my report needed to show that. He condescendingly said, "Your enthusiasm for Mexico is all well and good, and your research is obviously well informed, but now, about China…"

I was just pissed, so I asked him, "Why did you have me waste all my time for the last four months on this charade instead of just telling me to figure out how to open a plant in China?"

His response floored me. He said, "Well, I thought you'd have been smart enough to figure out that's where the best location for us would be. I didn't think I needed to spell it out for you. I guess I expected too much. You're just going to have to trust me on this one. I know better." At this point, I was eyeing the stapler on his desk as a good choice of something to throw at him.

That was two months ago. It's now nine o'clock on a Friday night and my team is scrambling to get all the last-minute preparations finished to present at our quarterly offsite that starts tomorrow morning. The transition team is number three of eight presentations scheduled for Saturday. We've made the case for China that he asked us to, but no matter how we do the math, it is more costly than Monterey. The national incentives for our line of business just aren't as strong in China, so we're going to present all of the data even though the final recommendation will be as Bill directed, China. In fact, the words "Bill's guidance has helped" and "As Bill instructed us," and "Bill has been instrumental in…" will be all through the presentation. If and when this thing blows up, I want to have been very clear with the leadership team who the brilliant mastermind was behind it. I don't want my name anywhere near it.

You in-Formation

1. What experience have you had working with a *Know-it-all*? What effect has that had on you? On the team? How did you respond? If you could do it over again, what would you change about your response?
2. When do you feel pressure to be a *Know-it-all*? What effect has that had on your working relationships? On your business? When is your expertise and knowledge most helpful? When is it unhelpful?

Your colleague's experience with an Apprentice

Leaders are fascinating to watch as they break in to new jobs, aren't they? Paula had recently been promoted to VP of Sales and Marketing from her previous director role in product development. As is usually the case, our two groups had been having a hard time working together, and sales numbers were down. Our division head thought that putting her into this role might help build a bridge and get underneath whatever was causing the struggle between us and the resulting downturn. Within the first two months of moving into her new role, Paula had met with all twelve of her direct reports twice, and somehow managed to sit in on four team meetings of groups launching new products within the next eight months. On top of that, she was able to continue working on all of her other assignments.

I couldn't believe she was able to do so much. I started to worry that she was spending so much time meeting with people that she was either hiding what she wasn't getting done, or working literally 24/7. I've been working in Sales and Marketing for the past six years and was pretty close to our previous VP. He never made time to meet with any of us. I remember a conversation I had with him just before his departure. He talked about not being able to keep up with all his responsibilities and that he was responsible for more work than any one person could handle. I totally understood why he couldn't meet with all of us regularly. Although it was difficult on us, we cut him the slack because of how insanely busy he always seemed to be. It made Paula's ability to meet with so many people so often even more strange.

I bumped into Paula when I was headed to a team meeting. She was headed in the same direction, so we got to walk and talk for a bit. "Hey, how's it going? Are you headed to the V4s3 team meeting? I hear you guys are doing awesome things over there."

A little surprised that she knew where I was headed and that she'd heard about the progress of our team, I responded, "Uh, yeah I am, actually." To be honest I felt a little guarded and wasn't sure how much to tell her. Was she checking up on me? Had I done something wrong? I quickly changed the subject. "So, how's the daily grind in your new position? You sure seem to be making the rounds with everyone. How do you do it? I can barely keep up with my own commitments let alone learn about everyone else's!"

She didn't blink or hesitate. "Well, in my last role I wasn't able to get the information I needed to make the best decisions, and it really made things much harder. Sure, I got the results, but I never saw at what cost. The constant conflicts among the product development teams and with Sales and Marketing just made for too much stress. The other thing I learned was that even when I did have good information, I didn't have the relationships I needed to actually do anything with it, so I was always working solo, which only perpetuated the very problems I was trying to solve. Before this opportunity was offered, I had begun to work on building relationships among my product teams and was seeing change faster than I'd expected. It was hard for me to leave just when I was seeing hope for change, so when I took this new role a few months ago, I made two commitments that ground everything I do. First, I assumed that I knew very little and that I had a lot to learn. Secondly, I decided that the best way to start learning was by building deep relationships with the people I am leading. I am committed to being curious about more than just results. I want to know what gets our people out of bed in the morning and what keeps them up at night. I don't know if you've heard yet or not, but I've decided to have an outside firm come in and take a look under our hood to help us learn more about what's working and where we're struggling. I think we have a lot to learn about ourselves, and I am convinced a formalized process will help us see some of our blind spots. In fact, I'd love it if you could be a part of the interviews and share your thoughts and concerns in the report. You'd even have a chance to give me personal feedback about how you think I'm doing. Would you be open to participating in something like that?"

Astonished, I responded, "I don't think anyone in leadership has ever asked for my opinion. I really appreciate that. Can I actually be honest?"

She laughed. "The truth is going to be the best thing for us. Honestly, we have a lot to learn from each other, and this is going to be a great start to that actually happening."

We said our goodbyes and I turned the corner to meet up with my team. I felt a foot taller as I headed into my meeting, and I felt a new sense of pride in the work I was doing. I couldn't believe someone in leadership was actually admitting she didn't know everything. Not only that, she was going around looking to dig up stuff just to find out how much she didn't know. What's up with that? I was oddly excited to be interviewed and wondered how I might respond if someone asked me how things were going in Sales and Marketing, and then it hit me. Maybe that would be a great question to start our meeting off with. Heck, if Paula can do it, why shouldn't I?

Everyone arrived and was seated. All eyes were on me. "I want to start off a little differently than we normally do. I want to begin with a question, and I want each of us to go around and answer it. Here's the question. In the last three to six months, what have you learned working on this team? And if you could change anything about the way we are working, what would it be, and why?"

You in-Formation

1. What experience do you have working with a leader or a peer who may not have all the answers? What are your assumptions about people who admit ignorance? Even if you don't express it outwardly, what thoughts and beliefs do you have about them when they don't know? Why?
2. How do you think about and approach your own humility? Are there any areas in your life where you could become more of an Apprentice? What will it cost you to make that shift? Who will you need to ask for help?

Your story from the future

Write a brief story about a member of your organization who experiences being an Apprentice in a way that strengthens his or her, and others, openness to learning. Assume that your Apprentice behavior motivated theirs.

Figure 2.0 summarizes the ten postures and their generative and degenerative forms. Use this as a quick reference guide and a discussion tool when seeking ways to bring about greater generativity.

	Degenerative ←	*Meta-Posture*	Generative →
1	**Terrorist:** People choose to become a Terrorist when they believe *forcing the hand* of others through fear is their only option. The choice to use fear and control to manipulate a situation for one's own agenda ultimately moves individuals and organizations in a downward, degenerative spiral.	**What will I choose to believe?** Belief is the coalescing force that summons people to action and allows them the freedom to act on the possibility they envision. Generative belief is choosing to trust in what's possible.	**Liberator:** People choose to become a Liberator when they believe in and invite the possibility others offer. The choice to use power and control on behalf of others instead of over them ultimately moves individuals and organ-izations in an upward, generative spiral.
2	**Arsonist:** People choose to become an Arsonist when getting themselves noticed at the expense of others fulfills their quest for visibility. The choice to create crises in an attempt to be watched ultimately moves individuals and organizations in a downward, degenerative spiral.	**How will I choose to be visible?** Visibility is the coalescing force that summons a generative future by enabling people to be the distinct and unique individuals that they are. Generative visibility is allowing others to be seen side by side with yourself.	**Orchestra Conductor:** People choose to become an Orchestra Conductor when helping others be seen fulfills their individual quest for visibility. The choice to diffuse individual crises and be seen as a member of the "symphony" moves individuals and organizations in an upward, generative spiral.
3	**Activity Addict:** People choose to become an Activity Addict when they pursue mindlessly repetitive activity in pursuit of illusory results. The choice to feel important by feeling busy ultimately moves individuals	**What will determine my actions?** Action is the coalescing force that summons a generative future by creating forward motion toward an intended	**Reflector:** People choose to become a Reflector when their pursuit of results is grounded in thoughtfulness. The choice to *go slow to go fast* moves indi-

115

	Meta-Posture		
	Degenerative		*Generative*
	and organizations in a downward, degenerative spiral.	outcome. Generative action builds on existing energy and intention.	viduals and organizations in an upward, generative spiral.
4	**Loan Shark:** People choose to become a Loan Shark when they disintegrate the parts of the system to perpetuate the organization's dependence on them to get things done. The choice to pit others against each other and necessitate a referee ultimately moves individuals and organizations in a downward, degenerative spiral.	**What degree of openness will I generate between people?** Openness is the coalescing force that summons a generative future by making people aware of where they fit into the larger system and how their presence juxtaposes others. Generative openness helps people connect their contributions synergistically with others.	**Integrator:** One chooses to become an Integrator by bringing people together and helping them better understand how to work with one another. The choice to create a place where people are open to others and their surroundings moves individuals and organizations in an upward, generative spiral.
5	**Narcissistic Evangelist:** One chooses to become a Narcissistic Evangelist when helping others learn means providing "pat" answers for every problem. The choice to have unwarrant-ed confidence in well-rehearsed answers moves individuals and organizations in a downward, degenerative spiral.	**How will I help others learn?** Learning is the coalescing force that summons a generative future by creating increased intellecttual capacity. Generative learning is characterized by finding the brilliance in everyone.	**Gold Miner:** People choose to become a Gold Miner when they help others learn by unearthing their unique wisdom. The choice to *see the gold from the soil* moves individuals and organizations in an upward, generative spiral.

	Meta-Posture		
	← *Degenerative*		*Generative* →
6	**Sniper:** People choose to become a Sniper when they exploit the difficulties of a perceived rival. The choice to *"kick others when they are down,"* either vengefully or opportunistically, ultimately moves individuals and organizations in a downward, degenerative spiral.	**How will I demonstrate regard:** Regard is the coalescing force that summons a generative future through the consideration of others. Generative regard is founded on the premise that people are worthy of response regardless of what is in it for the responder.	**First Responder:** People choose to become a First Responder when they meet a need of another without expecting personal benefit. The choice to regard others' needs before your own ultimately moves individuals and organizations in an upward, generative spiral.
7	**Prophet of Doom:** People choose to become a Prophet of Doom when their future thought is motivated by cynicism and hopelessness. The choice to find comfort in discouragement ultimately moves individuals and organizations in a downward, degenerative spiral.	**In what will I hope:** Hope is the coalescing force that summons a generative future through an act of faith. Generative hope motivates people to move even when all the odds are stacked against them.	**Optimist:** People choose to become an Optimist when they have hope in what they cannot yet see. The choice to en-courage others in even the most discouraging of circumstances ultimately moves individuals and organizations in an upward, generative spiral.
8	**Ingrate** People choose to become an Ingrate when they believe they are entitled to both the honor and contribution of others. The choice to *get what's mine* ultimately moves individuals and organizations in a downward, degenerative spiral.	**How will I honor others' contributions?** Honor is the coalescing force that summons a generative future through gratefully acknowledging the sustainable contributions of others. Generative honoring identifies the specifics behind the gratitude and its impact on the grateful.	**Grateful Host** People choose to become a Grateful Host when they assume a posture of indebtedness for others' contributions and celebrate all those who've benefited from the contribution. The choice to *keep expectations in check* ultimately moves individuals and organizations in an upward, generative spiral.

		Meta-Posture	
		Degenerative	Generative
9	**Auditor** People choose to become an Auditor when they look at people only as *problems to be fixed*. The choice to focus only on flagging what is wrong ultimately moves individuals and organizations in a downward, degenerative spiral.	**How will I hold others to account for their commitments?** Accountability is the coalescing force that summons a generative future by *calling people to account*. Generative accountability allows people to take deeper responsibility and ownership for the choices and decisions they make.	**Sage** People choose to become a Sage when they are more concerned with others' development than they are with finding fault. The choice of collaborative accountability ultimately moves individuals and organizations in an upward, generative spiral.
10	**Know-it-all (arrogance):** People choose to become a Know-it-all once they conclude they're right and have no need to hear from others. The choice of arrogance ultimately moves individuals and organizations in a downward, degenerative spiral.	**How will I remain humble?** Humility is the coalescing force that summons a generative future by allowing space for *other* people in the specified process or work. Generative humility is displayed in people who are able to appropriately walk the tightrope of expertise and novice.	**Apprentice:** People choose to become an Apprentice when they begin with a posture of *I don't know* versus *I already know*. The choice to humbly accept one's ignorance ultimately moves individuals and organizations in an upward, generative spiral.

Coalescing your stories from the future

Having just written ten stories from your future, it is important that you take the time to let the future "speak to you" about what you saw. Use the following tools to help you synthesize the themes and patterns in your stories. We begin with a brief example of how you might use this tool.

Learning from the Future: *Case Example*

A retail consumer products company desired to bridge the generational divide between their emerging and incumbent leaders. Facing excessive turnover among newer leaders and the impending retirement of many senior leaders it was important they close this gap quickly. Many of the long-term incumbent leaders struggled to pass on the knowledge and Experience to the emerging talent. They wanted to learn more about what motivated their rising leadership. Here's some of what they learned as they explored their generative future in the formation of stronger relationships between leadership generations…

1

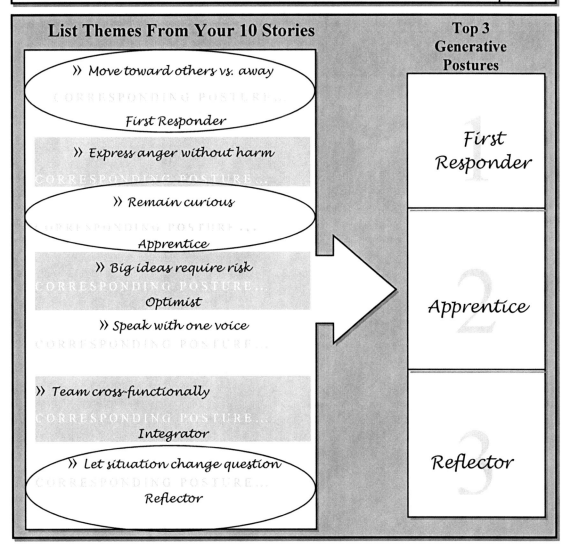

List Themes From Your 10 Stories

» *Move toward others vs. away*

CORRESPONDING POSTURE…

First Responder

» *Express anger without harm*

CORRESPONDING POSTURE…

» *Remain curious*

CORRESPONDING POSTURE…

Apprentice

» *Big ideas require risk*

CORRESPONDING POSTURE…

Optimist

» *Speak with one voice*

CORRESPONDING POSTURE…

» *Team cross-functionally*

CORRESPONDING POSTURE…

Integrator

» *Let situation change question*

CORRESPONDING POSTURE…

Reflector

Top 3 Generative Postures

First Responder

1

Apprentice

2

Reflector

3

OK, now you try it.

Learning from the Future: *Your Organization's Themes*
1. Re-read the 10 stories from the future you previously wrote after each question. As you read, write down recurring themes. (E.g. 5 of your 10 stories involve relationships with customers or as above, many of the stories involved conflicts in which people moved toward each other to pursue resolution)
2. List themes below, and consolidate where possible.
3. Identify a corresponding generative posture for each theme where there is a clear connection.
4. Circle most significant postures (based on either frequency or business requirements) and choose top three.

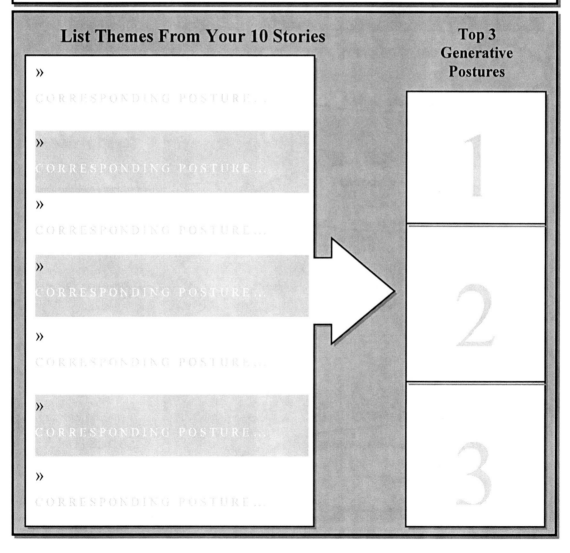

Reentry to your own story

These twenty vignettes portray the most dignified and depraved of organizational life. As the stories came off our keyboards and onto the page, we ached for the degenerative stories, and we cheered for the generative ones. For each degenerative story, we would exasperatingly declare, "Why do we do this to each other?" Indeed it is a mysterious question. We trust you were able to locate your own story in several of these vignettes–both types. We hope you honored your degenerative experiences, both those you have received, and those you have caused, with due grieving and resolve. We also hope you celebrated your generative experiences with due tribute, of the faces that have brought you delight in your organizational life and the faces to whom you have brought delight in theirs.

As you now prepare to build your own generative organizational life, we want to leave you with some reflections on these stories and their implications for the community from which you will invite ever greater generative life. Perhaps these thoughts might offer you some mile markers with which to navigate.

An unstoppable hunger for community

Each of these stories displays the human spirit's determination to find community. Even in the degenerative stories, where your colleagues reached the limits of their tolerance, they didn't give up the pursuit of meaningful community, an innate hunger within all of us. Some simply concluded they needed to look elsewhere for it. This resilient force is one to be revered. We are frequently amazed at how often we are told, especially by emerging leaders and our graduate students, how desperate they are for community. Paradoxically, they all tell us they have plenty of relationships, even relationships of depth and substance. In our overly digital, virtual, fragmented, and electronically connected world, where we can have hundreds of interactions with many people from many sectors of life, people still hunger for a consistent set of relationships. They want familiar relationships on which they can rely for support, encouragement, challenge, and care, to celebrate and grieve with and work with. *Work* with.

Our workplaces are meant to be meaningful sources of community. We all want this, and when this desire is thwarted in one area of our life, we look elsewhere. At the core of us is a desire to join a greater force for good that, when insulted to its limits, leads to defection as the only available option. When those you value in your community opt out, look for where their hunger for meaningful community was irreparably injured. You will likely find an accumulated collection of wounds littered along the path of their stories.

In the course of everyday organizational life

Notice that each of the stories takes place in the context of routine organizational life. These are the places that generativity comes alive. It is rarely in magnanimous moments where generative or degenerative experiences are remembered. Rather, they are most credible in the daily regimens of our workday. Every day, we are presented with hundreds of opportunities to reinforce these postures, either for good or for demise. Every interaction you have with a colleague presents you with the option of a generative posture. True, some interactions, and some colleagues, make it more of a challenging invitation than others. Still, it is always our choice. At their origins, degenerative postures have as their quest sustaining an impenetrable sense of control. Generative postures have at their core a desire to set people free to explore and create. One restrains; one releases.

Degenerative postures dehumanize

In each of the degenerative stories, the one common theme is that each of your colleagues felt like an object. They had been objectified as an obstacle, a threat, a nameless face, an interruption, or a means to an end by another. Once we have been objectified, we begin to lose ourselves to the prevailing agendas around us. We lose the essence of who we are and robotically step into behavior we would never otherwise condone simply for the sake of survival. "I am never like this at home," is an all-too-common lament we hear from people in organizations. The worst part of objectification is that once we have become objects, we make others objects. We become less able to see the human faces of our colleagues, and as we have been "done to," so we "do" in return. Notice in each of the stories how the speaker experiencing the degenerative posture often ends up resorting to a degenerative stance in return. The dark side of "people as assets" connotes that they are merely a means to selfish ends. The self involvement degenerative postures seduce us into becomes the fuel that perpetuates the mechanizing of people's hearts while serving our agenda. Excessive exposure to degenerativity callouses, and ultimately deadens the soul.

Generative postures dignify

By contrast, in each of the generative stories an element of latent greatness was liberated. Sometimes by surprise, but always with joy, people became more of themselves, more human, as they were dignified by another. When people are seen, honored, invited, invested in, respected, and challenged, they rise up. With a broadened horizon, they reach further beyond their self-imposed limits. They become willing. They become courageous. In our dignity, we are fully human, accepting of our flaws, proud of our gifts, curious and imaginative about future possibilities, and eager to contribute to realizing those possibilities. A leader's generativity toward those she leads manifests itself in a deep regard and fascination for all that it takes for the people she leads to be fully themselves and achieve all that they do on behalf of the organization. It is a leader's reverence for the privilege of stewarding the "becoming" of others that proliferates the beauty of generativity. Generative postures are what set the stage for a community's defining moments, both their deepest levels of satisfaction, and their record-setting performance.

The violence and waste of degenerativity

It is hardly ironic that many executives bemoan to us, "Our inability to keep up with customer demands is killing us." Degenerative postures kill. They kill more than performance. They kill our hope and confidence. They kill our spirit. And all the energy to survive the toxicity of degenerative postures is treasured capacity being wasted. If that energy is being consumed just to survive the degenerative environment, it is certainly not being invested in greater levels of competitive performance. Listen to the violent metaphors we often use to describe our organizational experience. Ever notice how often we use language that compares organizational life to warfare? "Dropped the bomb." "Nuked us." "Shot the messenger." "Take him out." You must have your own list. We named the degenerative postures after violent activities for a reason. Degenerativity is violent, and it *does* kill those we work with, along with their performance. We have become so accustomed to judgmental, self-serving, or shaming language in our organizations that it has sadly become second nature.[38] If the impact of every violent word spoken or violent act committed in the context of our organizations were visible and we could see the direct correlations to our retention rates or our EPS in real time, we would surely be shocked.

The implied "11ᵗʰ" question

If we were to add an 11ᵗʰ question to this list (and you may well have generated your own list of a dozen or so more), it would be a question that is implied through all ten of these. And that question is, "How will I struggle?" No human endeavor worth devoting oneself to will be without the requirement of suffering. Any leader who invests energy in the avoidance of pain will inflict much of it on those around him. Moreover, you will expend far more resources in the avoidance of pain than you ever will in contending with pain head on. You *will* confront pain and anguish in the pursuit of transformation. The important question of *how* you will do so is one you can prepare for in advance of pain's arrival despite the fact that pain is often unpredictable and capricious. All twenty vignettes, both generative and degenerative, have inherent struggles in them. The pursuit of generativity is not the *elimination* of painful organizational realities. It is the *choice* to embrace the pain that comes with community in a way that is restorative and caring, not in a way that perpetuates further suffering. And the painful paradox is this – the more generativity you realize, the more you will suffer. King Solomon knew this well when he said,"For with much wisdom comes much sorrow; the more knowledge, the more grief."[39] Finding sources of resilience and endurance to see transformation through is essential so that when inevitable struggles find their way to your doorstep, the refining messages of truth and grace that accompany them can be embraced without fear and defensiveness, but with humility and openness. Our colleague and friend, Don Sawatsky, Dean of NDG Leadership University, puts it well as he paraphrases Walter Brueggemann: "Expressed pain is seldom orderly. Indeed, one only needs to think of one's last domestic quarrel to see that this is true. The question that confronts all notions of order is,'What do we do with pain?' What we make of pain (and pain-bearers) is perhaps the most telling factor for the questions of life and leadership."
You will struggle. When you do, struggle well.

Generativity authenticates the "L" word

On occasions that feel too rare, we will hear people say, "I love my job." Recently one person who said this to us did so with such exuberance that we couldn't help asking in response, "Why do you love it so much?" She said without pause, "Because it loves me back." No one would argue that the desire to give and receive love is foundational to the human experience. It is so fundamental to being human that we simply take for granted its truism, yet for some odd reason, organizations dangerously assume that this basic need to give and receive love somehow stays home when people come to work.

What are the implications if the place where we spend nearly half our waking hours is bereft of the most fundamental need and desire we have?

What if we could say of the place where we spend so much of our lives, "It loves me back?"

True, there are many forms of love and some that should not be found in the workplace. But the basic care, regard, empathy, delight and support needed to lead well is indeed a profound form of love. It validates. It dignifies. It esteems. It elevates. It sustains. As such, it is an important form of love we all need as part of our work. What if when people got out of bed in the morning to get ready for work, they anticipated the experience of being loved and loving instead of anticipated the dread of being dehumanized or just a cog in someone's wheel? What if people didn't lose sleep terrified of a conversation they were going to have the next day with a boss, but rather could expect that even in difficult circumstances, they would know care? Many will dismiss these questions as inappropriate emotional focus for the capitalistic workplaces where productivity and competitive advantage are what matters. We kindly invite you to ask your HR executive for last year's turnover and retention cost analysis. Read the exit interview transcripts of those who left that you wish hadn't. These reports may offer you a different perspective.

To those of you who know this to be so, or even more directly, for whom it is real, can you say of your organization that it has loved you back? Can those you lead say that of you? To invite a generative life into your organization means to invite your organization to love well, to be loved by those who perform the noble work of your organization, and to love them back. The sooner we stop being afraid to admit this truth, the sooner we can get on with the generative organizational life we all inherently desire so much.

Let's get on with yours.

The Second Half
Choosing *Your*
Generative Organizational Life

How the Postures Work in Combined Formation to
Summon a Generative Future

"The future is not a result of choices among alternative paths offered by the present, but a place that is created—created first in the mind and will, created next in activity. The future is not some place we are going to, but one we are creating."

Unknown

PART FOUR

How the Postures Work in Combined Formation to Summon a Generative Future

In the first half of the book, our intent was to familiarize you with the ten postures in both their generative and degenerative forms. Our intent in this half of the book is to enable you to experiment with these postures to identify areas in *your* organization where greater generativity could help strengthen performance in your future.

Let's turn to an elegant and holistic view of how these postures interact with one another. The ten postures fall into four categories that are highly juxtaposed and correlated. As we discussed in the opening of the book, organizations are dynamic, open systems whose components interact among themselves. These categories are meant to illustrate how the archetypes of these postures combine in formation to strengthen or weaken performance through specific behaviors. None of the ten postures exist in isolation from one another, but rather are constantly in-formation and re-formation as our organizations adapt to new stimuli provoking change. Understanding the dynamic process in which these interconnected postures combine with one another to form generativity is key to realizing *trans*formation. As such, they are meant to help you identify how *your* organization's behavior forms to create generative or degenerative postures.

The four categories are:

- *Postures that Shape Meaningful Relationships*
- *Postures that Distinguish Individuals*
- *Postures that Shape Perspective*
- *Postures that Propel Forward*

There are natural, inherent tensions and synergies in these postures that serve to create balance among them if understood. Figure 3.0, *Choosing Postures of Generative Formation,* illustrates how these tensions are balanced inherently among the ten postures and how they combine to maximize both individual and collective performance. When these postures are juxtaposed well to one another, and their tensions are balanced, conditions for generative formation exist. But when one or more of these postures dominates its natural counterpart, degeneration ensues. For example, when an individual's need for visibility over exceeds his capacity to be open to others, the manipulation of the Loan Shark *(openness)* and the opportunism of the Arsonist *(visibility)* link up and create a degenerative force. By contrast, when one can balance the need for distinction with the need to fit into the larger whole, the generative systemic approaches of the Orchestra Conductor *(visibility)* and the Integrator *(openness)* join forces to maximize one's place in the greater system, and a generative force is created.

Another example of how these tensions between the postures work involves a self-righteous person who views himself as the guardian of the company's vision–in this case, the false humility of the Know-it-all *(humility)* and compulsive sense of accountability of the Auditor *(accountability)* create a degenerative force that we see frequently in environments characterized by dogmatic mandates to change in the face of great odds. By contrast, the humility of the Apprentice *(humility)* and the emphasis on growth opportunities instead of castigating errors evidenced by the Sage *(accountability)* result in a powerful generative force that leads to sustainably solved problems. In essence, the Know it all/Auditor in this example is the perennial critic and the Apprentice/Sage is the catalyst for positive change.

Similar tensions exist among the synergies. For example, there is a strong synergy between Belief and Openness–these are the generative postures of the Liberator *(belief)* and the Integrator *(openness)* serving as both a catalyst for freeing people's ideas and also keeping the big picture in mind so everything stays balanced and efforts do not get dissipated. The media company brought in by ONDCP in the example of the anti-drug campaign cited earlier served this role and was vital to creating a whole new generative approach that yielded immediate results.

The reverse of this synergy is that of the Loan Shark *(openness)* and the Terrorist *(belief)* using fear to divide and manipulate. This is a classic degenerative behavior and has more in common with Caesar conquering Gaul ("divide and rule") than with modern generative management practice. It is a constant source of amazement to us how frequently archaic degenerative behaviors like this one get rewarded in present-day companies.

Now that you get the general idea of how these interconnections between the postures work, let's take a closer look at how the specific tensions and synergies operate. After that, we'll have you do some work with the model to hone your agility with it.

Figure 3.0 illustrates the interrelationships among the postures.

Figure 3.0 Postures of Generative Formation and their Interrelationships

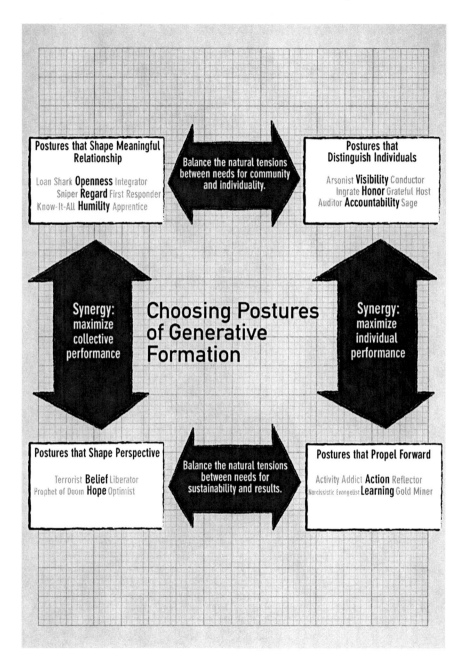

Generating Balance between the Tensions

The expression "striking a balance" is inherently flawed. What it suggests is not actually possible, nor is it desirable. To "strike" suggests a singular point in time that, once achieved, is completed. Achieving balance is a never-ending endeavor. Once a state of balance is realized, it is not sustained statically. It requires constant maneuvering and adjusting to sustain. When an individual, or a community, feels *off*-balance, it is unable to adapt. People are perpetually trying to regain equilibrium just to survive, because they want the inherent tensions of life eliminated. Balance, by contrast, enables adaptability and change, because it accepts that inherent tensions will always be present and are actually helpful to generating a future in-formation. The ongoing pursuit of balance enables generativity, while the grinding sense of being imbalanced leads to degenerativity.

Everyone has an innate need for both individuality and community; for relationship and individual expression. When these needs are overindulged to one degree or the other, degenerativity ensues. When an organization creates an environment of excessive Darwinian competition among its people, and people are pursuing their own gain at the expense of relationship, performance is weakened because the community is weakened and trust is eroded. When an organization balances the magnificence of its individuals by helping them enjoy the relationships they have with other magnificent people, relationships *and* results are strengthened and synergies among individuals' talents emerge. While this setup tends to be counterintuitive for many leaders, it is the *combination* of people's gifts that forms to achieve results greater than the sum of the individuals. When it works well, people's individualities are actually further distinguished, not less, as many people fear.

Organizations need to achieve meaningful results. They typically do so through the ongoing acquisition of knowledge ("information" versus in-formation) and skill, followed by the focused application of that knowledge and skill toward opportunities or problems. In the extreme, excessive results orientation causes cynicism and fear because people feel set up to fail. Organizations unrealistically gorge their people on ever increasing demands, and for many it feels gluttonous and terrifying to have to make dangerous leaps and painful sacrifices continually. This is the degenerative form of the pursuit of performance. Performance results must also be *sustainable* for the long-term health of the organization. We need people pursuing those results with optimism *(hope)* that those results are both achievable and worthy of achievement. Further, they should be pursued with a sense of confident liberation *(belief)* that they have a plausible chance of realizing those results, not fear that failure could be fatal. Thus the meta-postures of *belief* and *hope* serve to balance the meta-postures of *action* and *learning* to form sustainable results and a posture of generative formation.

When the tension between the desire for individuality and relationship becomes imbalanced, degenerativity spirals downward and the degenerative postures join forces. For example, Know-it-alls *(humility)* and Arsonists *(visibility)* combine in an all-out campaign to guarantee that the organization stands up and sees their brilliance, regardless of what destructive display is needed to turn heads. The countervailing powers of the Apprentice *(humility)* and the Orchestra Conductor *(visibility)* help the organization balance these tensions. In combination, they do so by graciously acknowledging both ignorance and the collective genius within the organization. In this context, one does not fear losing oneself to the greater whole. Rather, people trust that their visibility will increase as the visibility of others also increases. The painful irony of the Know-it-all/Arsonist combination is that the violent pursuit of connection and individuality gains neither. They end up being seen as a dangerous force to be eliminated and are therefore isolated from the rest of the organization. No connection. No visibility.

The Synergies and How They Generate Maximum Performance

When you combine a healthy distinction of individual contribution with the application of those talents toward generative learning and focused action, you maximize the contribution of every individual in the organization and ultimately the organization's contribution to its markets. The Sage *(accountability)* is vital in this connection, stimulating people through incisive questions, observations and statements regarding their contributions, to generate reflective behavior. Becoming a Reflector *(action)* entails thinking about and understanding how everyone's contribution fits together. The benefit here is that a true Reflector comes to understand how the collective contributions lead to results, generating an understanding of the balance of efforts and outcomes in the organization. This stance enables the Reflector *(action)* to differentiate between motion for motion's sake, as in the Activity Addict *(action),* and activity that has a payoff and delivers on the company's strategy. As the Sage *(accountability)* stimulates people to become Reflectors *(action)*, Reflectors themselves can become Sages, bringing their level of understanding to an issue and asking the sort of questions that can guide others.

The reverse of the Sage/Reflector relationship *(accountability/action)* is between the Auditor *(accountability)* and the Activity Addict *(action)*. Like the Sage, the Auditor seeks to hold others accountable for their commitments; however, the Auditor does it in a very literal sense by interrogating others and ferreting out any deviations from the plan. Audits have a chilling effect. They stifle initiative and place a premium on rote compliance. The act of auditing generates interrogative activity. Likewise, ensuring compliance creates internal work for the organization. As people become compliance focused, actual deadlines and real work can get lost in a series of increasingly ritualized steps that show sufficient progress to appease the Auditor's inquiry. These compliance activities invite and sustain the Activity Addict *(action)*, who confuses motion with progress. We have seen organizations suffer from an illness one of our colleagues calls *priorititis.*[40] The organization becomes locked in a destructive cycle of initiative and priority proliferation, coupled with audits that themselves become additional initiatives. At the end of the day, these organizations find that when they need to draw on their people to react to a market change, there is no energy, time, or performance capacity left, Everyone is addicted to dozens of rote activities, reinforced by enslaving audits that serve as the punishing device of accountability.

One of our clients really put his finger on this issue of accountability when he talked about helping junior managers shine in operations reviews. He was working in a company that placed a tremendous premium on personal accountability. The quarterly operations reviews caused a great deal of fear among managers, especially those less experienced. Our client said the default position for the more junior managers was to bring dense spreadsheets and cover every possible number–an Activity Addict *(action)* approach. Knowing this exercise in assembling useless piles of paper to be unhelpful, he said he wanted to see managers point out only those numbers that captured what was going on in the business unit that quarter, a Reflector's approach. He went on to tell his managers that the ability to find a few meaningful numbers in all that data was what "put the sizzle in the steak" for him in operations reviews. Sage advice, indeed.

Perhaps no pairing has a bigger impact on the organization than the combination of the generative meta-postures of hope and belief. The postures of the Liberator *(belief)* and the Optimist *(hope)* create the strong, meaningful, trust-based relationships that lead to a vibrant community aligned with a shared cause, pursuing collective results together. Let us think for a minute about what this statement actually means.

The Liberator *(belief)* allows people the freedom to respond to possibilities. One of our clients articulated this concept in a meeting when asked, "Does it mean we do whatever we want, to react to our competitors' steps and our consumer's needs? Isn't this a recipe for anarchy?"

He responded, "We have a vision for this company, and we also have a strategy and some specific goals in our markets. Think of these things as a set of clearly defined parameters in which we all work. But within these parameters, I want us to take advantage of the maximum freedom to creatively solve the challenges we meet. As long as you can make a case for it in the context of our strategy and our business, there are no barriers to what I'm encouraging you to think about and do."

The ability to make statements like that one comes from a truly optimistic vantage, a deep conviction that the glass can be filled if you just start pouring. This may seem highly idealistic, but in our experience, leaders who begin by saying "yes" and find a way to make that affirmation reality, inspire and energize their teams and engender a healthy, resilient environment in their organizations.

The degenerative equivalent of the Liberator and Optimist are the Terrorist *(belief)* and the Prophet of Doom *(hope)*. The Terrorist uses fear to drive the organization, and the Prophet of Doom is convinced that nothing can possibly go right. It might seem as if we have created these postures as caricatures, but they are based on a grim reality. Take for example the tenure of "Chainsaw" Al Dunlap as the CEO of Sunbeam in the 1990s.[41] Dunlap governed as CEO under the assumption that a huge number of people could be fired, to spruce the company up for sale. Certainly, anyone working for Sunbeam under Dunlap's regime would be motivated primarily by fear and would also have assumed that the company was on its last legs. Although Dunlap was an extreme example (and Sunbeam's share price plummeted as a result of his activities), the 1990s were filled with leveraged buyouts, which stripped value from organizations through firings and fire sales. The archetype of the grim-faced executive who assumes the worst of people and governs by threats and punishments is very much alive today in some organizations, though we would argue that this posture is so destructive that it cannot endure for long.

Dress Rehearsal

As you've seen, you can select any two generative or degenerative forms of any juxtaposed posture, across either the tensions or the synergies, to see how generative postures open the way to new possibilities. By contrast, degenerative postures act in concert to erect walls that imprison any possibility of enhanced performance beyond what already exists. Frequently, figuring out the degenerative postures you see in your own company and identifying how they are conspiring together can suggest how you can shift the posture, thereby changing results.

For the purposes of applying this knowledge to your own organization, we suggest you use the model to first locate postures in which you believe you are experiencing either inherently generative or degenerative behavior. To begin, we've created a dress rehearsal for you to hone your diagnostic eye by working several of these postures' continuums to identify both what the combinations might look like and what their implications would be on performance. Your ability to garner facility with the model will enable you to identify and architect generative transformation within your own organization.

When you identify generative postures and behaviors, it should be in the pursuit of sustaining and expanding them. And of course, when you identify degenerative postures and behavior, it should be in the pursuit of migrating them to their generative counterpart. By identifying these in the context of the tensions and synergies in which they reside, you will get a sharper view into your organization's system, and how you are perpetuating either generative or degenerative postures.

Below you will find an example of the Regard and Honor postures from the model depicted in juxtaposition to one another. We have illustrated how these combine both generatively and degeneratively. This will give you an idea of how we would like you to practice. After the example, we have provided two blank tools on which you can select postures to juxtapose to one another. Select postures that are in synergy or in tension to one another you feel reflect an actual tension or synergy within your organization. In the middle of each tool, we have created a space for you to imagine what these postures would combine to create (generatively or degeneratively), and then to imagine what impact that combination would have on performance. The purpose of working these pairings is for you to train your eye and mind on how to see the presence of generative or degenerative postures, and to imagine their effect within your organization.

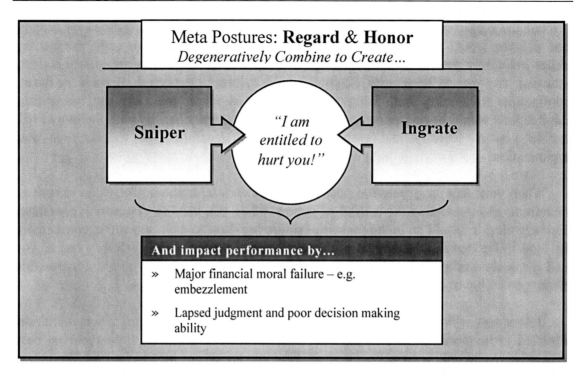

Meta Postures: **Regard & Honor**
Degeneratively Combine to Create…

Sniper → *"I am entitled to hurt you!"* ← Ingrate

And impact performance by…

» Major financial moral failure – e.g. embezzlement

» Lapsed judgment and poor decision making ability

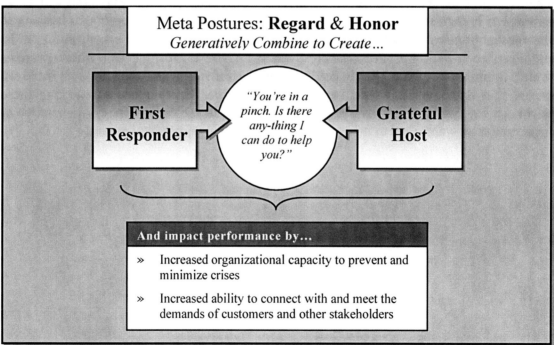

Meta Postures: **Regard & Honor**
Generatively Combine to Create…

First Responder → *"You're in a pinch. Is there any-thing I can do to help you?"* ← Grateful Host

And impact performance by…

» Increased organizational capacity to prevent and minimize crises

» Increased ability to connect with and meet the demands of customers and other stakeholders

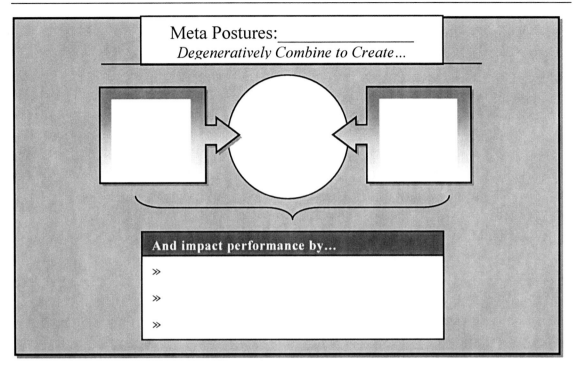

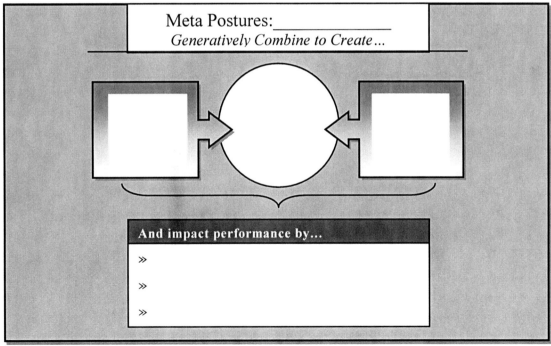

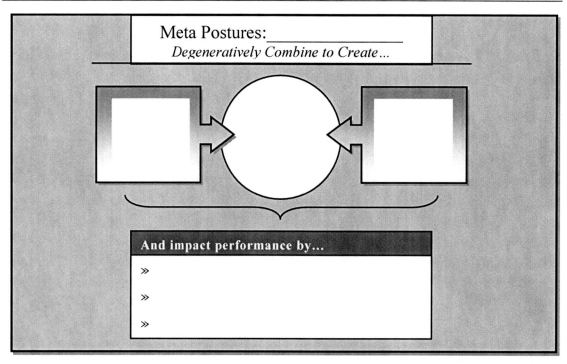

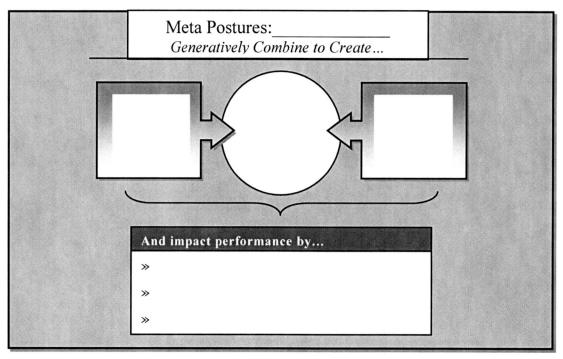

PART FIVE

Putting it All Together:
The Generative Work of Summoning Your Future *in*-Formation

"If we can recognize that change and uncertainty are basic principles, we can greet the future and the transformation we are undergoing with the understanding that we do not know enough to be pessimistic."

Hazel Henderson

PART FIVE

Putting it All Together:
The Generative Work of Summoning Your Future *in*-Formation

Having grasped the concept of the ten generative and degenerative postures, let us now turn our attention to the work of summoning your future *in*-formation. In most organizations, change processes like strategic planning and resource allocation (sadly, all too often the same process) are usually owned by a few, sometimes just the head of strategic planning and a small team. Department heads and business unit heads are given their "templates" to fill out and a due date by which to turn them in. Often these templates are accompanied with "reviews" by senior executives and multi-hour, sometimes multi-day presentations, inquisitions, and in the most degenerative cases, grilling sessions. These meetings have all the curiosity and future-focused passion of a funeral. They are laden with fear on the part of the presenters and predetermined conclusions on the part of the reviewers about whose will be good, whose will be lame, who will be given the requested resources, and who won't. When it's all over, someone puts it into a big document and then it gets reverently placed on a shelf to collect dust. People then return to business as usual. In some organizations, the priorities set in such a process do in fact drive decision-making and direction, but often not in a way that deeply engages those executing the work set forth in the plan.

Considering the four categories of postures in the model above, let's look at the impact each might have on any process intended to pursue a new future and that implies organizational change of some kind. After each section, there is a set of questions that an initiative team (for example, the strategic planning team or an organization design team), along with the executive team, should answer as a group. The implications of their responses should be carefully analyzed for strategic risk, and actions should be taken to mitigate those risks.

Strategic change processes, by their nature, require levels of sufficient trust and intimacy among those who are generating the ideas and plans and those who must execute them. Without courageous and candid conversations and dynamically sparring viewpoints between these groups, important interactions are reduced to cosmetic conversation where pleasantries and safe chatter are exchanged in public and fears, frustrations, schemes, and the "big ideas" are exchanged in private. It behooves those architecting the process to ensure the relationships among those engaged in forming and executing the plan can flourish *in*-Formation.

In the spirit of maintaining a posture of inquiry, you can use the following questions in any number of ways throughout a change initiative. Here are just some examples of contexts in which you may find these questions useful:

- Diagnostic and assessment phases of change initiatives
- Change/organization design sessions
- Initiative preplanning sessions
- To invite greater interaction during update presentations
- Implementation planning sessions
- As a feedback mechanism to gauge progress of an initiative
- As conversation-starters between key leaders whose leadership must guide the broader organization to a successful execution of the initiative.

The questions can help warranty effective stewardship of the resources allocated to achieve the initiative's anticipated results. Answers to the questions should be documented and analyzed for themes and important relational risks identified among key leaders and constituents. In section six, as part of a comprehensive tool for planning a generative future for your organization, we'll offer more specific ways to employ these questions as part of your overall change effort.

Postures that Shape Meaningful Relationship:
The importance of community and connection in shaping a dynamic future and maximizing limited resources

A client of ours shows a video to illustrate the connection between trust and risk. In this video, a mountain climber named Dan Osman climbs a nearly vertical stone cliff more than 400 feet high in only four minutes and twenty-five seconds, without any ropes or protective gear whatsoever.[42] He leaps from handhold to handhold with what appears to be an utter disregard for his own safety. With a vast yawning gulf below him and certain death if he slips, he actually seems to be enjoying himself as he ascends. The point here is that Osman was a trained athlete, confident in both his abilities and his preparation. An onlooker might conclude that he was utterly reckless, but to Osman, the level of risk was entirely commensurate with his level of trust in his ability, experience, and preparation, all three of which were considerable. Our client successfully made this vital point with his team: the greater the level of trust you have in your people, your capabilities, and your organization, the greater your willingness to take risks and sustain your level of commitment.

When ideas about the future, and the resources required to fund and execute it, are a zero-sum commodity that must be fought for in a contest of wills, wits, and political maneuvers, the future is often mortgaged before anything begins. When the future of a community or an organization has an inherent "loser" in it, the compromises are usually more significant than most care to admit. While it may sound Pollyannaish and naïve to suggest it could be any other way in our ruthless corporate battlegrounds, in fact, it is not. To the contrary, organizations that thrive globally and competitively in the future will have as their hallmark a culture of trust-based, respectful relationships at their core.

Questions for *Postures of Meaningful Relationship*

1. Who will most rely on you to be successful in their respective parts of the initiative? What agreements are in place between you and them to ensure your required contribution to their work is mutually understood?
2. Who will you most rely on to be successful in your respective part of the initiative? What agreements are in place between you and them to ensure their required contribution to your work is mutually understood?
3. With whom is there a risk of unnecessary competition in the process? What is fueling the competitive dynamic? What could be done to turn it into a posture of cooperation and collaboration?
4. What will this process require you to change? From whom in the organization might you get help with this change? Who do you fear being vulnerable in front of, when having to change? How can you strengthen that relationship so they can be allies in your pursuit of change?
5. Where will your own arrogance–your potentially excessive confidence in what you know–get in your way of seeing a different future? Who have you potentially caused to withhold trust from you because of a perceived insufficient degree of humility? What needs to happen to repair/restore/build those relationships prior to any change initiative so that you have their trust?
6. Whose arrogance has caused you to withhold trust? How does your withholding of trust in this relationship pose a threat to a successful change process?

147

7. If you had to relinquish all the resources you are seeking to fund/staff your part of this initiative, to whom would you want them to go? Why? Should your ideas or proposals not prevail in favor of others, how will you demonstrate regard and active support for their work? Whose plan/vision might you actively support by forfeiting some of your resource requests to help fund their initiatives? Why?

8. Where are there places of synergy in which investments you are looking to make coincide sufficiently with investments others are making, that warrant greater degrees of integration or collaboration? Are the relationships among those identified opportunities sufficiently strong enough to safely pursue such integration? If not, how will you strengthen them? What would it take for each of you to consider it unacceptable to wastefully duplicate investment dollars rather than maximize them through shared investments?

Postures that Distinguish Individuals
The importance of postures that unleash people's best talents and engage their deepest passion

A loss of one's individuality, the over-homogenization of one's distinctiveness blending into the sea of nameless faces in the organization, is the secret terror of any individual with the capacity to make great differences. Many organizations boast "high potential" development programs that attempt to identify the cream of the crop, but then isolate the candidates from the commoners in special, often clandestine processes designed to accelerate the development of their talent. While noble in intention, breaking off this group from community has two potential hazards. One, it breeds arrogance in those labeled as high potential and inadvertently can cause them to be less self-invested in their development, having the false sense that they've "arrived." Secondly, the rest of the people in the organization who could benefit greatly from their talent in the form of learning and role modeling have limited access to them. High-potential employees should be expected to contribute to the development of others, suggesting that giftedness is a privilege with which comes responsibility to the broader community.

While talent investments should always be asymmetrical (good stewardship would suggest that differences among people's degrees of talent be acknowledged and honored, not ignored or denied), they do not have to be to the detriment or neglect of some. In an environment where development is generative, regardless of the degree of talent one brings, its cultivation is seen as important and expected. Leveling the playing field of value allows greater respect for the natural distribution of talent in any organization. Formalizing "status" differences, deliberately or not, among people with differing degrees of talent only entrenches a "have" and "have not" culture. Those who feel like they are seen as "have nots" end up behaving that way–checked out, cynical, and resentful. Their sense of victimization sets them on a course to prove they are marginalized by withholding their participation, playing hard to get, and in the extreme, using passive-aggression to make others pay. Further, those who are labeled as the official "haves" gain an insatiable appetite for acknowledgment and visibility, and toxic levels of entitlement can proliferate as a result.

Having more or less talent than someone else should never equate to being more or less important than someone else. These are important distinctions not to be underestimated.

Here are some questions, again, to be included as part of the preplanning or actual planning processes of pursuing your organization's future and allocating the talent resources needed to achieve strategic aspirations.

Questions for *Postures of Distinguishing Individuals*

1. Do you feel we do a sufficient job at allocating our talent development resources? If not, how might we do better? What risks are being created by a shortcoming in this area?
2. Which segments of our employees would say they felt unacknowledged or "invisible?" What is causing them to feel this way? What do we need to do differently so that their contribution to this initiative can be optimized?
3. What do you do to ensure those you lead know you see their individual distinctiveness and invite their visibility? Do we have anyone at risk for feeling "cloned" into someone else's image beyond what he or she would want?
4. In what ways does our organization (through processes, culturally, programmatically, etc.) honor our people? In what ways do we dishonor our people? How do the ways we dishonor people threaten our pursuit of a new future?
5. Do our people feel accountable for the future of our organization? Why or why not? What needs to happen for every employee to feel deep ownership and accountability for the success of our future?
6. What capabilities will we need to successfully pursue the strategic aspirations we are setting out toward? Do we have a sufficient degree of those capabilities now?

Are they extant or latent? What are the risks of having too little?

7. Do we have an excess of certain capabilities in our organization that are becoming obsolete? Can we transpose them into capabilities we actually need? What happens if we can't?

8. In what ways can we use the process of future formation to build leadership capability in the organization?

Postures that Shape Perspective

The importance of postures that garner shared conviction and hope in a sustainable future

We have all had moments where we've come out of a meeting certain that we know where a project is headed, only to pass a colleague in the hall who informs us of an exactly opposite direction. This situation is confusing, to say the least, but it happens frequently. Given the variety of perspectives people have, two people can experience the same meeting in two totally different ways. We show up every day with biased perspectives about what we bring into the world, and it's that perspective that shapes what we believe and ultimately hope for in the world. Differences in perspectives can be seen in any company that has multiple disciplines within it–engineers versus planners versus finance people versus marketers, for example. When people in each of those disciplines attempt to translate the company's basic concepts around something like "return on investment," each can come up with a very different idea based on his or her discipline. Each of the disciplines has a series of assumptions on what "return on investment" is, based on that person's particular belief sets, and he or she will hold onto that perspective with almost religious fervor.

Perspective brings our world, and ultimately the future of our organizations, into focus. However, organizational focus that's grounded on limited perspective—that is, one pair of eyes—is not sustainable, because it fails to incorporate the vast array of components that make up an organization at any given moment. Compound that with a competitive landscape that is constantly changing, and you have one perspective on many parts, which are constantly changing. It's a recipe of forward movement predicated on reactionary moves and nonsensical formation. People in today's organizations want to know that when they show up to work they get to be a part of an experience larger than themselves. Time and again in our strategic assessments of organizations we hear comments such as "We need to approach this with one voice" or "We have too many versions of our story; we don't really know who we are becoming" or "We need to get aligned on true North."

Limited perspective decreases an organization's ability to make comprehensive meaning of its competitive landscape and internal operations as well and the meaning of the integration of those two to meet the needs of its clients in a way that is better than the rest. The integration of multiple perspectives toward a common future helps organizations harness collective meaning. It's that collective meaning that creates shared beliefs and hope toward a common future. While each meta-posture plays a distinct role in summoning a sustainable future, belief and hope often form a foundation on which the others rest. How an organization chooses to shape its collective perspective around these two postures will determine the future it pursues.

Ultimately, it is the collective harnessing of beliefs and hopes that allows an organization to both learn about and act upon its collective future.

Questions for *Postures the Shape Perspective*

1. What organizational perspectives do I hold? In what ways are my views limited? Who could help me see a broader organizational perspective as I look toward a sustainable future?
2. What do we believe to be true about our organization? (Who we are, what we do, where we are headed) What are we convicted about? Where do our beliefs align? Where do they differ?
3. In what ways do our shared beliefs inspire hope for the future? In what ways do our divergent beliefs create a sense of organizational victimization and hopelessness?
4. What are some of the degenerative beliefs I hold about my contribution, our organization, and our future? What are some of the generative beliefs that I hold?
5. What behaviors do our leaders exhibit that may be shaping perspectives counter to what we need for our strategy?
6. What are the general sources that are shaping the perspectives of our organization? How do the following contribute:

   a. Our public reputation
   b. Our recent results
   c. Our employee retention
   d. Our communication channels
   e. Our product and customer information and how we distribute and use it
   f. Our survey data

Postures that Propel Forward

The importance of postures that maximize contribution and encourage ever greater achievement

Some have said that wisdom is knowledge in action. If organizations are going to capitalize on the potential of their people and their market opportunities, they must increase their capacity to channel the wisdom that will move them into a future they pursue, as opposed to one that pursues them. Part of what will set organizations up to pursue and choose their future is linked with their ability to transform themselves in real time. As the complexity of competition increases, so does an organization's need to regularly transform itself. The ever-increasing iterative nature of strategy work and the allocation of resources toward that end have become more crucial than ever.

Organizations that regularly transform themselves are more likely to be the ones setting the pace instead of trying to keep up with it. We believe that one of the best ways an organization can become a pacesetter is by choosing to be an organization that continuously learns and has the ability to integrate its learning across its entire system and then act on the integrative learnings. In short, you must become *wise*.

Wisdom not only helps you keep up, it also moves you ahead, because it creates the capacity to anticipate. The closer you get to knowledge, both latent and extant, in your organization and the environment in which you reside, the more you're able to not just respond, but set up every aspect of your organization for success.

Organizations will not succeed unless they choose to act. Two types of action, mechanistic and creative, have the potential to summon the future of your organization. One is the result of history, personal experience, and repetition. The latter is the result of a belief and hope in a new future. One is not better than the other, and creating a balance between the two is crucial. Some of the most innovative moments in the history of humanity have come at times when individuals and/or groups of people began to see that something was not as it should be, felt they could contribute to a new way forward, were free to do so, and were compelled to act because they wanted to be a part of an even greater future. The balance of mechanistic action and creative action–knowing how to draw from your past to shape your future–propels forward motion with intention and confidence.

Questions for *Postures the Propel Forward Action*

1. Where do we see wisdom in our organization? In what ways are we knowledgeable but not actionable? How about actionable but not knowledgeable?
2. In what ways have we maximized the contributions of our people? In what ways have we hindered their contributions?
3. What are some of the ways we feel compelled to act? As individuals? As an organization? In partnership with other organizations?
4. When have we summoned our future mechanistically? (past-focused) What were the organizational implications? Would we do it differently in the future? How? Why?
5. When have we summoned our future creatively? (only future focused, ignoring the past) What were the organizational implications? Would we do it differently in the future? How? Why?
6. When were we able to accomplish something we set out to do? What were the implications? How did we do it? What did we learn from the experience worth repeating?

Obviously these questions will take years and many iterations to address. In the next section of the book we invite you to customize a set of questions to apply specifically to your organization.

Charting Your Course to the Future…One Posture at a Time

"The future is too interesting and dangerous to be entrusted to any predictable, reliable agency. We need all the fallibility we can get. Most of all, we need to preserve the absolute unpredictability and total improbability of our connected minds."

Lewis Thomas

PART SIX

Charting Your Course to the Future...One Posture at a Time

Congratulations. You have arrived at the starting line of your future. You now how enough perspective on the complexity of these postures to determine a course of action and you have enough insight into your own organization, and yourself, to choose a course of action through which you have a solid chance of realizing true transformation. Let's get to work.

Our rule of thumb on such endeavors is, "Wire it for success," meaning choose the low-hanging fruit and parlay small wins into larger transformative results. True transformation is indeed the result of many formative changes. They accumulate and compound. Sustainable transformation rarely shows up in one big earth-shattering event, unless of course it is indeed a calamity. Our suggestion, therefore, is to begin with one or two postures. First, select the posture you believe represents your organization's greatest display of generativity. It would be the posture that the majority of people in the organization would agree to, it is hoped, with some degree of enthusiasm: "Yes, that is us!" Second, if you choose to work on two postures, select the posture you believe is one of your organization's degenerative "dark sides." DON'T pick the one you think is the *worst* posture for you. Pick one that is problematic enough that the majority of people would recognize it as a problem, but not so toxic that seeing change would invite too steep a climb. In short, pick one that you believe has a reasonable shot of garnering commitment to change.

The following tool will guide you and your colleagues through the process of planning for transformative change. The goal would be to get your generative posture to an even greater pervasiveness in the organization and to reduce the unwanted and noxious consequences of your degenerative posture. For each step of this process, we provide you a brief illustrative example of how the tool can be used. Following each step, there are two blank templates provided for you to work through your identified opportunities.

Building Your Future in-Formation: *Instructions*

In the following pages we've created a toolkit to help walk you and your organization through building a generative future in-formation. There are 4 main sections of work for you to complete. At the beginning of each section we start you off with an example using the tool as a way to illustrate how you might pursue a generative organizational life. These are not the *right* answers, and yours will most likely have a unique look and feel. However, it is our hope that by seeing how others pursue generativity it may inspire you to discover your own approach. You may find the process needs to be iterative before you able to land on an approach that best suits your context. What is most important is that you *choose* to work the material by *choosing* to be in-Formation. Following each example there is an opportunity for you think about the generativity you desire to unleash in your organization. Below is an overview of the work in each of the four sections.

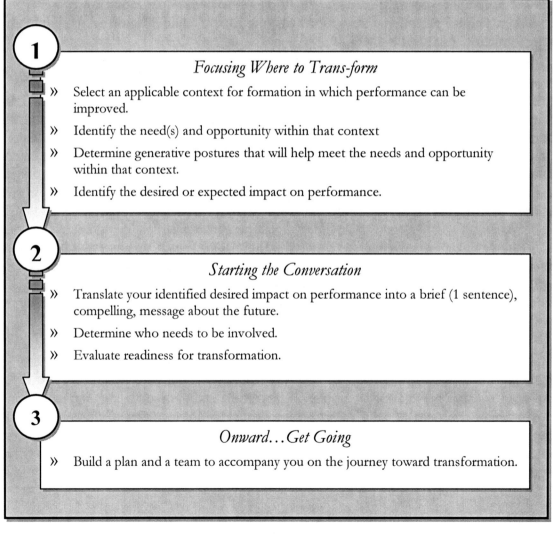

1

Focusing Where to Trans-form

» Select an applicable context for formation in which performance can be improved.

» Identify the need(s) and opportunity within that context

» Determine generative postures that will help meet the needs and opportunity within that context.

» Identify the desired or expected impact on performance.

2

Starting the Conversation

» Translate your identified desired impact on performance into a brief (1 sentence), compelling, message about the future.

» Determine who needs to be involved.

» Evaluate readiness for transformation.

3

Onward…Get Going

» Build a plan and a team to accompany you on the journey toward transformation.

Focusing Where to Transform: *Case Example*

A large biotech corporation was looking to increase the productivity of its R&D and commercialization processes. Their desire was to triple their product pipeline in an effort to capture global markets by running clinical trials around the world. Their ability to work collaboratively across multiple geographical, functional, and hierarchical boundaries would prove key to their ability to realize their desired growth. Here's some of what they learned as they explored their generative future in the formation of integrating multi-disciplinary processes.

1

Select Applicable Context

» *Build stronger collaborative relationships and processes between discovery, development, marketing, and commercialization.*

2

Identify Current Need(s) or Opportunity

» *Different therapeutic areas utilize different processes for commercialization, with no enterprise synergies*

» *Recently acquired startups have not been well integrated creating further confusion about development priorities*

3

More Conductors, Integrators, and Sages will help coalesce multiple parts of the organization into one cohesive whole.

4

Desired or Expected Impact on Performance

» *Increase product portfolio by 6 new products in 4 years and accelerate development timeline from 12 to 7 years*

Focusing Where to Transform: *Your Organizational Transformation*
1. Identify an area in your organization where you would like to see greater generativity. It can be a division, department, team, geography, etc. Or you can choose a specific process.
2. Identify current needs and/or opportunities that warrant increased generativity within that context. What behaviors are impacting the performance?
3. Determine generative posture(s) that could meet the identified needs or opportunity.
4. Identify what affect increased generativity could have on performance.

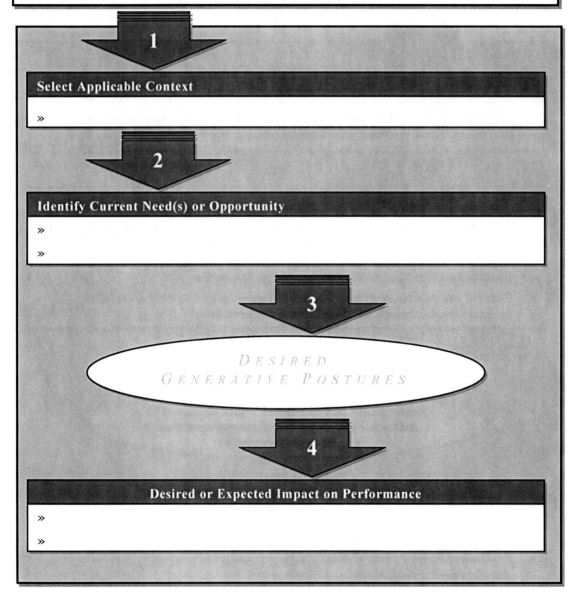

1

Select Applicable Context

»

2

Identify Current Need(s) or Opportunity

»

»

3

DESIRED GENERATIVE POSTURES

4

Desired or Expected Impact on Performance

»

»

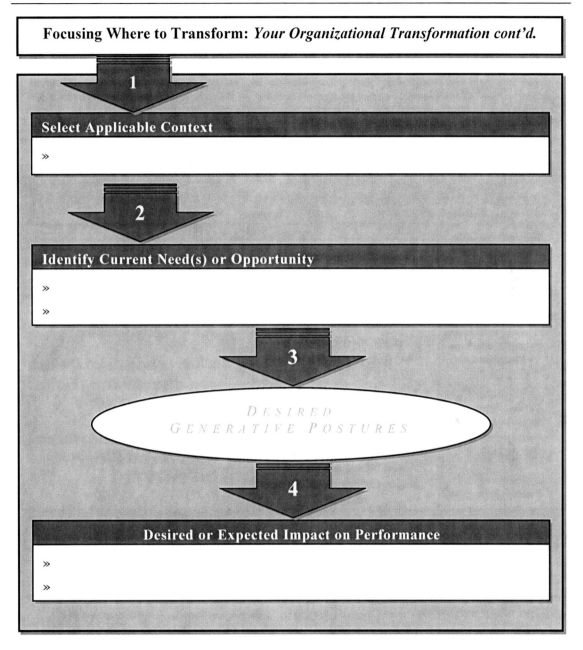

Focusing Where to Transform: *Your Organizational Transformation cont'd.*

1

Select Applicable Context

»

2

Identify Current Need(s) or Opportunity

»

»

3

DESIRED GENERATIVE POSTURES

4

Desired or Expected Impact on Performance

»

»

By now you've identified a couple of contexts that warrant greater degrees of generativity, corresponding generative postures that when developed have the potential to positively impact performance. With that work in mind, go back and re-read your stories from the future. Do you see any connections between the themes in your stories and your analysis of focusing where to transform? What do you notice?

Starting the Conversation: *Case Example*

A national Pittsburg based NGO dedicated to caring for disadvantaged youth in urban settings identified the need for more Gold Miners and Optimists as a way to accelerate the development of younger talent in order to expand their reach into 10 new cities. Having recognized the need to form alliances with existing organizations in some of those cities the need for mature managerial talent and the ability to manage complex relationships became apparent. Here's some of what they learned as they explored their generative future in the formation of pursuing expansion of their noble mission.

2

Compelling Message About the Future: Reach 6,000 disadvantaged youth in 10 western and north western cities within 5 years through alliances & increased capacity.

What stakeholders are required for desired future?	How will change impact the identified stakeholders?	Based on the people involved and the impact change will have on them what are the most critical questions to ask?
» *Julie L.* (Executive Director of PNW Urban Youth Alliance)	*Expansion of their organization while giving us access to targeted geographies*	» *How ready for growth is your organization?*
» *Daniel P.* (Midwest Regional Director for Community Outreach)	*Increased managerial responsibility will stretch his leadership capacity*	» *What concerns you most about stretching your own leadership?*
» *Regina T.* (Director of Human Resources)	*With limited resources she must devise creative strategies for developing talent*	» *How will you determine which capabilities to build first?*

What is the perceived readiness of those involved to talk about what really matters? If they are not prepared to talk how will you get them ready?

» *Julie - Very Ready*	» *Has been preparing her organization for growth and wants the alliance to work.*
» *Daniel - Minimally Ready*	» *Has been resistant to growth and fears his own inadequacy*
» *Regina - Moderately Ready*	» *Will have to switch from HR mechanics to talent strategist.*

Starting the Conversation: *Your Organization*

1. Briefly reflect on your work thus far. In light of what you learned from your previous work, what compelling message(s) do you hope to convey about the future.. In one or two sentences write out what that compelling message is. (Be as specific as possible)
2. With that message in mind, identify: who needs to be involved, how they will be impacted, and questions most relevant for that conversation (refer to section 5 for ideas for questions to ask).
3. In light of what is required to realize the transformation, how ready are they to make the journey? (E.g. Are there specific capacities that need to be developed?

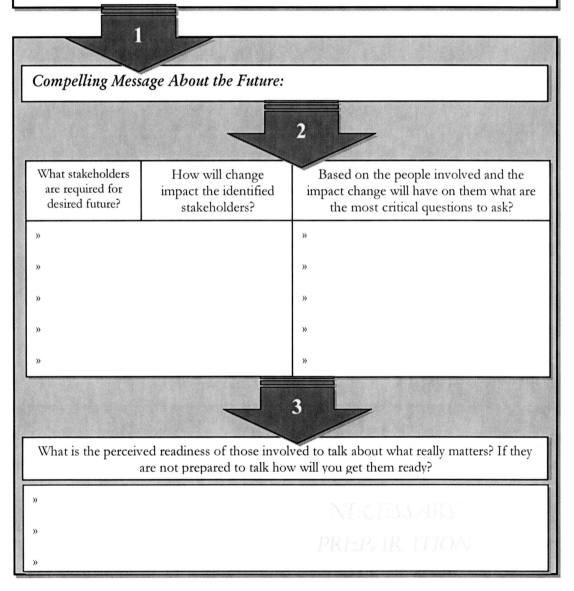

1

Compelling Message About the Future:

2

What stakeholders are required for desired future?	How will change impact the identified stakeholders?	Based on the people involved and the impact change will have on them what are the most critical questions to ask?
»		»
»		»
»		»
»		»
»		»

3

What is the perceived readiness of those involved to talk about what really matters? If they are not prepared to talk how will you get them ready?

»

»

»

Onward...Get Going: *Your Organization*

At end of the day all good ideas must translate into actual work if they are going to become something more than just a good idea. If you're going to *Get Going* in your organization you must begin translating the ideas behind the generative postures you hope to unleash in your organization into actual work. Thoughts on generativity are not truly generative until they are being lived out in the organizations, communities, and social networks in which you live. System-wide transformation is the result of cumulative *actions* that happen over time.

4

Who do you need to talk with about your organization's transformation?	What specifically to you want to discuss with them? Do you think they will be open to such a future? Why or why not?	Can your current relationship with them hold the required conversation? If not, what conversation can you have to strengthen the relationship?	Date Scheduled & Location

A Parting Refrain: The Contagious Nature of Generativity

"When great causes are on the move in the world, stirring our souls, drawing us from our firesides, casting aside comfort, wealth and the pursuit of happiness in response to impulses at once awe-striking and irresistible, we learn that we are spirits, not animals."

Winston Churchill

A Parting Refrain: The Contagious Nature of Generativity

Ever notice your inner reaction during the holiday season when you walk past the Salvation Army Santa, the Toys for Tots pile of toys in the lobby of your company, the Angel Tree of names of disadvantaged children in the entrance to your faith community, or the pile of food and other goods gathered for the food bank in your local supermarket? Most of us who are not Scrooge-like or blind to others' needs can feel our heart strings tugged. We want to participate. We want to help, and, it is hoped, not always out of guilt or shame. And the greater the accumulation of results that has preceded us, the more we want to join in. Why?

Generativity, and the *generosity* it ignites within us, is contagious.

There is an avalanche quality to bandwagonism. It's almost as if we can't stand the thought of *not* being a part of the greater community's efforts. Our longing for be-longing intersects with our naturally generative instinct to give and be among. We are compelled to leap into the action. It happens with the exciting and long-anticipated new products being developed in our organizations. It happens when one of our favorite colleagues gets a well-deserved promotion. It happens when a once-struggling region begins to turn the corner after an arduous struggle to climb back from red ink.

When something good is happening, we all want to fan the flame.

In one of our client organizations, a small team of engineers had an idea for a way to connect one of its new solar energy products to the struggling agricultural communities of arid east Africa. Team members figured out that if adapted, the product could help farmers there have more consistent growing seasons with more predictable crop yields. At first, the head of R&D was against the idea but told them they could, on their own time, explore the possibility. Once other teams of engineers learned of the first team's pursuit, many volunteered to stay late and help with the experiments. After about seven months, there were nearly forty engineers staying late and coming in on weekends to contribute to the development of the product. The manufacturing organization then got involved and figured out how to use lower-cost materials to manufacture the devices with sufficient quality at a minimal cost to the organization. The leadership of the organization made the decision to put it into production and manufacture 1,200 of the devices, enough to boost the crops of more than 600 farms. A year later, the farmers in those communities had raised enough money to be able to purchase more of the devices for other farmers in another region of the country, and the generative cycle continues. It began with a small group of engineers who decided they could make a difference. The forty engineers look back on that year as one of the best in their career, and most have said they learned and gained more than they ever contributed. The corporation has chosen not to promote the effort publicly because it believes it would be exploitative of those they are trying to help, a remarkable show of humility and a powerful generative story. Once a small ember was lit and others fanned the flame, transformation was inevitable.

Whose flame is waiting for your fan? Are you standing back, waiting for someone else to go first? What transformation–of yourself and of your world–awaits you?

Moving from a degenerative to a generative posture in your organization is akin to changing the world. The community is still there, the people are still there, yet everything is different. The good news is that once you get some movement behind the idea, momentum takes over, and the transformation of your organization becomes as contagious as a community's insatiable desire to fill the coffers of its food pantry.

Such transformation is comparable to grassroots movements that have transformed the societies of our world in the past hundred years. An example that comes easily to mind is *satyagraha*, the philosophy of nonviolent, passive resistance developed by Gandhi and applied so successfully in India. Many of the independence movements in our world have been violent campaigns "against" something, and they have been hobbled by degenerative results–the terror and eventual reversion to monarchy in France and the replacement of a tsar and emperor by brutal Communist dictatorship in Russia and China, respectively. Gandhi's ideas were generative in the best sense of the word. He insisted that his followers actually *be* the change they wanted to see in the world. He assiduously denounced violence and instead met every use of force by colonial British forces against the Indian independence movement with peace, dignity, and empathy for the suffering of his fellow Indians and an unswerving devotion to the vision of a free and democratic

India. It was a long, hard road, but Gandhi's movement spread in what the Internet age would call a viral fashion across the subcontinent, eventually becoming irrepressible. The movement from the beginning was a grassroots expression of the yearnings of ordinary people, and it successfully overthrew what had once been the most formidable of the European great powers.

Grassroots transformation of this magnitude can happen everywhere there is a strong yearning for it, from the community to the neighborhood to the boardroom to your office. The American Civil Rights movement is a perfect example. The Reverend Dr. Martin Luther King Jr. was an admirer of Gandhi and his methods. King recognized that Rosa Park's defiance of Jim Crow laws that included segregated bus seats in the South represented the broad yearning of all oppressed people in the United States. The Civil Rights movement, like Gandhi's movement thirty years before, simply refused to play by the rules, adopting a generative instead of a reactive posture. Again, the momentum forward became irrepressible, and it began with the resolve of one human being who believed there was something more to be had, that something generative could come from something degenerative, and he mustered the courage to fan the flames of desire among people who shared that desire. Transformation followed.

What irrepressible transformation is in-Formation, awaiting your future?

Turning Generativity Loose

As we have noted several times, systems, by their nature, are perpetually self-generating. Cultures proliferate their DNA, whether generative or degenerative. It is as true of biology as it is of corporations. Truly generative postures have a way of summoning further generativity. It's why some of the postures we have portrayed elicit positive, productive responses from people in the organizations where we are doing this work. It's why the movie *Pay it Forward* had such a dramatic effect on American society. It's why viral marketing has such an impact on advancing social causes. In our view it is the simple power of a generative posture reaching out into the world that invites the innate response within us.

Has your organization ever had a defining moment that led to great success? Did it begin with defining moments of individuals? What effect did it have on you and the people you lead? Our hunch is that it summoned belief and hope in yourself and in the people you led. Sometimes that's all it takes to move an organization out of a degenerative, downward spiral and into an infectious upward spiral of generativity, seizing one defining moment after another, parlaying them into generative transformation.

There is no greater force in all of nature than the collective will of the human spirit harnessed for good, united in a resolved pursuit of its own transformation. When momentum gathers behind this force, the world is changed.

We hope you have allowed your time with this material to intensify your dream of a generative future. Your story will reveal whatever you choose for it to reveal. You can infect the world with dark, degenerative contaminants that kill hope and performance or you can loose into the world the liberating power of generative elements that accelerate upward performance, heal torn communities, restore lost faith, and translate dreams into reality.

Your story *will* have a next chapter. You *will* begin writing that chapter today, intentionally or not.

Your story's next chapter is in-Formation. You get to choose what message it broadcasts to the world.

Choose well.

Choose now.

Choose a generative organizational life in-Formation.

And in so choosing, invite the world to the transformation it longs for you to begin…

and that you have longed to become.

With our very best hope,

Josh & Ron

[1] Dow Chemical – The Human Element, www.dow.com/ the human element

[2] Prahalad, C.K., The Fortune at the Bottom of the Pyramid, Eradicating Poverty through Profits, 2005, Wharton School Publishing

[3] Kotter, J.P. and Heskett, J.L. (1992) Corporate Culture and Performance, Simon & Schuster

[4] "Finnish Companies Exhibit Healthy Organizational DNA," Neilson, G. and Leino, T., BoozeAllen Web site, story posted 09/02/2004, http://www.boozallen.com/publications/article/659369?tid=934306

[5] Whyte, David Crossing the Unknown Sea, Work as a Pilgrimage of Identity, Riverhead Books, 2001

[6] Hamel, G. (2007) The Future of Management, Harvard Business School Press

[7] http://answers.yahoo.com/question/index?qid=20070522143252AAwbSXr

[8] "Another: Survey: Management, lack of opportunities top reasons why people quit", Austin Business Journal, 4/25/2008

[9] http://www.dol.gov/cfbci/turnover.htm

[10] Schein, E.H. (1985-2005) Organizational Culture and Leadership, 3rd Ed., Jossey-Bass

[11] Cummings, Thomas G. & Worley, Christopher G. (2005), Organization Development and Change, 8th Ed., Thomson South-Western

[12] Collins, J. and Porras, J.I. (1994) Built to Last: Successful Habits of Visionary Companies, HarperBusiness

[13] http://corporate.disney.go.com/corporate/complete_history_1.html

[14] "Why Toyota is Becoming the World's Top Carmaker," Newsweek, March 13, 2007

[15] http://en.wikipedia.org/wiki/Aikido

[16] Fortune,"Meet The 23,000% Stock," September 2003

[17] Gretchen Morgenson."Inside the Countrywide Lending Spree," New York Times, 8/29/2007

[18] Evelyn M. Rusli."Credit Fears Chill Countrywide Financial," Forbes, 8/9/2007

[19] Liz Moyer."Countrywide, Markets On The Ropes," and"Countrywide Is On Its Side," both Forbes, 8/16/2007

[20] www.marriott.com

[21] Barabba, Vincent P. Surviving Transformation: Lessons from GM's Surprising Turnaround, Oxford University Press, (2004)

[22] Whyte, David Ibid

[23] Senge, P. The Fifth Discipline: The Art & Practice of The Learning Organization, Currency (Paperback)

[24] Ryan, K. and Oestreich, D. Driving Fear Out of the Workplace: Creating the High Trust, High Performance Organization, Jossey-Bass.

[25] Winning Workplaces, 12/4/2007, accessed from www.winningworkplaces.org

[26] Nettesheim, U."Priorititis," Passages Consulting, 2007.

[27] Saul, J. The Unconscious Civilization, Free Press, 1999.

[28] http://en.wikipedia.org/wiki/Shawn_Carpenter

[29] Gilbert, D., Krull, D. and Malone, P."Unbelieving the Unbelievable: Some Problems in the Rejection of False Information." Journal of Personality and Social Psychology, 1990, 59 (4), 601-613

[30] Riehle, D. on open source software at http://opensource.mit.edu/papers/computer-2007.pdf

[31] Peterson, S.J. and Byron, K. Exploring the Role of Hope in Job Performance: Results From Four Studies, 2007, Wiley.

[32] Obama, Barack, The Audacity of Hope, Thoughts on Reclaiming the American Dream, 2006, Crown

[33] Romans 5:3-5, New International Version, Amplified Version

[34] Carucci, R., Leadership Divided: What Emerging Leaders Need and What You Might Be Missing, 2006, Jossey-Bass

[35] Michael, E., Handfield-Jones, H. and Axelrod, B. The War for Talent, 2001, Harvard Business School Press.

[36] Chambers, H.E., My Way or the Highway: The Micromanagement Survival Guide, 2004, Berrett-Koehler Publishers

[37] Collins, J. Good to Great: Why Some Companies Make the Leap... and Others Don't, 2001, HarperCollins

[38] Rosenberg, Marshall B Nonviolent Communication, Puddle Dancer Press, 2003

[39] Ecclesiastes 1:18

[40] Nettesheim, U."Priorititis," Passages Consulting, 2007.

[41] "How Al Dunlap Self-Destructed," Business Week, July 6, 1998.

[42] Free-Climbing Lover's Leap. Bear's Reach, 5.7. Speed solo. 400+ ft. in 4 min, 25 seconds. (YouTube Video)

ABOUT THE AUTHORS

Josh Epperson is a Consultant at Passages Consulting, LLC where he works with both small community-based NGOs and large multi-national corporations in a variety of industries. His work consists of large-scale organization and culture change, organization architecture, and leadership development. Some of his clients have included: Kleiner Perkins Caufield & Byers, McDonalds, Phase 2 Consulting, Gates Corporation, Cadbury Schweppes, Golden Key, Starbucks Coffee Company, TriHealth, Everett Washington USA, Microsoft, The CIA, The Atlantic Philanthropies, and MillerCoors.

Josh helps create and facilitate major simulation-based leadership interventions such as *The Leadership Crucible* (www.theleadershipcrucible.com). This is a 3-day in-depth immersion where participants, by assuming the leadership roles in several fictitious organizations in a fictitious city, are able to try on new leadership behaviors in a low-risk environment and get feedback on their styles of relating and leadership performance.

Josh holds an MS in Organizational Development from Pepperdine University's Graziadio School of Business and Management. His current research is focused on an organization's ability to create systemic interdependence and how to leverage that interdependence toward greater performance. Josh enjoys working in organizations, communities, and other groups that find themselves highly fragmented, stuck, and needing to create a common path forward. He is proud to be publishing this book as his first in which his beliefs about organizations and interdependence can be further explored.

Josh also holds an MA in Counseling Psychology from Mars Hill Graduate School in Seattle, WA, and an MA in Christian Studies. Previously he worked as a therapist helping clients with severe mental health disorders. His work and study in the field of behavioral sciences has greatly contributed to his life and profession in pursuit of individual and systemic transformation.

Ron Carucci is a seasoned consultant with more than 25 years of experience working with CEOs and senior executives of organizations ranging from Fortune 50 to start-up in pursuit of transformational change. Ron has worked extensively in the health sciences, bio tech, and healthcare provider sectors, and in the technology, financial services and retail food and beverage industries. He has led work on numerous large-scale merger integrations and subsequent culture change initiatives, and enterprise level global organizational redesigns.

Ron specializes in the areas of strategy formulation, global organization design, large-scale organization and culture change organizational change and executive leadership development, with a particular passion for developing emerging leaders within organizations. He has helped CEO's, their executive teams, and their enterprises re-design themselves, build appropriate talent strategies to ensure the current and next generation of leaders have the capabilities required by the organization, and help leaders and leadership teams architect and lead major transformations. He has been chief architect of several major leadership development simulations for organizations, including *The Leadership Crucible.*

Ron is a former faculty member at Fordham University Graduate School as an associate professor of organizational behavior. He serves as Chief Operating Officer and Graduate Professor of Leadership at Mars Hill Graduate School in Seattle, WA. He has also served as an adjunct at the Center for Creative Leadership. He is co-author of several books, including most recently *Relationships that Enable Enterprise Change* (Jossey-Bass 2002), and most recently the best selling, *Leadership Divided, What Emerging Leaders Need and What you Might be Missing (*Jossey Bass 2006) and has authored numerous articles and book chapters on the issues of organizational change. His clients have included CitiBank, MillerCoors, Corning, Inc, Bristol-Myers Squibb, Amgen, Deutche Bank, Gates Corporation, ConAgra, TriHealth, OhioHealth,

McDonald's Corporation, Starbucks, Microsoft, Sojourners, National Asian Pacific Center on Aging, Kliener Perkins Caufield & Byers, Cadbury Adams, Hershey Corporation, The Atlantic Philanthropies, the US Patent & Trademark Office, Price Waterhouse Coopers, Johnson & Johnson, ADP, and The CIA.

ABOUT PASSAGES CONSULTING

forward motion for leaders and organizations

PASSAGES
consulting

With offices in Atlanta, Kansas City, San Francisco and Seattle, Passages Consulting is proud to be a premier provider of consultation in strategic organizational change and executive leadership development to some of the world's largest corporations. With a unique understanding of the systemic nature of realizing sustainable change, and powerful approaches to help leaders achieve transformative results, we are passionate about seeing leaders and their organizations thrive amidst chaotic and challenging business conditions. Our proprietary methodology for organization assessment, our powerful approach to multi-level transformation when working with executives, and our acclaimed approach to building leadership capability through simulation, uniquely position us as a formidable resource when executives are pondering their next revolution.

For more information, visit us at www.passagesconsulting.com and learn how we might partner with you in the pursuit of your greatest aspirations.

ALSO FROM PASSAGES CONSULTING...

Visit us at www.passagesconsulting.com and enjoy our series **Musings from Gate 44...**

...inspiring and provocative perspectives about our clients from a consultant's most sacredly reflective places...the airport.

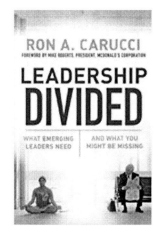

*Leadership Divided...*An innovative discussion on how you can attract, develop, and retain your promising emerging leaders by closing the relationship divide between them and the senior leaders that you need to mentor them.

LaVergne, TN USA
12 November 2009
163945LV00004B/13/P

The
Bird Feeder
Book

The
Bird Feeder
Book

*How to
Build Unique
Bird Feeders
from the
Purely Practical
to the Simply
Outrageous*

Thom Boswell

 A Sterling/Lark Book
Sterling Publishing Co., Inc.   New York

Design: Chris Colando, Thom Boswell
Production: Elaine Thompson, Chris Colando
Photography: Evan Bracken
Illustrations: Charlie Covington
Mechanical Drawings: Doug Stoll

Library of Congress Cataloging-in-Publication Data

Boswell, Thom.
    The bird feeder book : how to build unique bird feeders from the purely
practical to the simply outrageous / Thom Boswell.
        p.   cm.
    "A Sterling/Lark Book."
    Includes index.
    ISBN 0-8069-0295-7
    1. Bird feeders--Design and construction.   2. Birdhouses--Design
and construction.   I. Title
QL676.5.866 1993
598'.07'234—dc20

                                        92–40584
                                        CIP

10 9 8 7 6 5 4 3 2

A Sterling/Lark Book

First paperback edition published in 1995 by
Sterling Publishing Company, Inc.
387 Park Avenue South, New York, N.Y. 10016

Produced by Altamont Press, Inc.
50 College Street, Asheville, NC 28801

© 1993 by Altamont Press

Distributed in Canada by Sterling Publishing
    ℅ Canadian Manda Group, One Atlantic Avenue, Suite 105
    Toronto, Ontario, Canada M6K 3E7
Distributed in Great Britain and Europe by Cassell PLC
    Villiers House, 41/47 Strand, London WC2N 5JE, England
Distributed in Australia by Capricorn Link (Australia) Pty Ltd.
    P.O. Box 6651, Baulkham Hills, Business Centre, NSW 2153, Australia

Sterling ISBN 0-8069-0295-7 Trade
              0-8069-0296-5 Paper

Contents

Introduction

If you've never built a bird feeder or house, a wonderful adventure awaits you. Not only are they fun to build and a great way to ornament your yard, you'll get to watch them being used by a fascinating variety of birds you may barely have known existed. If you've already tried your hand at this craft or installed storebought structures, this book will inspire you to stretch the limits of your imagination and skills, and will even help you design your own.

There's something in this book for everyone, from children to experienced woodworkers. While most of the projects are constructed of wood, you'll be introduced to several other accessible materials and techniques as well. And while each project is explained with specific instructions, you are encouraged to adapt and experiment with these designs to suit yourself. Essentially, this book contains the "blueprints" for forty fascinating bird structures, yet it also serves as a manual that will equip you to exercise your own creativity.

Providing shelter, food and water for birds is a human pastime that extends far back into history. In medieval Europe, this was actually a way of harvesting birds to supplement their own meager diets. Native Americans used to hang gourd houses for purple martins who would chase vultures away from their meat drying racks. Gardeners like to attract certain birds to help control insect populations that can destroy vegetation. Martins, robins, wrens, thrushes, warblers, swallows and bats are all excellent exterminators and reduce the need for chemical pesticides.

Of course, there are other reasons for nurturing our feathered friends that are less self-serving. As human civilization continues to encroach on wilderness, we are obliged to provide habitat for species that have been denied their natural feeding and nesting sites. We can also lure species back into

refurbished areas they'd been forced to abandon.

Birding, or bird watching, is growing in popularity, especially in the U.S. and the British Isles. People have a natural appreciation and concern for birds. Sitings are compiled in "life lists," and copious field notes document behavior. The best bird structure designs are those which utilize this sort of information.

Constructing habitat for birds need not be such an exacting science, however. Many a bird will find comfort in even the most amateur of attempts at feeder or house building. Neither may it matter to you precisely which species comes to feed or takes up residence in your generically constructed house. The antics of sparrows can be just as much fun to watch as the flitting colors of a finch.

There are others yet who see these structures as an art form. A "house" need not be a "home," and a feeder or bath can be elaborately sculpted for the absolute delight of humans, yet be nothing more than a curious perch for birds. People who dabble with doll houses or miniatures will love the possibilities of art for the birds. In fact, some of the more detailed and exquisite structures in this book would be better appreciated indoors than out.

As you can see in our gallery (pages 30–49), most examples of this art form are houses instead of feeders. Curiously, feeders are more popular than houses. Maybe it's time to start elevating feeders to the level of art, too, as this book begins to do. Whether for function or fancy, you can take part in this enjoyable creative process.

"Eats Diner" by Randy Sewell

Design Considerations

Types of Feeders

There are several basic types of feeders, each designed to dispense certain feeds and to accommodate the feeding habits of different birds. These are some of the features to consider when choosing a design for your feeder:

1. Maximize the load capacity of the feed container for less frequent refilling.

2. Make the feed container easy to open to facilitate refilling.

3. If there's a roof, it should effectively protect the seed from rain and snow.

4. Provide drainage outlets in the feed tray to prevent stagnant pooling of water.

5. Incorporate a spill tray with a lip or plexiglass wall so birds can see the feed.

6. Provide adequate space for birds to perch and eat.

7. Make it as easy as possible to take apart and clean.

Here are the most common types of feeders, each of which has many design possibilities:

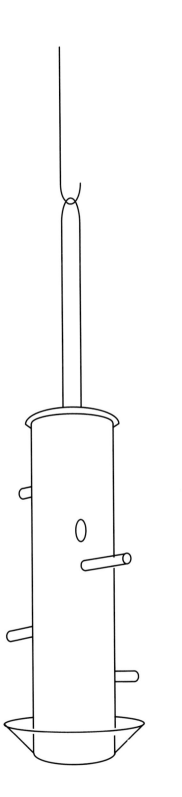

Ground or Open Tray feeders are among the simplest of approaches to dispensing feed. You can attract a wide variety of birds, such as cardinals, jays, sparrows, doves and chickadees, by scattering cracked corn or mixed seed directly on the ground. Choose a clearing of cropped lawn, dirt or patio and sprinkle seed over an eight-foot circle. However, constructing a simple post-mounted tray has several advantages for you and the birds. If you add a lip to contain the seed, allow for drainage with gaps in the lip or holes in the tray. This type of feeder should be mounted about five feet above ground and is very easy to refill and clean.

Roofed Tray feeders protect feed from the elements. The roof should be larger than the tray, and can be supported by a center post, peripheral posts, or even suspended from above. This open-air structure lends itself to all sorts of pavilion and gazebo-type designs, and is a highly functional feeder.

Hopper feeders are quite prevalent because they incorporate so many desirable features. The major feature, in addition to tray and roof, is a feed container that gradually dispenses feed through some sort of openings, usually onto the tray. The roof may cover both hopper and feeding tray, or the hopper only. Some of the walls might be transparent.

Tube feeders are very popular, usually clear plastic to display the feed, and mounted on post or by hanging. They have multiple holes with perches around the cylinder for feeding stations, and often feature a bottom dish and protective roof dome. They are easily refilled, and may incorporate metal-reinforced holes and perches that squirrels cannot chew.

Suet feeders require different structures because of the globular consistency of the suet. A plastic-coated wire cage works well. One-inch diameter holes can be drilled in a hanging log, post or stump and filled with suet. An inverted hanging cup (coconut half, yogurt canister or bell) packed with suet will attract chickadees. These can be hung from a tree or the eaves of a house, or fastened to a tree trunk. They are especially visited in winter, and attract woodpeckers, nuthatches and mocking-birds, among others.

Mesh Bag feeders are very simple and can also be attached to other sorts of feeders. Just fill a plastic mesh bag (such as onions are sold in) with nuts or thistle seed, and hang it to attract finches, buntings and chickadees.

Many birds prefer to light on a good vantage point and survey the situation before swooping down to feed or bathe. If there are no trees or tall structures in the vicinity of your feeder or bath, you can build a simple perch or two. Nail a short cross-piece on top of an 8'–12' pole and plant it nearby.

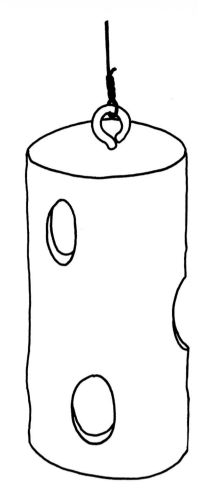

Types of Baths

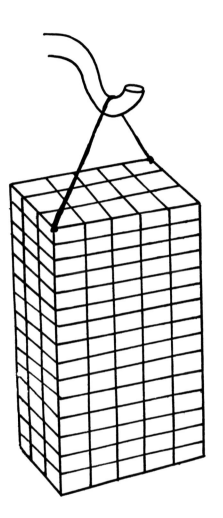

All birds need water for drinking and bathing. Most birds scoop water into their bills and tilt their heads back to drink. Others, like doves, can actually sip. Bathing behavior includes some fascinating variations as well. Many birds stand in shallow water and funnel it into and out of their feathers using complex body movements. Some take a quick dive and fly out while others fully submerge for a bit. Birds will also bathe in rain or dew drops.

Your bath will be visited more frequently if you place it near a feeder. It can be on or above the ground. When making or purchasing a bath, keep in mind that it should be shallow with gradual slopes so that birds can wade in to a depth of no more than three inches of water. The surface should not be slippery. Avoid ceramics if the water will freeze in winter because they will crack. Concrete works well and can be molded, especially when reinforced, into any shape on or above ground. You may want to incorporate one or more small pools in your landscaping. Even an inverted trash can lid will serve the purpose.

The sound of running water is especially attractive to birds. This can be achieved in several ways. Drip hoses and mist fountains are commercially available for this purpose. You can also erect a reservoir, such as a bucket, over your bath that has a tiny drip hole. This will, of course, require refilling.

Birds also need water during cold dry spells in winter. To keep the water in your bath from freezing, you can purchase an inexpensive electric water heater that is designed for bird baths. Scrub out your bath periodically with fresh water and a brush.

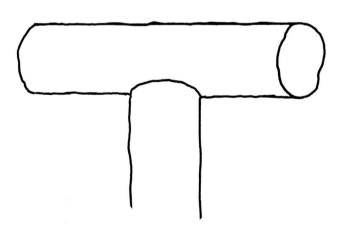

Types of Houses

When you consider how many birds take up residence in unlikely nooks and crannies, it would seem that they're not very particular about housing requirements. However, each species has its own specific needs regarding the dimensions of its living chamber, the size and position of entry hole, siting, etc. Also, it is surprisingly difficult to lure most bird species into man-made houses. Even the colors you paint your house will affect its habitability. Birds generally prefer natural muted hues, although purple martins are attracted to white.

The chart on the following pages lists guidelines for many common species, but bear in mind that birdhouse design is not an exact science. You can learn a lot simply by observing the behavior and nesting habits of whatever birds are common in your region. Build the chamber or platform according to the size of the bird you wish to attract. Place it in a site comparable to its preferred habitat. If it builds nests in the open, it should prefer a platform type of house. If it nests in a tree hole or other crevice, you will need to construct a chamber. Note which species are common to your area and alter your designs to accommodate them.

It must also be noted, however, that a number of designs are intended more for human amusement and decoration than bird utilization. Bird structures have become an art form in their own right, and are displayed in parlors and galleries as well as backyards and public parks. And who knows, maybe some odd bird will share your aesthetic and adapt its needs to your sense of whimsy.

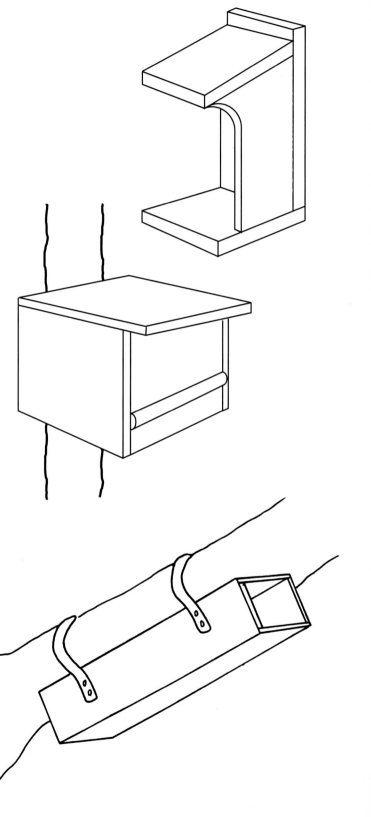

Most bird houses can be divided roughly into four categories, each of which offers numerous design possibilities:

Platform houses are preferred by certain claustrophobic species such as robins. They can be mounted on a pole, cradled in a tree or hung on a wall. They occasionally have one or two walls which facilitate wall mounting or act as a windbreak.

Open Box houses can vary significantly, depending on size, siting, and which part is left open. Barn owls can do without a roof when the box is inside a much larger structure. Kestrels and flycatchers like having one wall open. Bats need open floors for bottom entry. Mounting and siting will vary greatly depending on the species.

Enclosed houses are the most common since they appeal to the widest variety of birds. The floors of these chambers are recessed in the sense that the entry hole is above floor level. There is tremendous variance in all other design elements, mounting and siting.

Multi-Compartment houses have very limited appeal, being suited only to communal dwellers like purple martins and bats. Purple martin houses are mounted high on poles or rooftops. Bat houses are mounted high in trees or on poles. The number of compartments can vary greatly.

Some House-Nesting Birds

Species	Approximate Dimensions	Hole Dimensions
Bluebird (Eastern, Western, and Mountain)[1] Sialia spp.	Floor: 5" x 5" Interior height: 8" to 10"	Height above floor (centered): 6" (5" for Warbler) Diameter: 1-1/2"
Chickadee (Black-capped, Boreal, and Carolina)[2] Parus spp.	Floor: 4" x 4" Interior height: 8" to 10"	Height above floor (centered): 6" Diameter: 1-1/4"
Finch (House and Purple) Carpodacus spp.	Floor: 6" x 6" Interior height: 6"	Height above floor (centered): 3"–4" Diameter: 2"
Flicker Colaptes auratus	Floor: 7" x 7" Interior height: 16"+	Height above floor (centered): 12"+ Diameter: 2-3/4"
Flycatcher (Many varieties) Tyrannus spp., Myiarchus spp.	Floor: 6" x 6" Interior height: 14"	Height above floor (centered): 6"+ Diameter: 2"
Jackdaw (Corvus moredula)	Floor: 8" x 8" Interior height: 12"	Height above floor (centered): 6" Diameter: 6"
Owl (Barn) Tyto alba	Floor: 10" x 18" Interior height: 18"	Height above floor (centered): 4" Diameter: 6"
Owl (Saw-whet, Screech and Little) Aegolius acadicus, Otus asio and Athene noctua	Floor: 10" x 10" Interior height: 15"	Height above floor (centered): 10"+ Diameter: 3"
Pigeon (Street) Columba livia	Floor: 8" x 8" Interior height: 8"	Height above floor (centered): 4" Diameter: 4"
Purple Martin (Progne subus)	Floor: 6" x 6" Interior height: 6" (each compartment)	Height above floor (centered): 1-3/4" Diameter: 2-1/2"
Robin (American and English)[3] Tardus migratorius and Erithacus rubecula	Floor: 6" x 6" Interior height: 8" (open roofed platform)	No hole, open-sided roofed box
Sparrows (House and many others) Passer domesticus, members of Family Fringillidae	Floor: 10" x 10" Interior height: 15"+	Height above floor (centered): 6" Diameter: 1-1/2"
Wood Duck[4] Aix sponsa	Floor: 6" x 6" Interior height: 14"+	Height above floor (centered): 12"–16" (9"–12" for Kestrel) Diameter: 3" x 4" (oval) Add interior ramp covered with chicken wire
Woodpecker (Hairy, Red-bellied, Red-cockaded, Red-headed, and Yellow-bellied Sapsucker) Picoides villosus, Melanerpes carolinus, Picoides borealis, Melanerpes erythrocephalus, and Sphyrapicus varius	Floor: 8" x 8" Interior height: 24"	Height above floor (centered): 9"–12" Diameter: 1-1/2" (Hairy, Red-bellied, Red-cockaded, Sapsucker) 2" (Red-headed)
Woodpecker (Pileated) Dryocopus pileatus	Floor: 4" x 4" Interior height: 14"	Height above floor (centered): 10" Diameter: 4"
Wrens (House, Bewick's, Carolina, and others) Family Troglodytidae	Floor: 4" x 4" Interior height: 8"	Height above floor (centered): 4" Diameter: 1-1/4" (House), 1-1/2" (Bewick's, Carolina, and others)

[1] House will also serve: Tree Swallow (Iridoprocne bicolor), Warblers (Parula spp.), Spotted Flycatcher (Muscicapa striata)

[2] House will also serve: Brown Creeper (Certhia familiaris), Downy Woodpecker (Picoides pubescens), Nuthatches (Sitta spp.), Tufted Titmouse (Parus bicolor)

Height Above Ground	Siting Tips
5'–10'	On fence posts, stumps, utility poles, tree trunks, etc. Place around open fields or any grassy expanse (park, cemetary, golf course). Predator collar suggested.
6'–15'	Locate near large trees, Line with non-aromatic wood shavings.
8'–12'	Both birds primarily Western though sometimes found in East. Purple Finch prefers wooded site.
6'–20'	Site on tree trunk, line bottom with 3"+ of non-aromatic sawdust.
8'–20'	Prefers wooded site, natural-appearing house.
10'+	Away from human noise.
12'–20'	Locate near open fields/meadows to provide hunting range.
10'–30'	Near water if at all possible. Prefers open yard with few or no trees nearby.
10'+	Prefers a perch.
Above reach of cats	Prefers open area near well-maintained lawns for feeding.
12'	Habitats vary widely.
10'–20'	Locate on trees or buildings.
12'–20'	Wood Duck: Locate near (or above) water, line with 3"+ non-aromatic sawdust, predator collar suggested. Kestrel: Site on edge of field or meadow to provide hunting range.
12'–20'	Site on tree trunk, much prefers natural-looking house (bark lined, for example)
6'–10'	Locate among large trees. Natural-looking house essential.
6'–10'	Site on edge of woods, in fencerows, etc.

[3] House (nesting platform) will also serve: Barn Swallow (Riparia riparia), Phoebes, Eastern and Say's (Sayornis spp.), Various Thrushes (Cartharus spp.), Song Sparrow (Melospiza melodia), Pied Wagtail (Motacilla alba)

[4] House will also serve: American Kestrel (Falco sparvarius), European Kestrel (Falco tinnunculus)

Your birdhouse will be occupied only a few months each year by migrating birds. Wait until spring to clean out the house to allow winter birds like chickadees and bluebirds to use the old nesting material. To enable cleaning, design one panel of your house to be hinged or removable. It could be the roof, floor, or any wall. After you have removed all the old nesting material, pour boiling water over the interior to kill any remaining parasites.

Most houses will benefit from ventilation and drainage. Small holes or slots can be cut around the roof eaves for vents. Drill 1/8" drain holes in the corners of the floor.

The entry hole is a crucial part of any house. If it's too large it will invite intruders. If it's too small or high it will hinder access. If it's too low it will admit harsh weather. To discourage predators, you can cut a doughnut-shaped piece of 1 x stock that conforms to your entry hole and attach it inside to extend the portal. Roughen this tunnel with a rasp to accommodate the grip of bird claws.

Varying the shape and material of the roof is a great way to add interest to your birdhouse or feeder. Some basic shapes to consider are shed, gabled, hip, mansard, gambrel, pyramidal, conical and domed. Materials can include solid wood, plywood, bark-faced slab, cedar shakes or doll house shingles, tar paper, fiberglass shingles, sheet metal, copper, bamboo and thatch. Generally, the steeper the roof, the less it is prone to leaking. Just make sure the ridge is caulked to seal it. A flat roof requires the protection of an impervious sealant, as do the edges of plywood where the glue seams of lamination will separate.

Unwanted Guests

It's a jungle out there—and that's just the way it should be. As much as we might prefer well-mannered songbirds with exquisitely colorful plumage, nature's panorama reminds us that the weak must fall prey to the strong, and there is beauty in all creation. Swallows and swifts may clog our chimneys with their nests, but they also devour tons of bothersome mosquitos.

Ultimately, human intervention plays its part in this grand scheme. We are free to nurture and protect our feathered friends with food and shelter. And to do this effectively, we must learn how to counteract the competition and predation that would undo our efforts. Here, then, are profiles of the bird world's ten most unwanted list.

Sparrows

Most varieties of sparrow will nest almost anywhere, including your attic if they find entry. If you've built your house for a less common species, you'll want to discourage them from setting up housekeeping. Since they tend to nest earlier in the season than most birds, you can probably clean out their nests before your intended guests arrive. Also, they are much less likely to nest if you leave off the porch under your entry hole.

Sparrows will also be frequent customers at your feeder. This is really not a problem, unless your feed is limited or you're hoping to attract different birds. If you don't want sparrows, stock your feeder with red proso millet, Niger thistle and peanuts.

Starlings

There's no easy way to keep starlings from nesting in your birdhouse. Like the sparrow, the undesirability of the starling has mostly to do with its commonality. Your best bet is to build your birdhouse strictly to the specifications outlined in the chart on pages 14 and 15.

There's little competition at most feeders, however, since starlings are primarily suet-eaters. Keep this in mind when you stock suet for other birds.

Cats

Be aware of feline territories when you install a birdhouse or feeder. Let's face it, cats love birds, but assuming they're domesticated they will playfully torture a bird rather than consuming an honest meal. Mount your house, bath or feeder above leaping range. Install a predator barrier on tree or pole. Put a bell on your cat's collar. Eliminate low foliage where cats can hide as they wait to pounce, and keep grass mowed around feeders.

Dogs

Dogs aren't nearly as dangerous as cats, but can still pose a threat if you don't take precautions. You could perhaps verbally discourage your dog, or your neighbor's dog, but you'll most likely have success by fencing the bird zone away from dog territories. A dog's very presence can keep more timid birds from visiting your beautifully prepared sites.

Raccoons, Skunks and Oppossum

If you live in a rural or semi-rural environment, these predators may be looking for a quick meal. Follow the same precautions necessitated by cats, plus a tight mesh fence. You may also elect to control the threat by setting out traps. We would encourage the use of live traps, such as the Hav-a-hart brand. If you believe you must kill these animals, check with your local fish and game authorities and know what you're doing.

Hawks and Shrikes

An attack by these large birds on smaller birds would be natural and horribly fascinating, but

quite unlikely. If you'd like to create a defense for your smaller birds, provide them with lots of nearby places to seek shelter should they be assaulted. The most likely marauders are the sharp-shinned hawks in the eastern U.S. and Cooper's hawks in the western U.S. Do keep in mind that hawks are protected by laws, as well as nature's plan.

Squirrels

These cute little creatures are probably a bird's most prevalent pest. The squirrels' legendary attraction to bird feeders can become a consuming preoccupation for us as human hosts, but needs to be taken in perspective. You may as well expect a certain level of squirrel piracy as inevitable.

Since your goal is to keep squireels away from the birds' feed, let us look at a number of methods. Hang or post mount the feeder at least twenty feet from the nearest tree and six or more feet above the ground. The post should be slick metal. You can incorporate conical or disk-shaped baffles at least four feet up the post or on any wires used to hang the feeder. Any other barriers you incorporate into your design should be made of metal or tough plastic to prevent squirrels from chewing through them.

As a last, or even preventive resort, you can offer cracked corn or whole cobs of dried corn to distract squirrels away from the more expensive seeds intended for song birds mounted higher up. The corn can be dispensed on the ground or up in trees. Cobs of dried corn can even be spiked onto propellor-like squirrel feeders mounted on trees that keep squirrels occuped while providing humans with goofy entertainment. You may even find that squirrels are just as much fun to watch as most birds.

Predator Barriers

Birds will be much more able to experience the peaceful enjoyment of your feeder, house or bath if you install physical barriers to prevent the inevitable harassment of unwanted guests. These barriers are particularly effective against four-legged intruders.

Poles, posts and trees can be fitted with a sleeve of aluminum sheeting that will defy the traction of claws. It must be installed at least five feet above ground level. If you have a metal pole, it wouldn't hurt to grease it.

Conical foils can be constructed out of aluminum sheeting to fit both round and square posts. Join and attach the assembly with self-tapping sheet metal screws, which can be installed with an electric drill. Position the foil at least four feet above ground level.

If your bird structure is suspended, use heavy wire instead of rope. Squirrels can climb down and gnaw through rope. You can also install metal pie pans as baffles on the wire to foil dauntless intruders. The wire can be attached to another wire spanning two trees or man-made structures, but a feeder should be at least twenty feet from a tree or other tall structure to be out of jumping range.

Yet another way to impede cats is to spread chicken wire just above the ground beneath a feeder or house. This will compromise their ability to leap because they will be unable to build up speed on the ground.

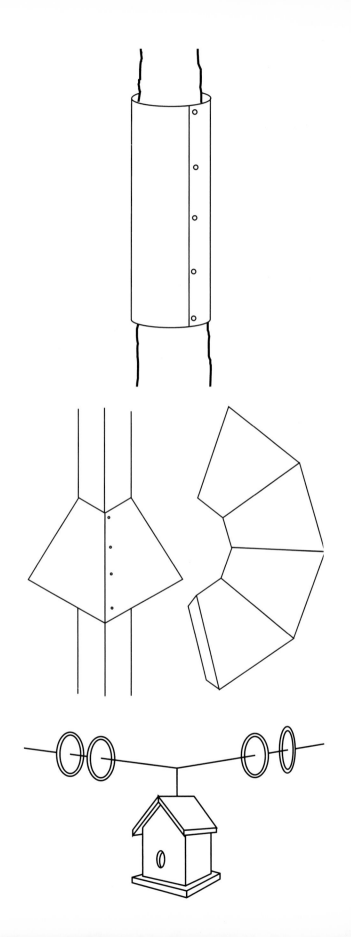

Mounting

Most birds will probably prefer houses that are firmly mounted on a post, tree or wall. Yet this does not rule out hanging, especially for feeders. Observe all siting specifications before planning how you will mount your structure.

If you hang something from a tree, wrap the branch with fabric or inner tube rubber where you attach the wire to prevent damage to the tree. Make sure the branch is strong enough to support the structure.

When mounting a house or feeder to the trunk of a tree, it is preferable to use a batten. This is a vertical plank, almost twice as high as the structure, which reduces the stress from the protruding center of gravity. Use galvanized screws, or a strong strap around the trunk, to attach the batten to the tree. Use galvanized hardware also when attaching a structure to a wall.

Posts can be metal or wooden. Use pressure treated lumber or cedar, whether square or round. Sink the post at least 18" using a post hole digger. Add gravel at the bottom for wood. Concrete isn't necessary, but pack the dirt well around the shaft. The top of a metal pipe can be threaded to fit a floor flange attached to the base of your bird structure. Wooden posts can be reinforced with metal L-brackets or wooden triangular braces at the top.

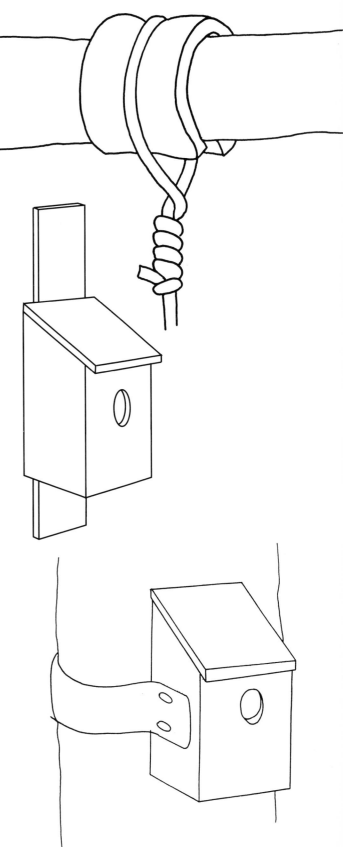

Siting

There are several things to consider when choosing an appropriate site for your feeder, house or bath. You will want to create an environment that is especially attractive to birds. Providing food, water and shelter is a good beginning. Placing these near trees, shrubs and flowers is another way to enhance a bird habitat. You should emphasize any of these elements which might usually be missing in the surrounding area. For instance, on the plains, introduce trees. In the desert, provide water. During winter, display food.

Birds prefer border habitat like where an open meadow or lawn meets the edge of a grove of trees. This allows unobstructed access and egress while maintaining proximity to food, nesting materials and safe haven in the forest.

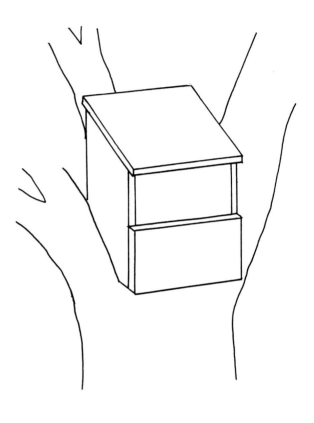

Feeders can be moved gradually closer to your house as birds get accustomed to using them. This will give you better views of the birds from your window. In fact, some feeders are designed for placement directly at your window for optimum viewing.

Orient the entry hole of a house away from prevailing wind-driven rain. To attract the more timid birds, houses and feeders should face away from the activity of people, such as sidewalks, driveways and children's play areas. Avoid sites that receive extreme sunshine. For the more open nesting boxes and platforms, a sheltered and reasonably hidden site is preferable. Refer to the chart on pages 14 and 15 for more specific site requirements.

If your yard lacks the appropriate vegetation, consider some creative landscaping to attract birds to your habitat. For instance, pyracantha has beautiful berries that birds love in winter months. Sunflowers are another sure bet. See what you can grow in your area.

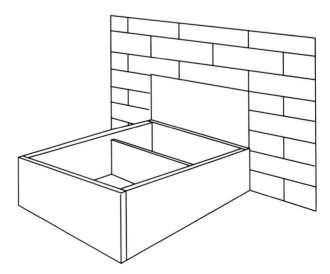

Construction Basics

Materials

There are no ideal materials for building bird feeders and houses. Moisture will eventually take its toll in the form of rot and rust, even undermining glue joints and finishes. Other factors such as sunshine, temperature fluctuation, toxic chemical components, expense and availability must also figure in to your choice of materials. Let's examine the most likely options.

Solid Wood is still a favorite choice, being both aesthetic and easy to work with. One disadvantage, however, is that it's commercially available only in 3/4" and greater thicknesses. If you have access to a thickness planer, this can be remedied. Otherwise you may encounter limitations having to incorporate such thick boards in your miniaturized designs. Another shortcoming of conventional lumber is the knots and other flaws that can complicate the assembly of small structures. It's worth the small extra expense to purchase the higher grades of lumber.

Many of the designs in this book call for pine, but you should feel free to substitute more rot-resistant or elegant species wherever you choose. These include cedar, redwood, cypress, and various tropical woods like banak. Locally you may find yew, black locust, fruitwoods and others. Western cedar is widely available and inexpensive, but its aroma may keep some birds such as chickadees from nesting in houses made of it. Clear-heart redwood is great to work with, but it costs at least twice as much as cedar. If you want to mix woods, be aware that stock thicknesses between species usually vary slightly, which can complicate accurate joinery.

Even though pressure-treated wood is rot-resistant, it should be avoided, except as mounting posts. The chromated copper arsenate with which it is treated doesn't belong with bird feed or tiny nestlings.

Plywood offers several practical advantages. It is strong, unlikely to warp, inexpensive and available in many dimensions. Of the many types, only marine- or exterior-grade plywood and oriented strand board are recommended for bird structures. The others either lack weather resistance or contain toxic substances. Still, with any plywood, care must be taken to seal any exposed end grain against weather.

Marine plywood is superior in that it has no voids, even in the inner laminations. Exterior plywoods are graded by letters which indicate the quality of both faces. For bird structures, use A-C or B-C, and face the better surface outward. Oriented strand board, not to be confused with particle or flake board, is all the same grade. Each of these plywoods is available in standard thicknesses of 1/4", 3/8", 1/2" and 3/4".

Plastics offer some unique possibilities. Tube feeders utilize PVC or clear plastic cylinders. Plexiglass is preferable to glass when used as windows in hopper feeders. Plastic sheeting can be curved and bent with heat, cut with fine-tooth blades, and joined with glues and bolts to form durable structures.

Adhesives usually need to be reinforced with nails or screws. Yellow carpenter's glue lacks water resistance but holds adequately when under roof and reinforced with metal fasteners. Two-part epoxy is expensive but sometimes necessary to bind critical junctures where no other fasteners can be used. Clear silicone caulk is quite effective in both sealing and adhering. A hot-melt glue gun is a handy tool for making waterproof seals, though the glue has relatively low adhesive strength.

Fasteners should always be corrosion-resistant. Nails and screws should be galvanized steel, stain-

Tools and Techniques

less steel, or brass. Hinges, latches or other hardware that is exposed should never be plated. Use solid stainless, aluminum or brass.

Finishes are actually used on wood more for structural and aesthetic reasons than to protect it from weathering. Unsealed wood expands and contracts as it exchanges moisture with the atmosphere, thus stressing the joints. Heat affects this process unevenly since only certain areas are exposed to sunlight, causing more stress. Even so, structural considerations need not overrule your appreciation for the beauty of naturally weathered wood. The small seams of bird structures will usually withstand these stresses.

Stains will help seal the wood while enhancing its look. A clear top finish can also be added, but must be compatible with the stain. Alkyd stains are oil based. Acrylic stains are water based, easier to apply and clean up, and longer lasting. Clear coatings include polyurethane, marine spar varnish, and penetrating oils which need to be reapplied every year or so. Exterior-rated primers and paints work well, but avoid those which contain mercury.

Any finish you apply must cover all surfaces of the wood, once all glue seams are dry. Pay close attention to all exposed end grain, especially on plywood. Let the structure dry thoroughly at least two weeks or until no odor lingers before letting birds use it.

Concerning the dimensions given in the materials lists, 1 x 12 is a stock size for dressed lumber which actually measures 3/4" x 11-1/4", whereas 1" x 12" means just that. Watch for the inch (") marks. Also, the exact dimensions of a finished component may not always be listed, but the stock needed to make the part is listed.

The projects in this book cover a rather wide range of difficulty. A child can make some, while others require an experienced woodworker. Most, however, are very manageable for anyone with moderate craft skills. In fact, building small-scale projects such as these is a wonderful and inexpensive way to develop your talents. You may soon become inspired to design your own.

Many of the projects require only simple hand tools: hammer, screw drivers, saws and a crank drill. Other tools will be required for specific projects: whittling knife, side cutters, pliers, files or chisels. A power drill and a coping saw will come in handy. All sorts of power tools will improve efficiency and accuracy if you have them, but are not absolutely necessary: jigsaw, hole saw, band saw, planers, routers, etc. However, a table saw is more or less required for about half the projects.

Most of the joinery used throughout these bird structures involves butt joints. Although they are the weakest of all joints, they are quite adequate for small structures, especially when properly glued, nailed and reinforced by other intersecting boards. Miter joints involve two beveled edges butting together, such as roof peaks, wall corners and molding that trims corners. Gluing is crucial since fasteners will not hold as well as with butt joints. However, miter joints seal all the end grain and present a neater appearance. Dado joints include several variations

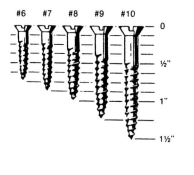
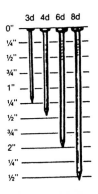

and are rarely used here. They generally require a table saw and are quite strong when accurately fit. Dado grooves are used for movable panels as well as the sort of multiple partitions found in martin houses.

To create a strong glue joint, there should be a minimum of gaps between the adjoining pieces. Cuts should be made smoothly and evenly, and the pieces should be held together tightly until the glue has dried. Good gluing technique is especially important for plywood, since fasteners won't hold well in the laminated grain. Always use plenty of glue for maximum seam strength. Excess can be wiped away after clamping, unless you plan to use stain, a clear finish or to leave wood unfinished. In that case, use just enough glue spread inside the joint without squirting and dripping outside the seams. Trim away any excess *after* glue has dried using a knife and sandpaper.

Screws hold better than nails but are compromised when penetrating end grain, and nearly useless in plywood endgrain. Unless the wood is very soft or the screws are very slender, holes should be pre-drilled to a diameter slightly smaller than the screws being inserted. You might also consider using corrosion-resistant threaded nails, but only for permanent joints since they cannot be removed.

To cut small entry holes in solid wood, a power drill with a spade bit can be used. A hole saw works nicely for larger holes and for plywood. A coping saw can be used if you lack a hole saw. A coping saw or jigsaw is also useful for cutting square holes or scroll cuts. Use fine-tooth blades and cut so that the non-splintering side is on the good face. Saw with patience and don't force the blade.

When joining walls to a floor or base, where water may collect, cut the wall panels so that their grain runs parallel to the base. End grain will then meet vertically at the corners rather than butting against the floor where water can wick up and increase rot.

Important: Be careful to read all of the instructions to understand a project before beginning to make it.

And finally, some important tips on safety. Operate all power tools with special care. Familiarize yourself with any appropriate safety techniques such as push sticks, jigs and feather sticks. Always wear eye protection and a dust mask when cutting or sanding. Ventilate your work space properly. Use common sense, and if you're unsure about something, don't try it. If you're tired, stop.

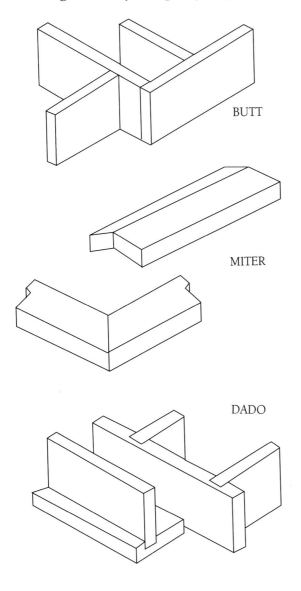

BUTT

MITER

DADO

A Versatile Mix

White Proso Millet

Fine Cracked Corn

Black Striped Sunflower

**Hulled Raw
Sunflower**

26

Raw Peanuts

Niger (Thistle)

Suet

Fruit Slices

Hemp Seed

27

Feeding Habits

Birds have high energy needs due to very high metabolic rates, especially the smaller species. They must eat the equivalent of between 40 and 75 percent of their body weight each day just to survive. Humans can play a very beneficial role in supplementing bird diets, particularly during severe weather such as droughts or prolonged snow cover.

The best time to start feeding birds is in early autumn. Certain flocks, like chickadees and juncos, will actually make their winter homes around good feeding areas. Because many birds will start to rely on the feed you put out, it is important to maintain your feeding program through the winter. If you must leave for awhile, taper off gradually or, better yet, ask a neighbor to take over while you're away. Come spring, providing feed is optional since natural food sources become abundant once again. There's no need to fear that birds will abandon wild foods just because they visit your feeder regularly. Providing water is a good year-round practice, though most critical during extremely cold weather.

There's not very much you can do to exclude ruffian starlings or gangs of sparrows in favor of the prettier songbirds. The best solution is to offer something to all. Set up a few different kinds of feeders, spaced apart, each with a different menu. Fill your feeders early to attract small birds like titmice, since starlings and blue jays eat later in the day. Sparrows often avoid hanging feeders. A ground feeder with inexpensive cracked corn, mixed seed or table scraps will divert many larger birds from the more expensive seed in elevated feeders.

Seeds are the most popular of feeds used to stock feeders. Although birds enjoy a great variety of seeds, which can even be mixed to suit the species in your area, sunflower seeds are the favorite of most birds. Chances are you live in a climate where you can grow your own sunflowers.

Nuts are also popular. Almost any kind will be eaten by birds, but unsalted peanuts are best. They can be strung up in their shells, mixed with other nuts in mesh bag feeders, or sprinkled almost anywhere. You'll enjoy watching nuthatches, titmice and downy woodpeckers perform their antics to get nuts hung right at your window.

Suet is hard fat trimmed from the kidneys and loins of beef or lamb. Birds love it plain during the cold months. For summer it can be rendered into "bird cakes." Melt small pieces in a pan and pour it over seeds, nuts, dried fruit, or almost any bird food, and let it cool. Or, try this alternative recipe: combine in a blender 1 part vegetable shortening, 1 part peanut butter, 1 part flour, 1 part cracked corn and 3 parts yellow corn meal. Insect-eating birds eat suet in winter when insects are scarce.

Cereal and Grain products are suitable when soaked or crumbled up for small beaks. Oats, breads, cakes, cookies, pastries, corn flakes and other variations appeal to birds.

Fruits and Vegetables such as dried peas and lentils can be served. Dried fruits such as currants and sultanas are favored by many species. Try a shish-kabob of apple, orange and other fruits to further delight bird palates.

Animal Products like small tidbits of meat, bones and cheese, along with other kitchen scraps are also worthy of bird consumption. There's almost no limit to supplementing a bird's diet.

When you opt for seed, buy in bulk. Store it in clean, dry containers with lids. Find a scoop to load your feeder, perhaps a plastic pitcher or milk jug with its bottom cut out. Clean your feeder periodically with hot water and mild detergent. Keep all feeding stations clear of old food scraps that rot and attract rats, causing infection and disease.

Feeder Fillers

White Proso Millet: Cardinals, Cowbirds, Finches (House, Chaffinch, Green Finch), Mourning Doves, Redpolls (Common), Sparrows (Field, House, White-throated), Wrens (Carolina)

Fine Cracked Corn: Blue Jays, Cardinals, Grosbeaks (Evening and Rose-breasted), Sparrows (Field, House, and others), Towhees (Green-tailed, Spotted, and Rufous-sided)

Black Oil Sunflower: American Goldfinches, Cardinals, Chickadees (Black-capped and Carolina), Grosbeaks (Evening and Rose-breasted),

Grackles (Common), Finches (House and Purple), Mourning Doves, Sparrows (Field, House, Chipping, and White-throated)

Black Striped Sunflower: Blue Jays, Cardinals, Chickadees (Black-capped and Carolina), Grosbeaks (Evening and Red-Breasted), Grackles (Common), Finches (House and Purple), Titmice (Tufted), Mourning Doves, Sparrows (House and White-throated)

Hulled Raw Sunflower: Mourning Doves, Sparrows (House)

Niger (Thistle): American

Goldfinches, Finches (House and Purple), Mourning Doves

Safflower: Cardinals

Raw Peanuts: Blue Jays, Chickadees (Black-capped and Carolina), Finches (House, Green and Purple), Goldfinches (American), Grackles (Common), Grosbeaks (Evening and Rose-breasted), Juncos, Nuthatches (Red- and White-breasted), Sparrows (Field, House and White-throated), Titmice (Tufted), Wrens (Carolina)

Suet: Blue Birds, Cardinals, Crows, Chickadees (Black-capped

and Carolina), Coal tits, Flickers, Goldfinches, Jackdaws, Juncos, Kinglets, Nuthatches (Red- and White-breasted), Thrushes, Titmice (Tufted), Warblers, Woodpeckers (Downy, Hairy, Red-bellied, Red-headed), Wrens

Fruit Slices: Blackbirds, Bluetits, Catbirds, Fieldfares, Orioles (Baltimore, Orchard, Spotted), Redwings, Robins (English), Tanagers (Scarlet, Summer, Western)

Hemp Seed: Finches (House, Chaffinch, Green Finch), Tits, Pipits

Wild Feeds

Wood Duck: Acorns, beech nuts, water plants

American Kestrel: Mainly insects, small mammals, reptiles

Northern Bobwhite: Seeds

California Quail: Seeds

Dove: Grass seeds, other seeds, and grains

Barn Owl: Rodents

Great Horned Owl: Skunks, rats, squirrels, grouse, weasels, snakes and insects

Eastern Screech Owl: Worms, crayfish, mice, small birds, insects

Chimney Swift: Flying insects

Hummingbird: Flower nectar, tree sap, some insects

Woodpecker: Acorns and other tree fruit; some insects

Flicker: Ants, insects, berries

Eastern Kingbird: Insects

Eastern Phoebe: Mainly insects

Least Flycatcher: Insects

Swallow: Mainly insects

Purple Martin: Insects

Blue Jay: Acorns, beech nuts, tree mast, insects, birds' eggs, nestlings, voles and mice

Black-billed Magpie: Insects, seeds, berries, eggs, mice, carrion

Crow: Animals, vegetables

Tufted Titmouse: Mainly insects; also seeds and berries

Bushtit and Chickadee: Mainly insects; seeds and berries

Eastern Bluebird: Insects; also berries, fruit and seeds

Western Bluebird: Insects, spiders, invertebrates; berries

Thrush: Insects, invertebrates, berries and seeds

Brown Creeper: Insects; seeds

Nuthatch: Insects, spiders, nuts, seeds and berries

Wren: Insects, invertebrates; sometimes seeds

Blue-gray Gnatcatcher: Mainly insects; other invertebrates

Kinglet: Insects, spiders and some berries

Robin: Earthworms, grubs, larvae, insects, spiders; berries, fruit, seeds

Cardinal: Mainly seeds and fruit; also insects and spiders

Mockingbird: Wild berries, seeds, insects and invertebrates

Brown Thrasher: Insects, small invertebrates, some fruit and seeds

Cedar Waxwing: Mainly berries and seeds; also insects

Warbler: Mainly insects and spiders; sometimes seeds and berries

Yellowthroat: Insects

American Redstart: Insects, spiders, fruit and seeds

Grosbeak: Insects and fruit; seeds and berries

Bunting: Insects, spiders, berries and seeds

Towhee: Seeds, fruit and insects

Dark-eyed Junco: Mainly insects and seeds

Finch: Mainly seeds and fruit; also insects

Oriole: Mainly insects and spiders; also fruit and seeds

Brown-headed Cowbird: Grain, seeds, berries and other fruit; some insects

Common Grackle: Insects, grass seeds, worms, eggs and young birds

Eastern Meadowlark: Insects, grubs, grass and weed seeds

Blackbird: Insects and seeds

Sparrow: Insects, seeds and fruit

Red Crossbill: Pine seeds, other fruit and seeds

Pine Siskin: Seeds and some insects

Common Redpoll: Mainly insects and fruit

"Everyone Needs a Home" (series) by
Don Bundrick

"Boyds in the 'Hood" by Don Bundrick

Three **Bird Houses** by Marshall Fall

"Cross Birdhouses" (series) by Charles Ratliff

Gallery

Three *"Gourd Houses"* by Harold Hall

Opposite, *"Lighthouse"* by Fox Watson & the students at Juvenile Evaluation Center, Swannanoa, NC

36

"Bluebird House"
by Paul Sumner

Three *"Nuthatch Houses"* by Paul Sumner

Bird Houses by Susan Starr

"Standing Birdhouse" by Bryant Holsenbeck

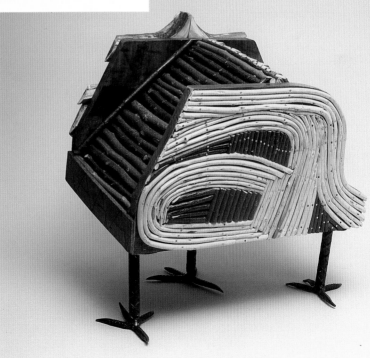

"A-Frame Birdhouse" (front and back views) by Bobby Hansson

Bird Houses by Barry Leader

Bird Baths by Debra Fritts
(Photos by Sue Ann Kuhn-Smith)

"If That Mockingbird Don't Sing" (left and detail) and *"Nature Gets The Exxit"* (middle) by Mana D. C. Hewitt

"Closed Doors" (open and closed)
by Mana D. C. Hewitt

"Global View" (open and closed)
by Mana D. C. Hewitt

"Ironclad Monitor" by Randy Sewell

"Tar Paper Fishing Shack"
by Randy Sewell

"Oasis" by Randy Sewell

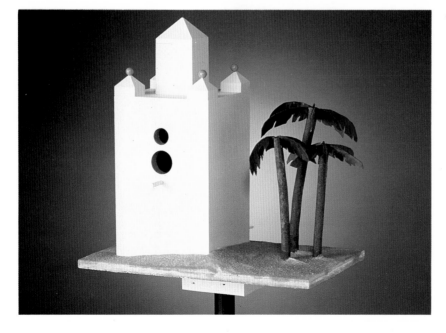

46

"Radio World"
by Randy Sewell

"Java Jive" by Randy Sewell

"Silo Birdfeeder"
by Randy Sewell

"Lewis' Reptile Farm"
by Randy Sewell

Wall Feeder & Bath by Carol Costenbader

Amorphous Environ by David Renfroe

48

Gallery

"Sunflower Birdhouse" by West Olive Folk Art

"Country Bird Feeder"
by Bruce Malicoat

Twig Tent Feeder

What could be more simple—an A-frame roof over a feeding platform. The materials and construction may vary, but they're all within reach and easy to assemble. This is a great way to start feeding—and watching—birds.

Feeders

Mosaic Twig Feeder

Once you get the knack of splitting twigs, the possibilities for mosaic ornamentation are endless. This wall-mounted feeder discourages squirrels and mice, yet is easily refilled to attract all sorts of birds.

Twig Tent Feeder

Materials List

	1 x 12 x 12" Pine base
2	1-1/4" dia. x 12" Twigs
1 or 2	16" V-shaped twigs
	1" dia. x 9" Twig
3–4	Coffee cans
	Bundle of broom corn
6	1-3/4" Wood screws
	Twine
	Glue and assorted nails

Step One You can saw one V-shaped twig in half, or use two the same size, for the roof frame. They are glued and screwed to the base from the bottom. The 9" twig is glued and screwed between both apexes to form the roof ridge.

Step Two Saw the two 12" twigs in half, then glue and nail them around the edge of the base to form a lip for the feed tray.

Step Three Open and flatten coffee can barrels, then nail them over the roof frame, overlapping the peak. For a more natural look, tie broom corn over these tin panels with twine. This can be replaced as the birds eat the broom corn seeds. Mount this feeder on a post.

Mosaic Twig Feeder

Materials List

2	1 x 12 x 12" Pine
	1 x 8" x 10" Pine
2	10" V-shaped twigs
	1" dia. x 9" Twig
	1-1/4" dia. x 12" Twig
	1" dia. x 12" Twig
	1-1/4" dia. x 8" Twig
	1/4"–3/8" Assorted Twigs
	Juice can
	Large hinge
2	4" Steel L-brackets
6	1-3/4" Wood screws
	Glue and assorted nails

Step One The 8" x 10" base and V-shaped uprights are joined in the same manner as the previous feeder. The 9" twig is screwed to the apexes of the uprights. The 8" twig is split in half, then glued and nailed to the side edges of the base. The 1-1/4" x 12" twig is split, and half is attached to the front edge of the base to complete the lip.

Step Two The juice can is opened at the top end, then punctured with a can opener around the bottom edge of the cylinder to spill seed. It is screwed to the center of the base. The base assembly is then attached to the bottom edge of one of the 12 x 12" panels with glue and nails. It is reinforced with two L-brackets.

Step Three The other half of the 1-1/4" x 12" twig is glued and nailed to the front edge of the roof. The 1" x 12" twig is split for the side edges. Trace a pattern on the roof panel. Split the assorted twigs with a hunting knife and mallet for the mosaic. The smallest twigs may be left whole. Those to be bent can be boiled first. Cut each to the appropriate length, then predrill and nail them into the pattern. The roof will be hinged to the back.

Bark-Faced Feeder

This classic design has been embellished with a woodsy mix of twigs, mosses and lichens. It is a highly functional feeder that will attract frequent flyers, and it's easy to make.

Materials List

	1 x 5" x 7" Pine base
	6-1/2" x 10-1/2" Bark-faced slab
2	1-1/4" dia. x 5" Twigs
2	2" x 11" Bark-faced slabs
2	2" x 5" Bark-faced slabs
4	#10 Wood screws
	Eyescrew
	Glues and assorted nails

Step One Glue and nail the two 2" x 5" slabs to the 5" edges of the base, flush at bottom. Glue and nail the two 2" x 11" slabs to the long edges of the base, completing the feed tray.

Step Two Glue the two 5" posts to each end of the base, reinforcing with screws from the underside. Glue and top screw the roof slab to the posts. Install the eyescrew top center.

Step Three Attach all the woodsy ornamentation with clear silicone sealant.

Thatched Twig Feeder

Here's yet another variation using all natural materials. This post-mounted feeding pavilion features a thatched roof with ornamental wattle railings and sub-roofing.

Materials List

	8" x 16" Log slab
4	1/2" dia. x 12" Forked branches
	Lots of assorted twigs
3	1" dia. x 17" Twigs
	Bundle of straw
	Tie wire
	Glue

Step One Trim 1" of bark off the non-forked end of each post branch. Drill slanted 1/2" holes for these four corner posts into the log slab, about 5" and 10" apart. Glue the posts into place, rotating the forked tops to accept the roof frame.

Step Two Attach four main twig members to the forked post tops with tie wire. The smaller end members should be V-shaped to form a roof peak. Attach smaller V-shaped cross pieces to the longer side members with tie wire. Weave the smaller twigs lengthwise through these cross pieces to form a peaked roof frame.

Step Three Insert 3/8" dia. x 10-1/2" twigs into pre-drilled and glued holes in the corner posts for two pairs of top and bottom rails. Wire on a few upright slats, then weave smaller twigs through these to form wattled railings. The upright slats could also be pre-drilled and glued into the railings.

Step Four The thatched straw is wired to the wattled roof frame. Lacquer it thoroughly for longer life. Split the 17" twigs that will be wired through the thatch to the frame to form the roof ridge and eaves caps. Add whatever ornamental bracing and decoration you like with more twigs.

Bird Cage Feeder

Grapevines are a wonderful material to make this charming cage, complete with trapeze. See how many pretty birds try out the swing, swoop down for a tempting morsel, then fly the coop, evading jailbird captivity.

Materials List

An armful of grapevines
A small spool of tie wire
8" dia. Plastic tray (potted
*   plant saucer)*
Side cutters

In place of grapevines, you can use
willow or other flexible material.
Tie wire can be found at most any
lumber yard or hardware store.

Step One Roll grapevines into circles A, B, C and F as shown.

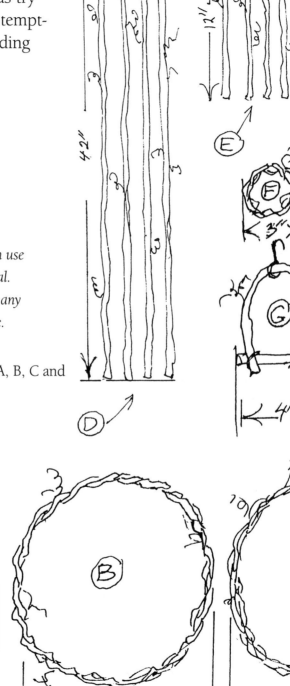

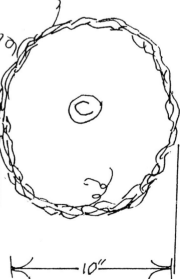

Step Two Wire four bottom bars E with tie wire to C.

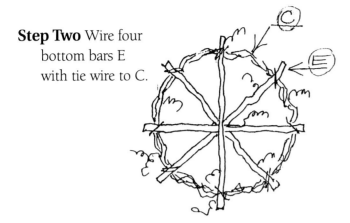

Step Three Wire 42" D bars to *inside* of C at joints of C and E. Install only 2 D bars as shown.

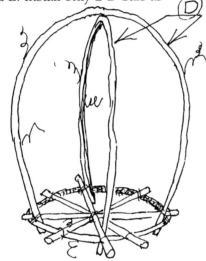

Step Four Place B inside D bars 4" from C. Cage bottom wire in place, then insert A 11" from bottom and wire in place.

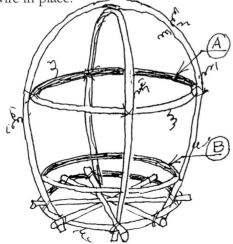

Step Five Wrap extra small vines around bottom C and, if desired, around B and A as shown in photo. Place plastic tray in bottom for seed.

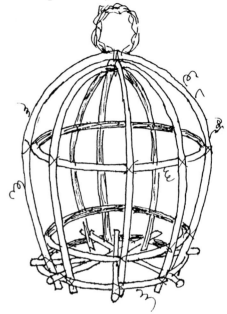

Step Six Install last two D bars just as first two were installed. Wire F circle to top, and hang swing inside center.

59

Traditional Slant

Here's a new slant on a classic birdfeeder design, fashioned out of durable cedar. It's fun to make, and features a clever lift-off roof panel for easy feed loading.

Materials List

2   *1 x 7-1/4" x 18-1/4" Cedar*
2   *1 x 7-1/4" x 17-1/2" Cedar*
     1 x 7-1/4" x 5-3/4" Cedar
3   *1 x 2-1/2" x 4-1/4" Cedar*
     1 x 2" x 4-1/4" Cedar
2   *1 x 1" x 5-3/4" Cedar*
2   *1/2" x 1-3/4" x 10-1/8" Cedar*
2   *5/16" x 6-1/8" Dowels*
2   *3-1/4" x 4-5/8" Plexiglass*
     4" x 9-1/4" Copper flashing
2   *Rubber bumper knobs*
     Glue and assorted nails

Step One Cut a 45° bevel on each upper corner of the 1/2" cedar pieces. Drill a 5/16" hole, 1/4" deep, below each bevel. Insert the dowels with glue as you glue and nail the 1/2" stock, centered and flush at the bottom, to the 5-3/4" x 7-1/4" base plate.

Step Two Rip cut a 45° bevel on the two 1 x 1" strips. Glue and nail these pieces on the open edges of the base to complete the feeding tray.

Step Three Rip cut intersecting 75° bevels on one long edge of two of the three 2-1/2" x 4-1/4" blocks. One of these will be affixed to the removable roof panel. The other supports the two spear-shaped walls, along with the square block opposite, just above the plexiglass slot. Rip cut 45° bevels on the two top long edges of the 2" x 4-1/4" base block.

Step Four Cut the two spear-shaped walls from the 17-1/2" lengths of cedar. Cut a 1/4" deep groove in both lower slanted edges of each wall. Glue and nail the walls to the two side blocks and base block as shown in the drawing. Attach the rubber knobs to the base bevels, then insert the plexiglass. This assembly can now be inserted into the center of the feeding tray, and glued and nailed in place.

Step Five Rip cut a 15° bevel off one short edge of each 18-1/4" roof panel to intersect as a peak. Place both panels in position, remove the fixed side, then mark the position of the upper beveled block to be attached to the removable panel. Glue and nail the block in place.

Step Six Put both panels back in position, and glue and nail the fixed side. Bend the copper in half lengthwise, then lay it over the roof peak. Bend, clip and crimp the ends, then nail them to the removable panel.

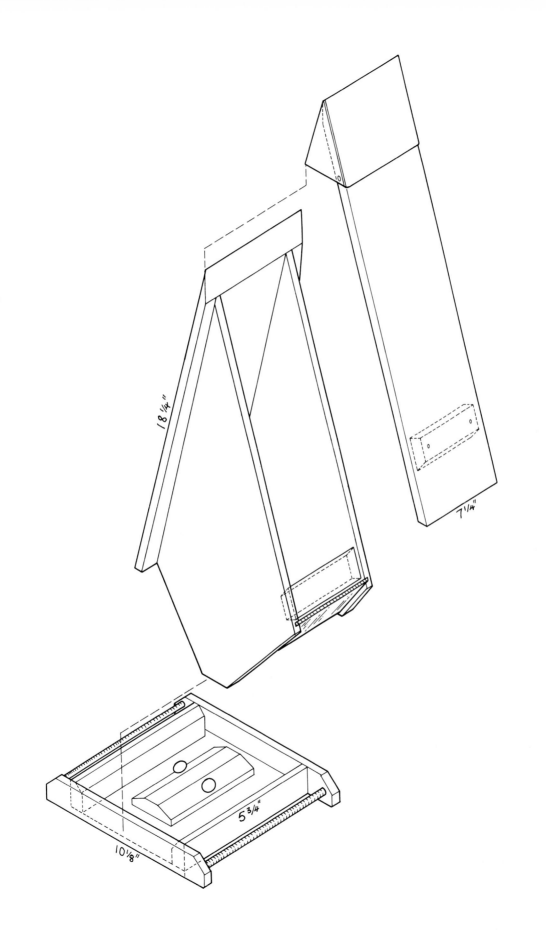

18 1/4"

7 1/4"

5 3/4"

10 1/8"

Pyramid Canopy

So elegant and simple, this redwood and copper feeder needs no glue or fasteners. The brass chain does all the work. Just hang it, fill it, and watch the birds feed.

Materials List

3	1 x 9-1/2" x 11-1/4" Redwood
	12" x 13" Copper flashing
2	1/2" Split key rings
5	7/8" Brass S hooks
6	5/8" Brass S hooks
6	Brass eyescrews
3	8-1/2" Brass chains
3	4" Brass chains

Step One Straight cut the 90° notch 1-3/4" into one long edge of each redwood block. Mark another 90° angle from the center of the opposite long edge. Undercut 35° bevels along each diagonal line. Drill a 1/4" hole in each roof panel centered near the apex. (See Diagram 1.)

Step Two Cut a triangle with flanges from the copper flashing. (See Diagram 2.) Fold along the dotted lines to create a triangular tray with double thick rims. Drill 1/16" holes through the double thick upper corners of each rim.

Step Three If you wish to glue the roof sections together, do so now. However, the sections will hang neatly in place without glue once the chains are installed.

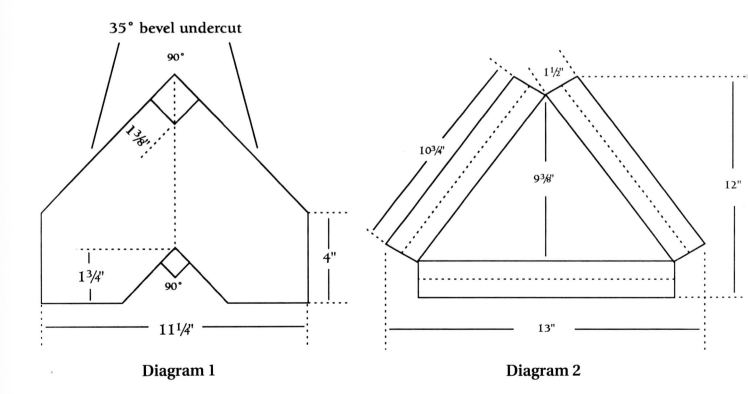

Diagram 1

Diagram 2

Step Four On the inside surface of the roof panels, pre-drill and insert eyescrews 5/8" in from each edge of the bottom outside corners. Insert and crimp a 5/8" S hook through each of the six corner holes in the copper tray. Insert and crimp a 7/8" S hook through each of these smaller pairs of S hooks. Open both end links of the 4" chains, hook them on each pair of eyescrews, then crimp them closed. Insert the top of each large S hook through the center link of each chain and crimp it closed.

Step Five Join one end of each 8-1/2" chain with a split ring. Pass one chain through each roof hole from the underside. Insert and crimp an S hook through the other end of each chain. Add another S hook to this one. Suspend the structure from this top S hook. Pass a split ring through each chain 1/2" above the apex of the roof, or join them with single chain links (as in the photo).

Plentiful Pagoda

Three tiers of tempting treats await your famished feathered friends. With an oriental flare, this ingenious design features top-loaded feed that trickles down to fill all levels.

Materials List

> 3/4" x 17" x 17" Plywood
> 1/2" x 12-5/16" x 12-5/16" Plywood
> 1/2" x 7-15/16" x 7-15/16" Plywood
> 1/2" x 3-13/16" x 3-13/16" Plywood
>
> 4   1/2" x 7" x 13" Plywood
> 4   1/2" x 6" x 8-5/8" Plywood
> 4   1/2" x 6" x 4-1/2" Plywood
> 4   1/4" x 1-1/2" x 17-1/2" Cedar
> 4   5/8" x 4-5/8" x 18" Cedar
> 4   5/8" x 3-3/8" x 12-1/4" Cedar
> 4   5/8" x 3-3/8" x 8-1/4" Cedar
> 4   5/8" x 3-5/8" x 4-1/2" Cedar
>
> Glues and assorted finishing nails

Step One In each corner of the 3/4" plywood base, drill a 1/2" drainage hole centered 1" from each edge. Measure 7" from each corner toward the center, and drill four more 1/2" drainage holes. You may wish to cover each hole with a 1" circle of window screen, which you can affix with clear silicone.

Step Two Miter cut all the short edges of the 7" x 13" wall panels for corner joints. Rip cut a 37-1/2° bevel along one long edge of each panel for roof joints. Dado cut a 1/2" groove, 3/16" deep, 1" from the top on the non-beveled side. Using a hole saw, cut three equidistant 2" holes centered 1-1/4" up from the bottom edge of

each panel. (The holes need to be lower than those pictured.)

Step Three Centered 1" from each edge of the 12-5/16" square, drill 1-1/4" holes in each corner, then four more between these. Centered 1" from each edge of the 7-15/16" square, drill 1-1/4" holes in each corner, then a fifth hole in the center. Drill a 3" hole in the center of the 3-13/16" square. Cut the remaining wall panels in the same manner as the bottom tier, with 2" holes centered 1-1/4" from the bottom edge.

Step Four Using glue and nails, join the top four wall panels, inserting the 3-13/16" square into the dadoed groove at the top. Let dry, then glue and nail this assembly to the center of the 7-15/16" square. Join the middle tier of walls, inserting the top assembly into the groove. Let dry, then glue and nail this assembly to the center of the next larger square, and so on down to the bottom. Varnish this plywood assembly thoroughly before attaching the cedar roof panels.

Step Five Mark a 55° line from each bottom corner of all cedar roof panels to form the trapezoids. The top cap sections will be triangles. Set your table saw blade at 52-1/2°, and cut along each of these lines. Each tier is then glued into place, nailing the top edges into the wall bevels, and angle nailing the bottom corners to reinforce the seams. You can use clear silicone in place of glue for durable roof seams.

Step Six You may wish to bevel the 1/4" cedar lath for the tapered look shown here. Miter the corners, then glue and nail each strip to form the lip of the foundation.

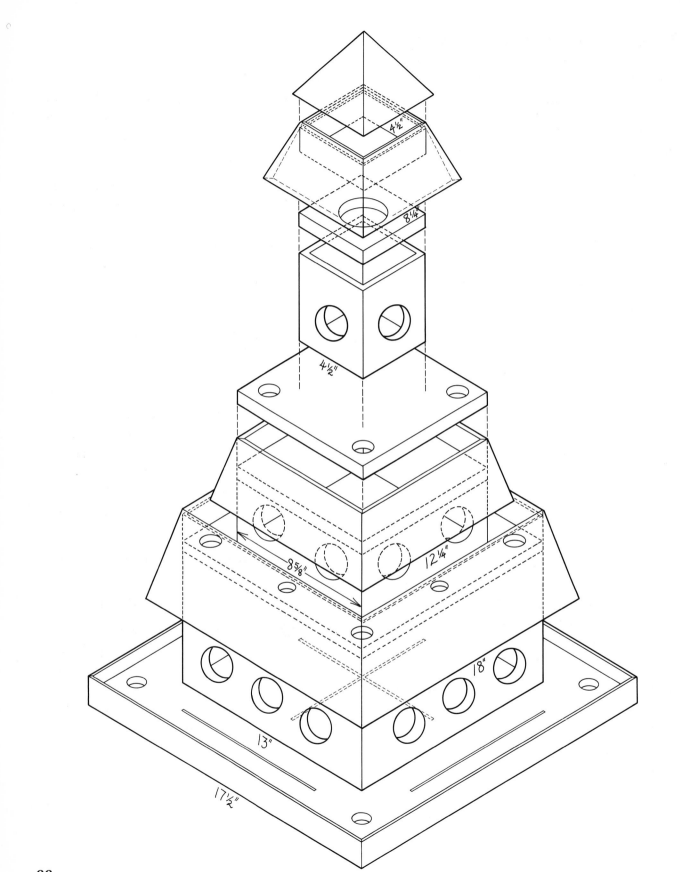

4½"

8¼"

4½"

8⅝"

12¼"

18"

13"

17½"

English Country Gazebo

This Old World way station for hungry birds has natural appeal as a landscaping ornament. The hexagonal, double-roofed pavilion can be made of cedar, redwood or pine, then left to weather.

Materials List

2   *1 x 9" x 20" Solid stock*
6   *1 x 5" x 11" Solid stock*
6   *5/8" x 1-1/2" x 9-3/4" Solid stock*
6   *5-1/2" x 11-1/4" x 11-3/4" Triangles of 1/2" solid stock*
6   *4" x 7-1/2" x 7-1/2" Triangles of 1/2" solid stock*
     3/8" Solid stock scrap
     Glue and assorted nails

Step One Lay the two base planks side by side, then trace a hexagon with 9-3/4" sides that fills the area. Cut off the outside corners.

Step Two Miter cut both long edges of all six 5" x 11" wall panels at 60° to form the hexagonal chamber. Using a jigsaw, cut the arched window openings in each panel. The bottom sill is centered 2-1/4" from each bottom edge. The openings measure 2-1/4" x 6".

Step Three Join the six walls with glue or clear silicone. Use large rubber bands to hold them together while they dry. Small brads can be tapped in to reinforce the seams after the glue is dry.

Step Four Apply glue to the bottom rim of the chamber as well as the center seam of the base planks, assemble upside down and top nail the base to the chamber. Then pre-drill and add wood screws for reinforcement. Let dry.

Step Five Miter cut the 9-3/4" rail section at 60° Drill 1/2" holes through the center lengthwise for decoration. Glue the adjoining edges, then nail into place. By inverting the structure, you can lay the base over the rails and top nail them. Angled corner nails will reinforce the corner seams.

Step Six All twelve roof sections will need to be miter cut at 52-1/2° along intersecting edges to form the hexagonal cones. Join them by applying a large bead of glue or silicone to each seam, then leaning the sections together and pressing them into alignment. Let dry, then sand the seams smooth. The eaves can be trimmed neatly after joining. Each roof section can be glued and nailed into place. You may also wish to add a decorative spire. The stem should be inserted and glued into the apex.

Step Seven Cut the six arch-shaped stoops from the 3/8" stock. They should measure 2" x 4". They are simply glued and nailed onto the sills.

Step Eight Cut the window trim from solid 3/8" stock. They will measure 3-1/2" x 7-1/2" before cutting. You can gang half or all at the same time depending on whether you use a band saw, a jigsaw or coping saw. Use glue and small brads to secure them in place.

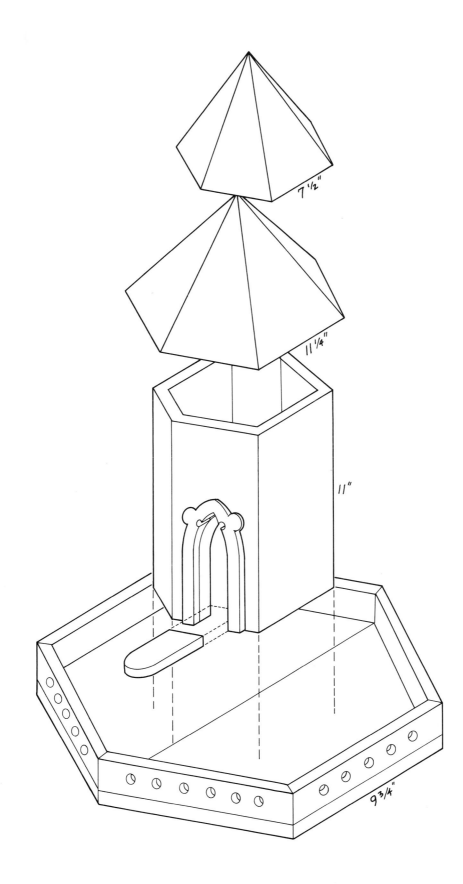

7'½"

11 ¼"

11"

9¾"

Wishing Well

This nostalgic feeder exudes country charm, and it can be constructed many ways—from a rustic romp to a cooper's dream. No matter, a bird's only wish will be that you keep it well stocked.

Materials List

	1/2" x 6-3/4" dia. Plywood
	1/4" x 11-1/4" dia. Plywood
12	1/2" x 2" x 4" Pine
2	3/4" x 3/4" x 11" Pine
	1-1/2" x 1-1/2" dia. Dowel
	1 x Scrap
	1/4" Scrap
	1/4" x 10" Dowel
	5-1/2" Metal rod
	8" Nylon string
	1-1/2" dia. Wooden spool
	5-1/2" Heavy wire
	Large eyescrew
2	#8 Wood screws
	1-1/4" dia. Screen
	Glue and assorted nails

The well shown here is basically a cylindrical bucket with a conical roof. This can be constructed using various materials and techniques. It could also be a square or polygonal shape. The structure could even be purchased ready-made. It's entirely up to you.

Step One Find some reasonably tight-grained or furniture grade stock for the bucket slats. The 2" x 4" pieces will need to be bevel cut on the long sides at 30°. Using large rubber bands or a circular clamp, glue these slats together into a cylindrical barrel shape. Let dry.

Step Two The bucket shown here was taper cut on a machinist's lathe. All you need to do with your polygon is round off the exterior. You can whittle before sanding if you want it really rounded. Also sand the top and bottom rims.

Step Three Cut the floor of the bucket to fit snugly after tracing the interior shape onto the 1/2" plywood. Wedge into the bottom with glue and tack it in place. Cut a 3/8" hole in the center, then glue or tack the screen over it for drainage.

Step Four The two 3/4" support posts are glued to the sides, nailed at the bottom, and screwed from the inside bucket rim. You may want to notch them as in the photo. If your bucket is tapered, the top should be beveled slightly to join with the roof disk. Drill a 1/4" hole halfway into one post, 1-1/2" from the top, before joining. Glue and nail the roof disk to the posts.

Step Five Taper the 1-1/2" dowel at the top before gluing it to the center of the 11-1/4" plywood disk. Cut triangles from the 1 x and 1/4" scrap. Glue the 1 x triangles like spokes around the tapered dowel (see photo). Layer the triangular 1/4" shingles over this substructure with glue. Let dry, then insert the eyescrew at the apex.

Step Six Cut the 10" dowel into a 9-1/4" shaft and a 3/4" handle. Drill holes into one end of each to accommodate the metal rod. Bend the rod into a crankshaft, then glue it into both dowels. Drill a 1/4" hole through the undrilled post, 1-1/2" from the top, then insert the shaft. You may glue it in place, or leave it free to turn.

Step Seven The bucket shown here was lathe-turned. You can make a reasonable facsimile from a wooden spool, or purchase one from a hobby store in the doll house department. The 5-1/2" wire handle is bent and inserted into pre-drilled holes. Tie the nylon string to the shaft, wrap it, then dangle it to tie onto the bucket handle. Stain the assembly to your taste.

Covered Bridge

These quaint country crossings may be disappearing from rural landscapes, but they're due for a revival in bird feeder architecture. This perfectly adapted design will experience heavy traffic from birds on the wing, and built out of cedar, may last as long as its predecessor.

Materials List

2	1 x 7-5/8" x 27" Cedar
	1 x 7" x 24" Cedar
2	1 x 7" x 8-5/8" Cedar
2	1 x 2-1/2" x 8-1/2" Cedar
	1 x 4" x 4" Cedar
	1-1/2" x 1-1/2" x 6' Cedar post
4	1/2" x 1/2" x 22-5/8" Cedar
2	1/2" x 1/2" x 5" Cedar
28	1/4" x 1-1/2" Dowels
	Cedar shake shingles
4	#10 Wood screws
8	#8 Wood screws
	Glues and assorted nails

Step One Rip cut 45° tapered bevels on all long edges of the two 27" roof panels. Cut the 45° roof peak and rounded arch out of both 7" x 8-5/8" blocks at once. Mark the arch with a compass.

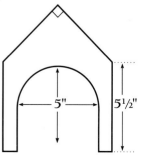

Step Two Drill fourteen 1/4" holes along one face of each 22-5/8" rail. They should match up on 1-1/2" centers and be 1/4" deep. Rub glue around each dowel tip before tapping it into the bottom rails. Rub glue on the upper tips before tapping the top rails onto them. Let dry.

Step Three Glue and nail the rails to the arch blocks to form the walls. They should be flush at the bottom and at the corners. Let dry.

Step Four Glue this assembly to the 24" base, clamping or weighting for tight seams. After seams are dry, reinforce the arches with four #8 screws from the underside corners. Glue and nail the 5" lip molding inside the arch thresholds.

Step Five Using clear silicone sealant, glue both roof panels atop the arches. After seams are dry, reinforce the roof to arch seams by top nailing. The shingles are attached one row at a time from the bottom, also using silicone. If you use non-cedar shingles, such as available for doll houses, you should add two coats of polyurethane to protect them.

Step Six Cut both scalloped braces from the 2-1/2" x 8-1/2" pieces at the same time on a band saw or jigsaw. Cut a decorative bevel on the edges of the 4" square post block.

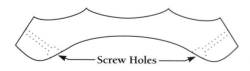

Step Seven Attach the post block, bevels down, to one end of the post with two #8 screws. Attach the block to the center of the base with two #8 screws. Attach both scalloped braces to base and post with countersunk #10 screws.

Cascading Post

This modern design sports multi-level feeding decks that Frank Lloyd Wright might have engineered. The top-loaded feed spirals down around the post, and it's all under one roof. An intriguing blend of function and aesthetics.

Materials List

	3-3/4" x 3-3/4" x 5" Pine block
4	1/4" x 4" x 16" Plywood walls
	1/4" x 3-3/4" x 10-1/8" Plywood partition
	1/4" x 14" x 14" Plywood roof
2	1/4" x 8" x 8" Plywood decks
2	1/4" x 4" x 6" Plywood braces
	1/4" x 2-1/8" x 3-3/4" Plywood floor
4	1/4" x 7/8" x 8-1/4" Plywood
4	1/4" x 7/8" x 4-1/4" Plywood
2	1-1/2" Threaded posts
2	Matching capped nuts
	Glues and nails

Step One It should be noted that this entire structure can be built around a pressure-treated 4 x 4 post, the upper 5" of which would be encased. A squirrel barrier would then be advisable. Also, you are encouraged to substitute solid 1/4" stock in place of plywood if you can find it. This is not crucial so long as you thoroughly caulk, prime and paint the plywood structure to withstand the elements.

Step Two If you are not building this around a 4 x 4 post, procure a 1" steel pipe (threaded at the top end), and cut a snug hole in the bottom center of the pine block.

Step Three Cut 22-1/2° angles across the tops of the wall panels. In one of these panels, cut a 5/8" x 3" slot, the sill of which is centered 5" up from the straight bottom. In another panel, cut the same slot 11" above the straight bottom edge.

Step Four Wood glue and rubber bands (for clamping) will be used to join the walls around the pine block, with successive butt joints. However, as you join these, you must also glue in place the central partition as well as the 2-1/8" x 3-3/4" floor of the upper chamber (see drawing). You may wish to pre-glue the floor and partition assembly. Note that the partition is aligned off-center toward the lower chamber, and rests on the pine block inside the four walls. The walls should be turned so that the bevels alternate, creating two planes for the peaked roof. Sand all surfaces flat and square with a sanding block before joining.

Step Five Cut a V-slot 7/8" in from each corner on the long edge of the two 4" x 6" pieces. These K-shaped braces will support the decks. (Rather than joining these separate pieces to the main trunk chamber, you could cut the two non-slotted walls to include this irregular shape intact.)

Step Six Cut the 4" x 4" upper decks out of one corner of the two 8" x 8" deck pieces. Cut all eight 7/8" strips that form the lips of the decks. Sand all of these surfaces flat and square.

Step Seven Glue one pair of decks at a time. Lay the trunk chamber horizontally each time and add weights to all appropriate members so that all seams dry tightly. Sand the seams of the entire assembly once it has dried.

Step Eight Cut the 14" square roof panel diagonally with a 52-1/2° beveled angle. Using

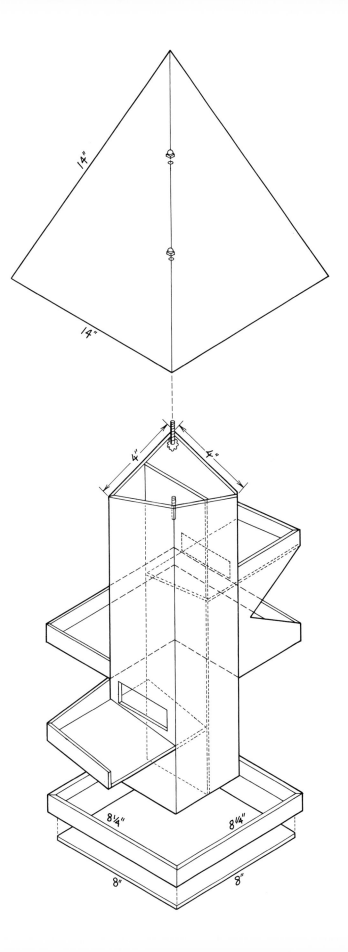

14"

14"

4" 4"

8¼" 8¼"

8" 8"

shims to support these angled panels, glue them together along the long beveled seam. (You can glue a triangular block into the center if you wish to brace them.)

Step Nine Epoxy the two threaded posts inside the opposite high corners of the trunk chamber. They should extend 1/2" above the corner rim.

Step Ten Lay the roof over the center of the trunk chamber. Carefully mark the points where the threaded posts meet the underside ridge. Drill snug holes to accommodate the posts.

Step Eleven Thoroughly caulk, prime and paint the structure according to your own taste.

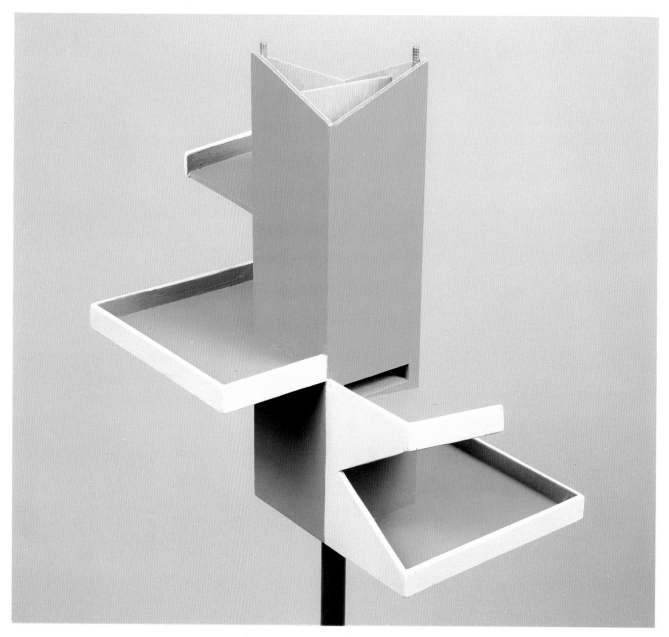

Birdie Can-teen

A child can make this simple feeder with hand tools and minimal supervision. And in addition, it is a very functional feeder that can be decorated many different ways.

Materials List

	1 x 11-1/4" x 11-1/4" Pine
	1 x 7-7/8" x 7-7/8" Pine
4	1/4" x 1-1/2" x 8-3/16" Lath
	3-7/8" Dia. coffee can
	16' Clothes line
2	#6 Wood screws
	Glue and assorted nails

Step One The pine squares can be cut with a hand saw. Find the center point in both pine squares. Mark two points in each, 3" apart in the center and parallel with each other, and drill 1/4" holes in all four points.

Step Two The lath can be glued and nailed in successive butt joints around the base, flush with the bottom, or mitered from 8-7/8" lengths if you prefer.

Step Three Cut four openings in one end of the can with a can opener, hammering back the triangular flap with a screwdriver and hammer flush with the can's bottom. The top should be removed.

Step Four Paint the can and both plates as you wish. Let dry. Screw the can to the center of the bottom plate from the top, punching holes in the can with a nail and hammer near the perimeter of the circle.

Step Five Run the clothes line (preferably plastic coated, to defy squirrel traction) in a long U shape through the top, into the can and through a bottom hole, back up through the other bottom hole and through the top. This can be hung from a big tree or other high places.

Bird Feeder

This bird likes nothing better than to hang around and feed her fellow fowls. They will visit often to perch on her wings and sample the fruit or bread scraps *du jour*.

Materials List

      1 x 3-1/4" x 9-1/2" Pine

2   3/8" x 2-3/4" x 8" Pine

      3/8" x 2-3/4" x 3-1/2" Pine

3   1-1/2" Nails

      Eyescrew

      Glue

Step One With a coping, jig or band saw, cut the outlines of the body, wings and tail as shown in the photos, or as you prefer. Whittle the edges into pleasing tapers, except where the wings and tail will join the body.

Step Two On a table or band saw, cut a 3/8" notch into the body's tail about 1" deep. With a coping or jig saw, cut a 3/8" x 1-1/2" slot through the belly area. Whittle and sand these junctures until all pieces fit snugly. Glue them in place and let dry. Whittle and sand the tail joint.

Step Three Prime and paint the bird as you wish with outdoor paint. This bird has an antique finish. Keep in mind that you may want to wash the bird periodically.

Step Four Using a same size nail, drill holes into the top of the body as shown in the photo. Snip the heads off three nails and glue them into these holes with epoxy. Install the eyescrew wherever the piece will balance with food spiked on it.

Cardinal Dispensation

They say that gluttony is a cardinal sin. See how often you have to refill this tempting see-through feeder, and you may discern which is nobler: man or bird.

Materials List

2   *2 x 9" x 10" Pine*
     1 x 4-1/2" x 4-1/2" Pine
4   *1/4" x 1-1/2" x 4-5/8" Lath*
2   *4-1/2" x 5-3/8" Plexiglass*
     Sink stopper
     Eyescrew
     Glue and assorted nails
     Clear silicone sealant

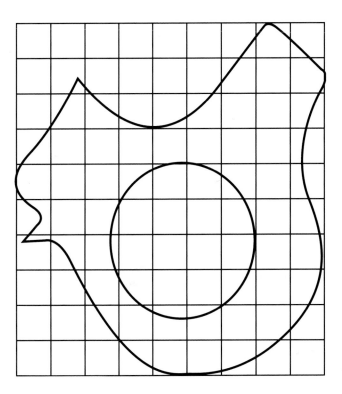

Step One Trace a bird pattern on one of the 2 x pine blocks. Cut it out with a jig or band saw. If you have access to a hole saw, cut a 4-1/4" circle out of the center. Otherwise, trace and cut the circle with a jig or band saw. The bottom of the circle should be 1-3/4" from the bottom edge of the bird.

Step Two Lay this cut piece on top of the other 2 x pine block, then trace the circle and the outline. Cut this block to match. Glue and clamp them together. Let dry, then sand the seams smooth.

Step Three Lay a plexiglass rectangle over one of the holes, leaving a 3/8" opening for seed spill. Trace a C-shaped outline around the hole that has a 5/8" margin. Cut this shape gently with a fine tooth coping saw. Trace and cut the other pane the same.

Step Four Cut the 1 x pine square diagonally into two triangles. Miter cut the short edges of the lath, then glue and nail them to the short sides of both triangles, flush with the bottoms. Glue and nail these wings to the body, with the top surface flush with the circle bottoms. Let dry.

Step Five Using a hole saw or coping saw, cut a hole in the top of the bird through to the feed chamber, big enough to accept the sink stopper snugly.

Step Six Paint the entire assembly to taste. Topcoat with a sealant to preserve the center glue seam.

Step Seven Pre-drill the nail holes through the plexiglass. Run a bead of silicone around the curved edges, then nail them into place. Install the eyescrew.

Catfish Windvane

Reminiscent of primitive American folk art, this whimsical windvane features a unique advantage in bird feeding comfort. No matter which way the wind is blowing, the cat's head always shelters our dainty diners from the elements.

Materials List

          1 x 12 x 28" Pine
    2   1 x 5-1/2" x 6-1/2" Pine
          1 x 7-1/2" x 8-1/4" Pine
          1 x 5-1/2" x 8-1/4" Pine
          1 x 4-1/4" x 4-1/4" Pine
          1/4" dia. x 1-1/2" x 8" Lath
          5' Heavy wire
    2   2" Lag screws
          16d Nail
          1-1/4" dia. x 6'–8' Post
          Glue and assorted nails

Step One First, build the head. Cut 80° bevels around the 4-1/4" x 4-1/4" face block to join with the flared sides. The face surface will then measure about 4" square.

Step Two Mark points on both 5-1/2" x 6-1/2" side blocks, 1-1/4" in from each corner on the same long edge. Draw lines from these points to the opposite corners, then cut along these lines at 90°. Bevel the 4" edge at 80° on both blocks.

Step Three Mark points on the 5-1/2" x 8-1/4" bottom block, 1-3/8" in from each corner on the same long edge. Draw lines from these points to the opposite corners, then cut along these lines at 90°. Trace this shape onto the 7-1/2" x 8-1/4" top block, with the 5-1/2" edge flush with one 7-1/2" edge. Trace and cut at 90°. Bevel the 5-1/2" edges of both blocks at 80°. (The overhang on the top block is a rain-shed.)

Step Four Glue and nail the head together. Let dry, then sand all the seams. Using a coping or jigsaw, cut wavy lines along the outer edges of the top and sides to suggest tufts of fur.

Step Five Using a jig or band saw, cut a fish body outline from the 28" board. Save the scrap. A tapered neck area should extend about 4". The bottom edge of the neck must be flat to join with the head, and angled parallel to ground level. A hole, slightly larger than the 16d nail should be drilled about 2" deep, perpendicular to the bottom neck edge. This will keep the feed tray level.

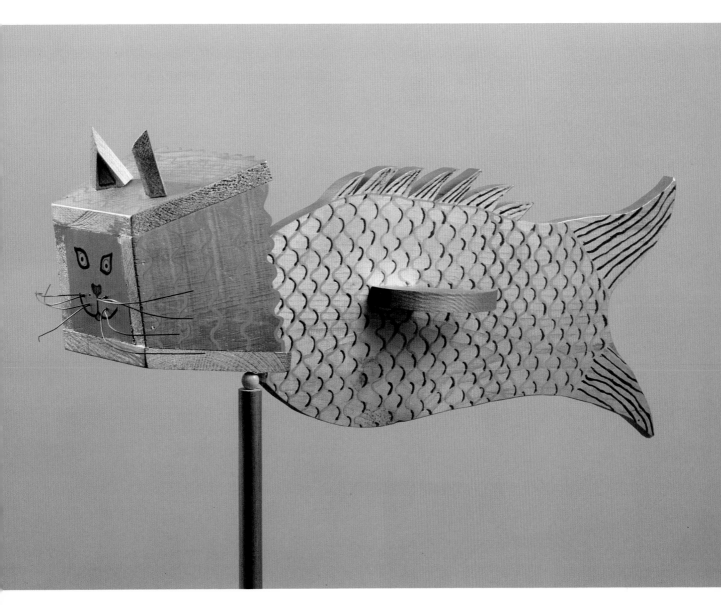

Step Six Cut curved side fins from the scrap, then glue and nail them to the body. Bevel cut two triangles to make ears about 2-1/2" tall. Glue and nail them on.

Step Seven Glue and nail the neck into the head. Reinforce this joint with two 2" lag screws from the underside of the head. Cut the lath into two 4" lengths. Glue and tack these to the bottom edge of the head, forming a lip for the feed chamber.

Step Eight Prime and paint for exterior use to your taste. Cut the wire into four 15" lengths. Bend these in half, then insert into small whisker holes drilled into the face.

Step Nine Hack saw the head off the 16d nail after hammering it halfway into the post.

Window Box

If you've ever wished that birds would come right to your window to feed, now you can sneak a peek through the tulips. Refill the feed simply by raising your window and opening the flower bed lid.

Materials List

	1 x 11-1/4" x 14" Pine
	1 x 7-1/2" x 21-5/8" Pine
	1 x 6-3/4" x 21-5/8" Pine
	1 x 5" x 23-1/2" Pine
2	*1 x 4" x 8-1/2" Pine*
2	*1 x 7/8" x 7-3/8" Pine*
	1 x 7/8" x 14" Pine
2	*1/4" x 1-1/2" x 24" Lath*
2	*1/4" x 1-1/2" x 5-3/8" Lath*
9	*1 x 4" x 4-1/2" Pine*
9	*5/16" x 4-1/4"–7-1/4" Dowels*
2	*2-1/2" Hinges*
	Glue and assorted nails

Step One Mark a point 3-13/16" from each end of the 6-3/4" x 21-5/8" side piece on the long bottom edge. Draw and cut a line from each of these points to the upper corners. Cut a long notch 1/2" x 10-1/2" centered into the bottom edge, or cut 2 or 3 notches (as in the photo). Lay this piece on top of the 7-1/2" x 21-5/8" side piece, trace the diagonal edges to the bottom corners, then 3/4" lines perpendicular to the bottom edge. Cut along these lines. Cut a 60° bevel on one short edge of each 4" x 8-1/2" side piece.

Step Two Glue and nail the notched side to the two 4" sides, with the bottom (notched) edge flush with the 4" beveled edges. Join the other big side opposite to form the window box, then join it to one long edge of the 11-1/4" x 14" tray base.

Step Three Lay the 5" x 23-1/2" lid on top and mark the screw holes and outline of the hinges. Chisel the hinge area out of the lid edge to recess them flush. Clip 1/8" off each corner for drainage. Install the lid with hinges.

Step Four Miter the corner edges of all the lath, then glue and tack them around the lid edge flush with the bottom. Miter the four edges of the 1 x 7/8" strips where they join, then glue and nail them to the tray edge.

Step Five Cut each flower and leaf piece from one of the 4" x 4-1/2" block. Drill 5/16" holes into the lid, the flower bottoms and through the leaf centers. Join them with glue. Paint to your taste.

Step Six This feeder can be attached with steel brackets on top of your window sill (as shown), or lower so that the flower bed is flush with the sill.

Breakfast Tray

Start their day off right with a bountiful banquet. This feeder is easy to stock, delightful to watch, and a real treat for almost any of the bird persuasion. What mother wouldn't drop her worm in favor of this early bird special.

Materials List

	3/4" x 17" x 23" Plywood
2	1/4" x 1-1/2" x 24-1/4" Lath
2	1/4" x 1-1/2" x 18" Lath
2	1 x 12 x 14" Pine
2	1 x 3" x 14" Pine
	1 x 4-7/8" x 11-1/2" Pine
2	1" Hinges
4	#10 Wood screws
	Vase
	Cup and saucer
	Bowl
	Flatware
	Glue and assorted nails
	Epoxy

Step One The only component you must build is the cereal box, but you may prefer to make this oversize tray rather than incorporate a ready-made cafeteria tray. Bevel each edge of the 3/4" plywood at 45°. Cut the bottom corners off each lath strip at 45°. These will butt against each other at each tray corner. Glue and tack the lath to the tray bevels. Drill a 3/16" hole at each corner for drainage. Prime and paint for exterior use.

Step Two Cut a 5/8" x 6" slot centered in the bottom edge of one of the 12 x 14" box panels. Glue and nail the 1 x 12's to the 1 x 3" panels to form the box. Let dry, then sand the seams. Prime and paint the box and lid, decorating it as you wish. Epoxy the box to the tray, then reinforce with #10 screws from the underside into the box corners. Install the lid using the two hinges.

Step Three All the other table items should be fastened in place with epoxy. For periodic cleaning, use a whisk broom or you can even hose it down.

Country Storefronts

This replica of quaint village shops might appeal more to you than window shopping birds, but the goods spilling onto the sidewalk are sure to get their attention. Stock each bin with different feeds, and see which birds stop by on their way through town.

Boswell's Feed & Seed

City By-Merchantile

Country Storefronts

Materials List

1 x 12 x 24-1/2" Pine
1 x 10" x 24-1/2" Pine
4 *1 x 6-3/4" x 12-3/4" Pine*
1 x 7" x 24-1/2" Pine
1 x 2-5/8" x 24-1/2" Pine
1 x 4-5/8" x 26" Pine
1 x 7-1/16" x 9" Pine (optional)
4 *5/8" x 6-1/4" Dowels*
1/4" x 1" x 25" Lath
2 *1/4" x 1" x 11-3/8" Lath*
1/4" x 15" x 24-1/2" Plywood
13-1/4" x 24-1/2" Plexiglass
1/8" Scrap plywood (optional)
24-1/2" Continuous hinge
Cabinet knob
Glue and assorted nails

Step One Rip cut a 60° bevel along one long edge of the 10" x 24-1/2" piece. To cut the peak in the side and interior walls, the pitch is 30° and centered 4-3/4" from one edge. Cut the 2-5/8" x 24-1/2" strip with 60° bevels on both long edges.

Step Two With glue and nails, join the back and four parallel walls onto the 12 x 24-1/2" base, securing them with the narrow top strip across the shorter roof slope. If you wish to add the optional slanted floor baffles, bevel cut the short edges at 45°, then glue and nail them into place.

Step Three Cut the roofline and all windows and doors out of the 1/4" plywood sheet. Cut and attach optional trim pieces cut from 1/8" scrap plywood. Paint this panel. Lay the plexiglass sheet beneath this panel, cut semi-circles inside the doorways, then put both in place over the front of the walls. Pre-drill, glue and nail into place.

Step Four Cut 60° bevels on both long edges of the 7" x 24-1/2" roof panel. Secure this to the other roof strip with the long hinge. Install the knob near the bottom edge center.

Step Five Cut 60° parallel bevels along both long edges of the 4-5/8" x 26" awning panel. Cut the tops of the four dowel support post with a 30° bevel. Glue and nail these pieces into place. Signs cut from 1/8" scrap can be hung with small eyescrews. Tack the lath lip into place, then paint the rest of the assembly.

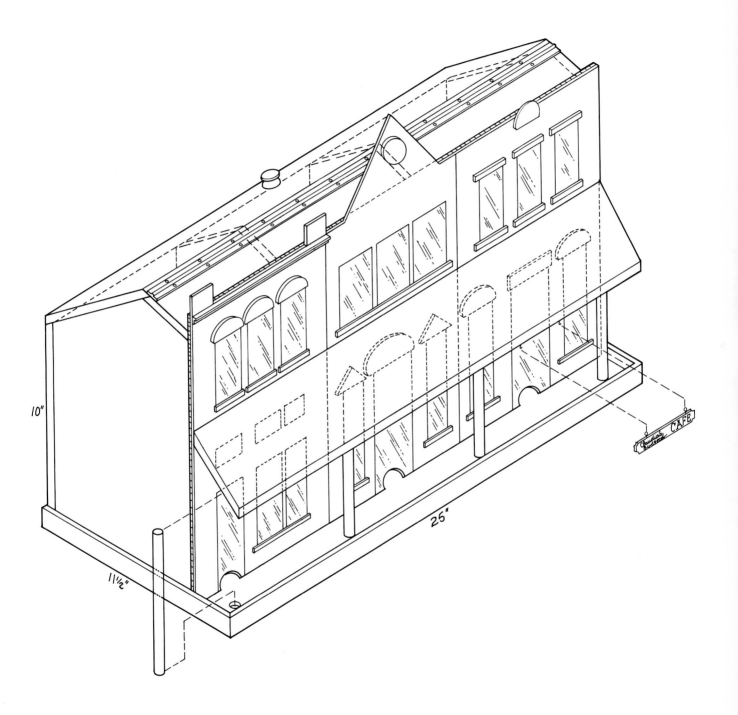

10"

25"

11½"

Charlie's Architect CAFE

Flying Aces Hangar

After a tough day of aerial acrobatics, your plumed pilots will be happy to taxi down this runway for a snack. A hinged loading door in the rear lets you keep this feeder well stocked.

Materials List

	1 x 12 x 24" Pine
2	*1 x 6 x 12" Pine*
2	*1 x 8-1/8" x 9-1/4" Pine*
	1/2" x 12" 1/4-round Molding
	12-1/2" x 14-3/4" Aluminum sheeting
2	*3" x 4" Aluminum sheeting*
2	*1" Hinges*
	Cabinet knob
	1/4" x 1" x 4" Lath
	1/4" x 5/8" x 5" Lath
	1/4" x 1" x 6-1/2" Lath
	1/4" x 8-1/2" Dowel
	3-1/2" Heavy wire
	3" x 3-1/2" Stiff cloth
	Toy airplane
	Glue and assorted nails

Step One Cut a 4-1/2" x 5-3/4" front doorway out of one of the 8-1/8" x 9-1/4" wall pieces. Save the cut-out. Draw a line 7/8" above the top doorway edge and parallel to it. Everything above this line will be the arc area. Trace the arc neatly, lay this piece over the other same size piece, then cut the arc in both. Cut a 3-1/2" x 5" hole, centered 4-1/2" up from the bottom edge, in this second wall.

Step Two Glue and nail these arc-top walls to the 6 x 12" side walls, butting the side pieces inside the end pieces. Glue and nail the two 1/4-round strips to the top edges of the side walls, rounded faces out and flush with the arc. Let dry. Glue and nail this assembly to one end of the 24" base.

Step Three Cut a 3-3/8" x 4-15/16" rectangle from the front door cut-out. Round the top inner edge for clearance. Cut a fan shape out of each 3" x 4" piece of aluminum. Tack a straight edge of each fan to the opposite side edges of the door panel, flush with the outer door surface. Glue and tack the 4" lath strip to the inside top of the door opening to act as a door-jamb. Install the knob, then hinge the door in place.

Step Four Tack the aluminum roof sheet into place. If you want extra strength, cut and bend a section of stove pipe instead, and pre-drill the nail holes. Leaving a 1" stem, bend the 3-1/2" wire into a question mark and close the circle. Sharpen the stem to a point with a file.

Step Five Cut converging tapers on opposite edges of the cloth. Glue or stitch the funnel-shaped wind sock around the wire hoop. Drill a hole 3/4" into one end of the dowel that is 1/32" wider than the wire stem. Whittle and sand this end of the dowel to round it. Drill a 1/4" hole in the base, then glue the dowel in place. Also glue the airplane in place.

Step Six Cut the wings from the 5/8" x 5" lath. Paint them, along with the 1" x 6-1/2" sign. Paint the entire structure to your taste, then glue and tack the wings and sign above the doorway.

Step Seven To avoid drainage problems and soggy feed, you can either mount the structure to slope away from the chamber, or add a 1 x 7-3/4" x 12" raised floor before attaching the chamber to the base.

Intergalactic Snack

To boldly go where no bird feeder has gone before…That is the mission of this stylish seed shuttle. It is a shining tribute to the birds that first inspired man's flight—a spacecraft with real star quality.

Materials List

    1/4" x 16" x 16" Mahogany plywood
    1/4" x 10" x 14-1/2" Mahogany plywood
3 *3/8" x 9" Dowels*
    7/8" x 1" dia. PVC pipe
    Glues

Step One Cut the base plate from the 16" square plywood, following the diagram. All edges are cut at 90°. Save the scrap.

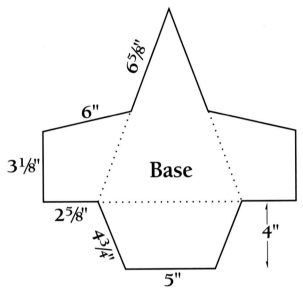

Step Two Cut the two sides of the fuselage from the 10" x 14-1/2" plywood with a 42° diagonal cut. Trim these into isosceles triangles with 90° cuts. Bevel the third sides at 48°. Then go back and cut another 3/32" at 42° halfway down each long edge to open up a slot for the top fin.

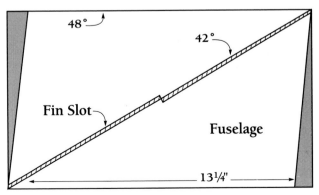

Step Three Cut a kite-shaped top fin from plywood scrap. Then cut a 6-1/8" x 4-5/8" x 4-5/8" triangle from scrap. (The dotted line shows the glue seam with the fuselage.) All edges are cut at 90°.

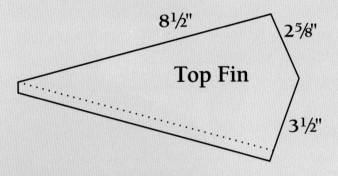

8½" 2⅝"

Top Fin

3½"

Step Four Run a good bead of glue along every edge to be joined as you assemble the fuselage to the base. Weights can be leaned against the sides and rubber bands clamped around the nose. Let dry, then glue the top fin into the slot, and the triangular baffle into the fuselage.

Step Five Cut three 5/8" x 5" strips from plywood scrap. Miter them and glue them to the rear of the base to form a lip for the feed tray.

Step Six Cut the PVC in half lengthwise to form two radar dishes. Drill a 3/8" hole in each one. Sharpen the ends of the dowels in a pencil sharpener. Glue the radar dishes onto two of the dowels. Glue the dowels in place with silicone sealant. Caulk all the other seams with silicone after the dowels have dried. Prime and paint for exterior use. This feeder can be hung or post mounted.

Lighthouse Lunchbox

If you're a coastal dweller, this feeder could be the perfect yard ornament. You may even wish to install a working beacon which will draw extra insect snacks for night birds.

and nail the end panels onto these ends. Trim and sand excess flush with sides after the glue has dried. This tray will hold excess feed, but could also be a wider base with a lath lip.

Materials List

	1 x 6-1/2" x 21" Pine
2	*3/8" x 3-1/2" x 21" Cedar or redwood*
2	*3/8" x 3" x 10" Cedar or redwood*
	1 x 4" x 14-1/2" Pine
2	*1/4" x 3" x 14-1/2" Plywood*
2	*3-1/2" x 10" Plexiglass panels*
	3" x 19" PVC pipe
	4" x 4" x 4" Pine block
3	*1/4" x 2-1/2" Dowels*
	Scrap plastic packaging or bottle caps
	Scrap of window screen
	Shingles
	Glue and assorted nails
4	*#10 Wood screws*

Step One Bevel cut both long edges of the 6-1/2" x 21" pine base at 45°. Glue and nail both 3-1/2" x 21" side panels to these beveled edges. Sand both short ends flush, then glue

Step Two Cut two 5" blocks from the 1 x 4" pine. Cut two roof-peak tapers at the top of each block. Cut three tapered braces, each 3-1/2" long parallel to the grain, from the remaining 1 x 4" to match the roof-peak angles. Glue and nail the two 1/4" plywood roof panels onto these three braces, spacing them (as shown in the photo) so as to fit either side of the two upright blocks.

Step Three You can mill your own shingles from 1/8" stock, or purchase doll house shingles. Apply successive beads of silicone across both roof panels, and apply each layer of shingles, staggering them, from the bottom up.

Step Four Cut two 3/8" grooves into each of the upright blocks, stopping 3/4" short of the bottom edge. These will hold the plexiglass. Bevel cut and chisel an indentation on the outside of one block to accommodate the 3" PVC shape. Using a hole saw, cut a 1-1/2" hole through this block and into the PVC while they are standing together. Glue and bolt them together. Cut three 1" holes spiralling up the cylinder for feeding stations. Cut a 1/4" hole 1" below each of these.

Step Five Glue the cylinder assembly 3" from one end of the tray, reinforcing with two wood screws up from the bottom and into the block. Attach the other block the same way, inserting the plexiglass in place to determine spacing. Remove the plexiglass, drill two 3/8" drainage holes between the blocks, and glue circles of screen over them. (The photo shows dowel pegs for roof alignment, but these are optional.) Cut a rounded notch in the roof to fit around the cylinder.

Step Six This beacon was lathe-turned from a 4" block of wood. Another effective approach would be to join concentric circles of wood with a cross-cut section of a plastic bottle in the middle. The bottom must fit neatly inside the cylinder to act as a stopper.

Step Seven After painting the structure, the dowel perches can be glued into place. Sections of curved plastic packaging can be glued under the feeding holes with silicone or epoxy. If you prefer, glue bottle caps into these holes and pack suet into them for the winter months.

Tropical Island

Birds can snack after bathing in this tropical paradise. Pipe in a little reggae or calypso music, and they may never want to leave.

Materials List

	1 x 12 x 14" Pine
	1 x 8-1/2" x 10-1/2" Pine
2	1/2" x 13" Copper pipe
6	1" Styrofoam balls
6	Paper clips
	Aluminum sheeting scraps
2	#9 Wood screws
	Clear silicone sealant

Step One Cut an irregular oval out of each pine piece using a coping, jig or band saw. Using a router, sander or hand tools, round off the top edges of these pieces if you want a naturally tapered beach and greenery. Cut a 5" circle out of the center of the smaller piece to cradle the feed. Using a bead of silicone and woodscrews from the underside, join these two pieces.

Step Two Bend each copper pipe gently into curved palm trunks. Use tin snips to cut palm fronds out of aluminum sheeting. Leave 3/8" x 1" stems that will be glued into the pipes with silicone. Straighten one end of each paper clip. Insert these straight ends through the styrofoam balls until the looped end is flush. These wire stems will be inserted with the frond stems. Paint the trunks, fronds and coconuts with enamel before gluing them into place with silicone.

Step Three Drill two 1/2" holes slanted into the island base. Silicone the trees into place and let dry. Paint the island well with enamel to seal it against the rotting effect of water. You can either float the island or rest it on a brick inside your bird bath.

Seed for Sail

You'll have more than gulls circling this vessel of victuals, eager to sample the catch of the day. Hang a few mesh bags full of thistle seed over the sides, fill the hold with tasty morsels, then run signal flags up the mast that say "good eats."

Materials List

1 x 4" x 24" Pine

1 x 2-5/8" x 3-3/4" Pine

1/4" x 1" x 7" Pine

1 x 2" x 4" Pine

6 *1/8" x 1-3/4" x 25"–28-1/2" Poplar*

1/4" Lath scrap

1/2" x 36" Dowel

1/4" x 17" Dowel

2 *1/4" x 13"Dowels*

1/4" x 11" Dowel

1/4" x 7" Dowel

5 *1/4" x 3-3/4" Dowels*

4 *Eyescrews*

Nylon string

7" x 13" Canvas

Toy bucket, anchor and chain

3 *1" dia. Screens*

Glue and assorted nails

Step One Cut the curved hull bottom with an 80° bevel all around. Cut the stern block as shown in the diagram. The 2-7/8" bottom edge should be cut on an 80° bevel. Glue the stern block on top of the hull bottom. Let dry.

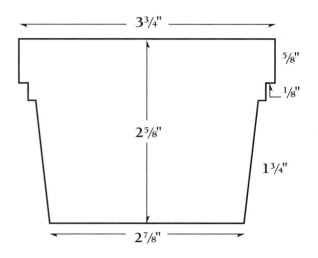

Step Two Each end of the 7" bow stem should be cut at parallel 45° angles. Cut one end of two 1-3/4" x 25" strips at 45°, then bevel the insides of these edges slightly to join with the bow stem. Run a good bead of glue on the lower stern, hull bottom edges and lower bow stem. Tack the side strips to the stern, then clamp them to the bow stem, which gets glued to the hull bottom. Let dry.

Step Three Sand the bow joint down to a taper before attaching the next side strips. Glue, tack, clamp, and let it dry. Sand the new bow joint before attaching the last strips. After they have dried, sand the bow and trim the top edges flush with the stern block.

Step Four Glue the 2" x 4" block, centered 15" from the stern, to the hull bottom. Glue a brace cut from 1/4" scrap over this, resting across the middle side strips. Enclose the bow with two triangular pieces of scrap if you wish.

Step Five Drill a 1/2" hole through the center brace and into the block to support the mast. Drill three 1/4" drain holes across the bottom, then glue the screens over top. Drill a 1/4" hole into the bow stem to support the 7" bow sprit. Drill a 1/4" hole at each corner of the stern and both sides of the center brace to support the 3-3/4" posts for the tarp. Glue all these dowels into place.

Step Six Drill a 1/4" hole through the mast, 7-1/2" up, for the 17" boom. Drill a 1/4" hole 3" from the mast top for the 3-3/4" yardarm, and another 9-1/2" from the top for the 11" yardarm. Glue these dowels into place. Install an eyescrew next to each tarp support post, then rig the boat with nylon string.

Step Seven Glue each long edge of the canvas around a 13" dowel. Let dry, then drape it over the boom. The dowels can either be tied or glued directly onto the tarp posts. Mount this feeder on a post.

Victorian Gazebo

Nothing quite matches the charm of turn-of-the-century architecture. This feeder could serve as an attractive focal point in a formal garden, at the same time luring colorful creatures to feed.

Materials List

	1 x 11-1/4" x 11-1/4" Pine
	1 x 10" x 10" Pine
4	9" Triangles of 1/2" plywood
	1/4" x 4-1/2" Dowel
	3/8" x 8" Dowel
	1/8" x 5-1/2" Dowel
10	5/8" Wooden beads
4	3/4" x 3/4" x 5-1/2" Pine posts
4	3/4" x 1-1/16" x 1-1/16" Pine blocks
4	1/2" x 3/4" x 8" Pine
4	1/4 x 1-1/2" x 11-5/8" Lath
3	1/4 x 3/4" x 8-1/2" Lath rails
18	1/4 x 1/4" x 3" Lath ballisters
8	1/4 x 3/4" x 2-3/4" Lath scrolls
	Doll house shingles
	Aluminum sheet scrap
	Clear silicone and assorted nails

Step One Cut and sand the two foundation plates from 1 x 12 pine. Cut a 5" circle out of the center of the smaller plate using a jigsaw, and sand.

Step Two Rip cut (from 1 x stock) the four 5-1/2" square posts, then cross-cut each post into a 3" and a 2-1/2" length. Next, rip cut the four 1/2" strips (from 1 x), each measuring 8" long. These will be butt joined to form the top frame that supports the roof. Finally, rip a 5" length of 1 x into a 1-1/16" width, then cut four 1-1/16" blocks to go on top of the posts.

Step Three Miter cut four 11-5/8" lengths of lath to form the lip around the base. Next, rip cut three 8-1/2" lengths of lath to a width of 3/4" for the rails. Miter cut all but the two ends which will join the posts at the opening of the feeder. Out of a 13" length of the same lath, rip four 1/4" strips, then a fifth strip from what would have been the fourth 3/4" x 8-1/2" rail. Cut these into eighteen 3" ballisters.

Step Four Measure and glue the four 3" sections of corner posts into place, then glue the three rails around the top. Let dry, then wedge and glue the ballisters into place. Let dry. Reinforce the corner posts with a nail or screw from underneath. Then glue and top nail this assembly onto the bottom plate with the two grains running perpendicular. Glue and nail the mitered lath lip around the perimeter. A small drainage hole can be drilled in each corner.

Step Five Glue the 1-1/16" blocks onto the 2-1/2" upper post sections. Glue and nail the roof frame together with butt joints. Let dry. Drill 3/8" holes, each 1/2" deep, into the centers of the upper and lower post sections. Cut the 3/8" dowel into four 2" lengths, thread two wooden beads over each one, and join all the post sections with glue. While the glue is wet, align the roof frame over the posts and glue it in place onto the post blocks.

Step Six Two of the three sides of each 9" roof triangle can be bevel cut for tighter joinery. Lean these roof panels together, joining them with silicone. Let dry, then glue onto the roof frame.

Step Seven Sharpen one end of the 1/4" dowel to a point. Drill perpendicular 1/8" holes through the center of this dowel, then insert two 2-3/4" lengths of 1/8" dowel through the holes. Glue in place. Cut the letters N, E, W and S from

aluminum sheet, and silicone them onto the ends of these small dowels. Glue two beads, pre-drilled with 1/4" holes, onto the main dowel either side of these small dowels.

Step Eight Using a coping or band saw, cut the eight scroll pieces from lath. They can be glued into place after they are painted. Drill a 1/4" hole at the apex of the roof. Glue the weather-vane assembly into this hole.

Step Nine Apply successive beads of silicone onto two opposite roof panels, and apply each row of shingles from the bottom tier up. Let dry, then trim the diagonal edges with a coping saw from the bottom up. Apply shingles to the other two roof panels, let dry, and trim. Paint the entire piece to your taste. Apply two coats of polyurethane to the roof shingles.

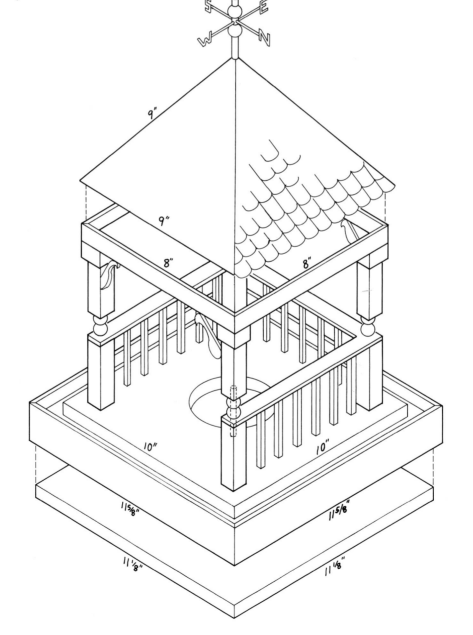

Castle Keep

This aviary compound features all the amenities: house, rooftop bath and turret feeders, proving that a bird's home is his castle. Fortify your feathered friends in this medieval marvel.

Materials List

4	1 x 12 x 10" Pine
2	1 x 8-3/8" x 8-3/8" Pine
4	1 x 5" x 20" Pine
4	1/4 x 1-1/2" x 20-1/2" Lath
4	2" x 12" PVC pipe
	7-3/8" x 7-3/8" Plastic tray
8	1/2" x 1/2" x 8-3/8" Pine
4	1 x 3-1/2" Circles of pine
33	3/4" x 3/4" x 1-1/4" Pine blocks
	3-1/4" x 4-3/4" Pine door
4	1/4" x 6-1/4" Dowels
	Aluminum sheet scrap
4	Small eyescrews
	9" Chain
	3-1/2" x 4-1/4" Wire mesh
	Glue and assorted finishing nails

Step One It should be noted that, depending on the dimensions of the rooftop tray (or baking pan) you find, the size of the castle can be adapted accordingly. So find your bird bath tray first.

Step Two Miter cut the 1 x 12 pine to 10" lengths (or to fit other tray) to form the castle walls. Cut square notches in the top edges for battlements. Rip cut eight 8-3/8" pine strips 1/2" square. Miter cut these to recess into the top and bottom of the castle walls. Glue and nail the bottom tier of these, recessed 3/4" from the bottom edge of each wall.

Step Three Glue and nail the four wall sections together. Cut the two 8-3/8" square panels from 1 x pine. Glue and nail one of these, recessed 1/2" from the top of the battlement cutouts. Glue and nail the remaining mitered 1/2" square strips above this panel into place.

Step Four Cut the 2" PVC pipe into 12" lengths. Cut a 1/2" x 1-1/2" slot in one end of each pipe. Pre-drill and screw, at top and bottom, each pipe to the walls at the front and back corners.

Step Five Cut four mitered 5" x 20" planks from 1 x pine to form the blue moat. Glue and nail, from the inside bottom edge of the castle walls, these moat planks into place. Glue and tack the lath lip into place around the perimeter. Finally, insert the 8-3/8" square bottom panel into place, and secure with glue and angled nails.

Step Six Cut four 5-pointed asterisk shapes from the 3-1/2" circles of 1 x pine. Also cut four 1-1/2" circles of pine. Rip cut 3/4" strips of 1 x pine, to be cut into 33 blocks of 1-1/4" lengths. Glue five of these onto the tops of each asterisk. Glue and screw the 1-1/2" circles beneath them. Drill 1/4" holes into the top centers to accommodate the dowel flagstaffs.

Step Seven Cut the four lengths of 1/4" dowel. Notch one end with a fine coping saw blade. Cut long triangles of aluminum sheet to wedge into place as flags. Glue these flags into place.

Step Eight Cut a 3-1/4" x 4-3/4" door from 1 x pine. Round off one end. Glue and nail into place. Glue the remaining nine blocks into place around the doorway. After these are

painted, the wire mesh and eyescrews with chain will be installed. Drill the bird house entry hole above the door.

Step Nine Paint as you wish. The mortar lines can be added with a small-tipped paint pencil. The turret tops are removable in order to load seed into the turret towers. Drainage holes can be added to the moat.

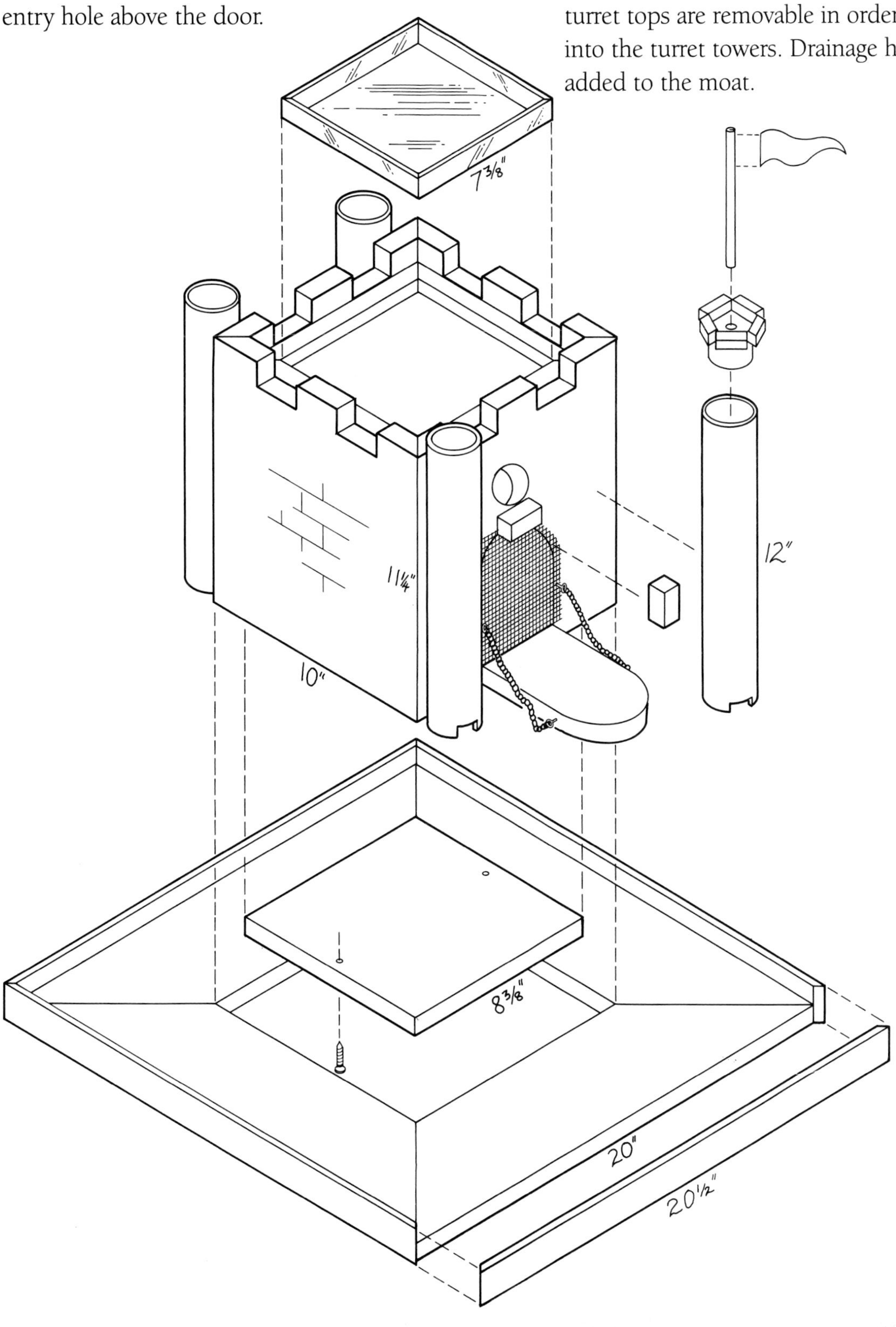

7³⁄₈"

12"

11¼"

10"

8³⁄₈"

20"

20½"

Carousel Cuisine

Fanciful animals orbiting a seed dispenser—how could a hungry bird resist? And what if the saddled species were all sorts of birds? Then again, you may elect to display this spectacular feeder indoors with nuts and candies for our own kind.

Materials List

2   1/2" x 16" x 16" Mahogany plywood
8   1/2" x 7" Dowels
    1/2" x 13" Dowel
8   3/16" x 7" Dowels
    3/16" x 2" Dowel
8   1/4" x 6-5/8" x 9-1/2" x 9-1/2" Plywood triangles
8   1/4" x 1-3/8" x 6-3/4" Mahogany plywood
8   1/4" x 3/8" x 6-15/16" Mahogany plywood
8   1/4" x 3-1/2" x 3-3/4" Mahogany plywood
8   4" x 5-1/4" Medium acrylic safety glazing
8   1/2" x 1/2" x 6-3/8" Molding
    1-1/4" Wooden bead
    3/8" Wooden bead
    Toothpicks
    Glue

Step One Cut two identical equilateral octagons from the 16" square plywood. Draw the four intersecting lines from each pair of opposing points on both pieces. Mark 4-3/8" in from each of these points along all eight spokes to determine the centers of the support posts. On one piece, draw four more intersecting lines between the midpoints of each edge. Mark 3" in from each edge along these bisecting spokes to determine the animal mounting posts.

Step Two Line up both hexagons, the piece with more lines drawn on top of the other. Drill 1/2" holes through both pieces on the centers marked for support posts. Drill 3/16" holes on the centers marked for animal mounting posts. Drill a 1/2" hole in the very center of one of the hexagons. With a compass, mark a 6" circle in the center of the other hexagon and cut it out with a jigsaw.

Step Three Each of the eight support posts must be rip cut with two 1/8" grooves 135° apart. See the diagram to make a jig that will facilitate these two cuts. Fill the lower ends of these grooves with 1-1/4" lengths of toothpicks, glued flush with the bottoms to act as stops for the acrylic panes.

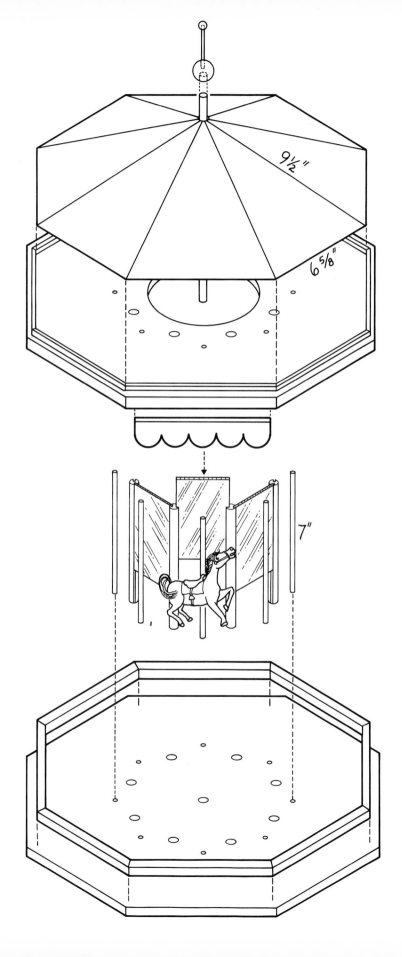

9½"

6⅝"

7"

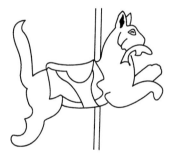

Step Four The lip on the lower hexagon can be made with 1/2" stock—square or rounded, half-round or other mouldings. Miter cut the ends at 67-1/2°, then glue them around the perimeter. Cut five rounded scallops into one edge of each 1-3/8" x 6-3/4" piece. Miter cut the ends to 67-1/2° and glue around the outer edge of the other hexagon. (Glue the top edges flush if you plan to install outdoors, since drainage will be a factor.) Miter the 3/8" strips the same way, and glue on as trim.

Step Five Paint all dowels and both hexagons, except the 1/2" ends of dowels to be glued, before joining. The acrylic panes can be cut using an inexpensive plastics cutting tool with a straight edge. Glue and tap each dowel into the bottom hexagon. Insert the acrylic panes as you go so as to align the support posts before they dry. You must also insert all dowels into the upper hexagon and tap into place before the glue dries. Let everything dry.

Step Six Miter cut one long edge of each roof triangle at 70°. Lay the panels together over tape strips, edge to edge, bevels up. Run a good bead of glue down each seam, fold the panels into a cone and tape the last seam. Let dry, inverted. Drill a 1/2" hole at the apex from the underside. Glue the 1/2" center post into the base. Check the fit of the roof over this post, then trim if necessary and sand all edges and seams.

Step Seven Drill a 1/2" hole 3/4 of the way into the larger wooden bead. Drill a 3/16" hole in the top, and into the smaller bead. Glue this assembly together, then onto the apex of the roof. Paint the roof and spire. Pennant may be glued to the spire's shaft.

Step Eight Using the patterns, or your own imagination, cut the animals out of 1/4" plywood with a coping or band saw. Paint them as you wish, and glue them to the posts.

Baths

Materials List

An armful of grapevines
A small spool of tie wire
8" dia. Plastic basin (potted plant saucer)
Side cutters

15"

⊢ 16" ⊣ —G

Ⓗ
⊢ 4" ⊣

20"

Step One Make thin wreaths and cut all pieces as shown.

Ⓔ Ⓕ

12" 8"

curved 28" length
21" length
Ⓒ

8"

Ⓓ

Ⓐ

Step Four Weave extra vines around A for desired thickness.

Step Two Wire G to A 6" from bottom of A. Wire E pieces as shown from G to A.

6"

Step Three Wire D to center of G. Shape B and wire D to center of B. Wire each end of D to A as shown. Shape E and wire to center of B and bottom of A. Repeat with E as many as needed. Bend C and wire to A & E as shown.

Ⓗ

Ⓗ
Ⓐ

Ⓖ
Ⓑ
Ⓒ

Ⓔ

Ⓓ
Ⓖ
Ⓑ
Ⓒ
Ⓓ
Ⓔ

Top view

Ⓐ

Ⓓ

Ⓑ

Ⓒ

Ⓔ

Step Five Wrap small grapevines for thickness desired and attach H to top of A. Use 8" clay or plastic flower pot tray for bath basin.

112

Wall Hanging Bath

Not all bird baths sit on pedestals. This woven basket cradles a basin and belongs on a vine-covered wall next to a garden. It could also be used as a feeder.

Swimming Pool

Even birds need a recreational splash now and then. And what fun you'll have watching them do back flips and belly flops off the high dive. Sprinkle some seed around the patio furniture, and watch them frolic.

Materials List

	1/2" x 12" x 24" Plywood
	3/4" or 1" x 12" x 24" Plywood
2	1/4" x 1-1/2" x 24-1/2" Lath
2	1/4" x 1-1/2" x 12-1/2" Lath
	1/4" x 1-1/2" x 6" Lath
	3/4" x 3/4" x 1-3/8" Pine
	3/32" x 46" Brass rod
	1/16" x 40" Brass wire
	3-3/4" dia. Dome from plastic bottle
	3/4" x 1" dia. Dowel
	5/16" Wooden bead
2	7/8" x 3-1/4" Grosgrain ribbon
	Polyurethane (can be water base)
7	#9 Wood screws
	Glue and brads

Step One Use a jigsaw to cut a kidney-shaped hole through the 3/4" plywood to form the pool basin. Then, using a coping saw, cut a taper into each side of the 1-3/8" pine block to form the pedestal for the table. Glue the sanded pedestal onto the deck, reinforcing it with a wood screw from underneath. Glue the deck onto the 1/2" plywood base, reinforcing it with the six remaining screws from underneath.

Step Two Miter the edges of the four long lath strips to fit around the base and deck. Glue

114

and tack the lath around the edges. Cut the 6" lath piece into the following: (2) 5/8" x 3-1/2" diving boards, 3/4" x 1-1/16" lifeguard seat, 5/8" x 5/8" step, and a 1-1/2" dia. circle. Drill a 3/32" hole through the center of this circle, another into the pedestal, another through the 3/4" section of dowel, and another into the wooden bead. Glue the dowel into the top of the dome. Let dry. Using glue in all joints and seams, assemble the patio table with a 4" length of brass rod.

Step Three All the furniture is soldered together using brass rod for the ladders and vertical supports, with brass wire for the chairs, hand rails, and seat back. They are painted silver after assembly. The high dive and lifeguard chair stand 3-1/8" tall. The low dive is 3/8" above the deck. The chair back frames are 2-1/2" long and 1-1/8" wide. The chair seat frames are 2" long. Each piece of furniture is glued into 3/8" deep holes in the deck. The ribbon is glued or sewn to the chair frames. After painting everything, coat the basin with 2–3 coats of polyurethane.

Drive-Thru Bird Wash

Falcons and Thunderbirds have been zipping through these automated tunnels of suds for years now, emerging clean and glistening. Isn't it time to offer this dandy device to all the dirty birds in your neighborhood?

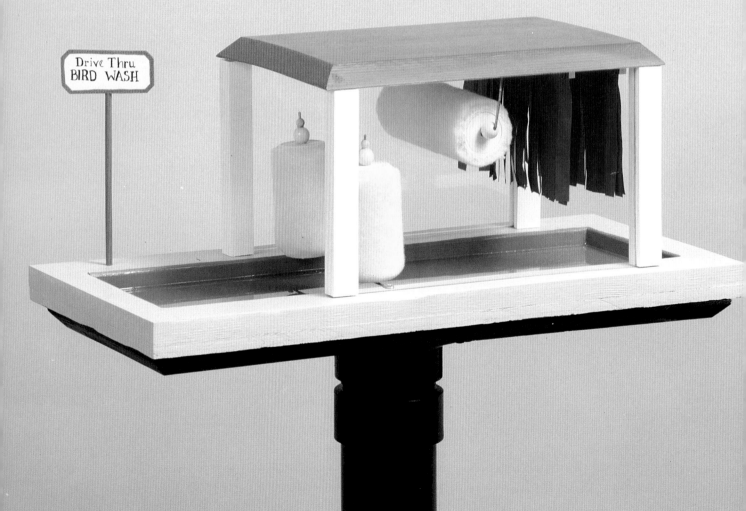

Materials List

    1 x 10-7/8" x 24" Pine

    1/2" x 10-7/8" x 24" Plywood

    1 x 9" x 13-3/4" Pine

  4 *3/4" x 1" x 7" Pine*

  2 *7" x 11-3/4" Plexiglass*

  2 *1/4" x 3/8" x 7-1/4" Pine*

  2 *4-3/4" x 7-1/4" Rip-stop nylon*

    6-1/4" Paint roller

  2 *4" Paint rollers*

  6 *3/4" x 1-15/32" dia. Pine disks*

    3/32" x 14-1/4" Brass rod

  2 *3/32" x 7" Brass rods*

  4 *5/8" Wooden balls*

  2 *5/16" Wooden balls*

    1/4" x 8" Dowel

  4 *1/4" x 1-3/4" Dowels*

    1/8" x 1-1/2" x 3-3/8" Lath

  8 *#8 Wood screws*

    Glue and assorted nails

    Small wire staples

    Polyurethane (can be water base)

Step One Cut a 6-1/2" x 21" hole in the center of the 24" pine. Rip cut a 1/4" deep groove down one 3/4" face of each 7" pine post to accept the plexiglass. Cut a 45° bevel on all four edges of the pine roof block.

Step Two Drill a 3/32" hole through the center of each pine disk. If you can't find a dowel that fits snugly into the paint roller, cut the disks from 1 x stock with a hole saw. Glue the disks into the rollers flush with the ends.

Step Three Bend the 14-1/4" rod into a tall C-shaped rectangle, the long back of which will be tacked to the ceiling with staples. The long side measures 7-1/4". The bracket bends 90° down to 2-1/4", leaving 1-1/4" on each end to bend 90° through the wooden bead and into the disk. Bend both shorter rods into L-shapes, the long stem of which measures 5-1/4". Bend the shorter ends into tight eyelets to accept the mounting screws. Slip the rollers onto the stems, and glue the wooden beads on top.

Step Four Cut 4" slits into the nylon to make fringe. Tack these strips to the 1/4" x 3/8" x 7-1/4" pine, then glue and tack them to the ceiling 1-1/4" and 3-1/2" from one edge. Tack staples over the roller support rod 6-1/2" from the same edge. Screw the two upright rollers 3/8" from the edges of the basin, and 10" from one end of the 24" pine.

Step Five Drill a 1/4" hole 1" into the center of one end of each 7" pine post. Drill four 1/4" holes through the 24" pine that form a 8-3/16" x 12-3/8" rectangle. The holes closest to the rollers should be 2-1/8" away from the roller mounting screws.

Step Six Glue a 1-3/4" dowel into each post. Fit the plexiglass into the post grooves, then glue the posts to the base, tapping the dowels into place. Glue and top nail the roof on to the posts. Let dry.

Step Seven Glue the 24" pine base to the 1/2" plywood foundation, reinforcing with the six remaining screws from underneath. Flatten one side of the top inch of the 8" dowel, then glue it to the lath sign. Drill a 1/4" hole in the base, and glue the sign in place.

Step Eight You may want to paint as you assemble, or paint everything after assembly. After painting, apply 2–3 coats of polyurethane to the basin.

Houses

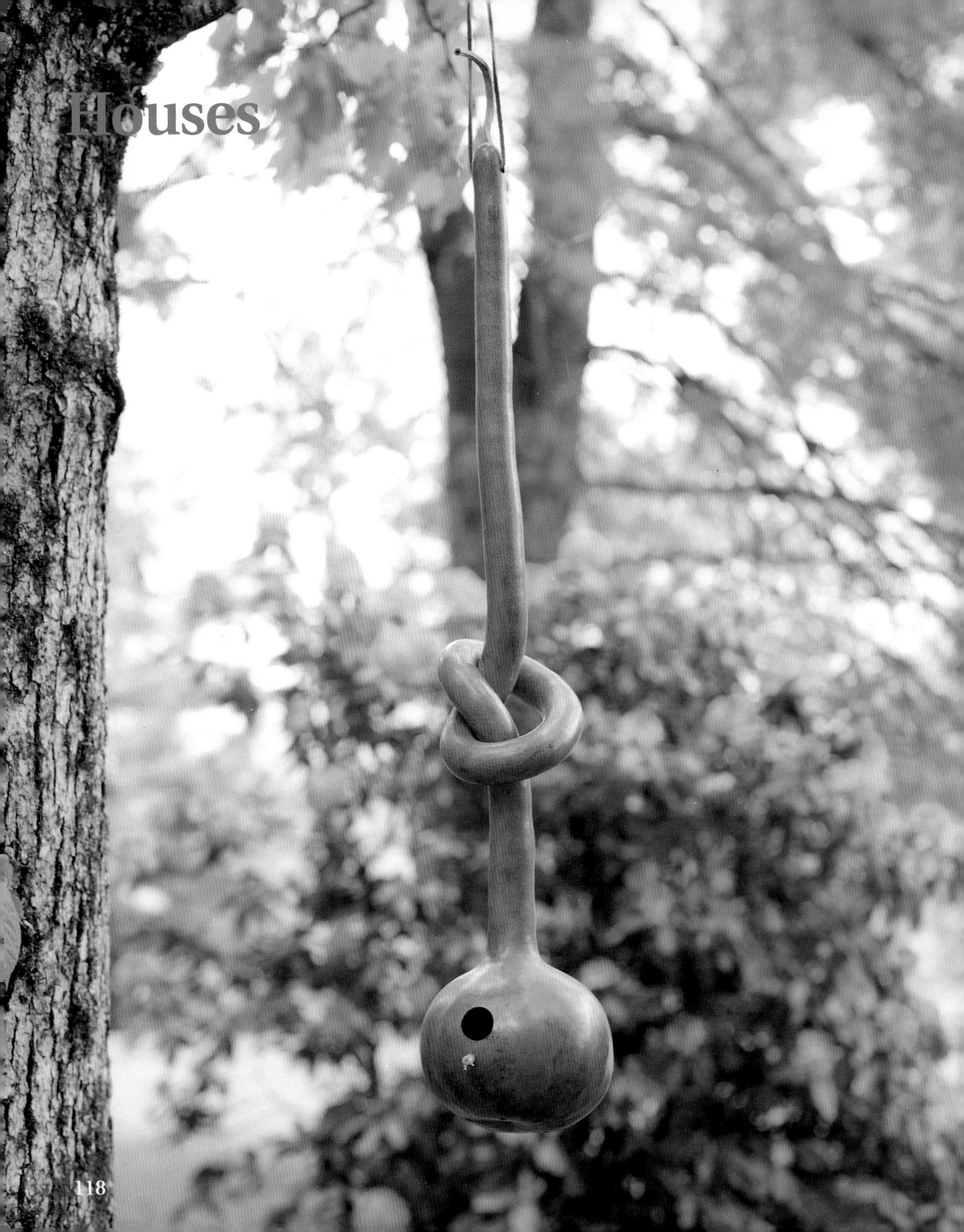

Acorn Gourd House

Gourds make wonderful bird houses. Different ways of cultivating various species add to the design possibilities. Hang this giant acorn from your tallest oak.

Materials List

Dipper gourd
Bottle gourd

Step One Select a medium-sized dipper gourd with a tapered bottom for the chamber. Cut off the neck of the gourd at a point just above the largest part of the ball, and clean out the seeds. Save the stem to use for the perch.

Step Two Drill an entrance hole about 1-1/4" dia., or start with a sampler hole and enlarge it using sandpaper wrapped around a pencil. Drill a smaller hole just big enough to accept a piece of the gourd stem for a perch.

Step Three Select a bottle gourd of the same size but with a flatter bottom for the acorn's cap. Cut this gourd just below the widest point. Use the bottom piece for the cap. Drill a small hole in the center of this part.

Insert the stem as the stem of the acorn.

Step Four Fit the cap over the house section and glue them together. Wood burning or painting the cap to look like a real acorn cap will be effective for a natural look. Wood stains of different hues will also enhance the bird house. When you are satisfied with the look you've achieved, spray with a clear coat of acrylic finish.

Thatched Gourd House

Birds may have to evict the gnomes before setting up housekeeping in this elfin-looking abode. Either way, you'll enjoy hanging this enchanting shelter in your yard.

Materials List

Pear-shaped gourd
Spare gourd
Broom corn
2' Raffia
Glue

Step One Select a medium-sized, pear-shaped gourd that is tapered downward to a flat bottom. Drill a 1-1/4" hole in the side of the gourd for an entrance hole. Carefully clean out the seeds. A piece of coat hanger with a small hook on one end is helpful in the cleaning process. Cut off the stem and use it for a perch, gluing it into a pre-drilled hole.

Step Two If you decide to stain your gourd, do so now. Add a coat of clear acrylic after the stain and glue have dried.

Step Three The roof is made from broom corn stalks cut to about 3"–4". Most craft stores carry broom corn. Three layers, glued progressively higher up the gourd, should be enough. You can use a hot glue gun to attach the rows of broom corn.

Step Four The porch roof is cut from the neck of another gourd and glued on. Since the apex of the roof will look ragged from the tips of the broom corn, a cap should be made from the top of another gourd and glued securely on top.

Step Five The thatch is held in place with a band of some natural material like raffia. Dried flowers would add a nice touch, tucked through the raffia band.

Grapevine Summer House

This decorative birdhouse, with its husky vines and coiled tendrils, offers breezy shelter for nesting birds. It can be hung under a porch roof or eaves to keep out rain. It can also be built around a gourd for use in colder climates.

Materials List

An armful of grapevines
A small spool of tie wire
Side cutters

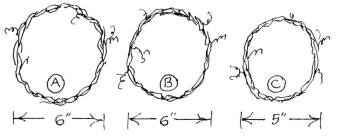

Step One Make thin round wreaths and cut all pieces as shown.

Step Two Start with eight 32" stays and add as many as you desire.

Step Three Start with eight 6" roof vines and add as many as you desire.

Step Four Attach E to C as shown.

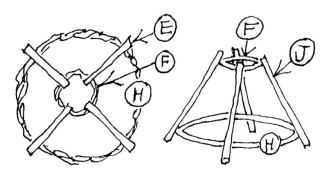

Step Five Attach four rafters as shown, then add more.

122

Step Six Bend I into tear drop. Attach ends of E 5" from top of tear drop.

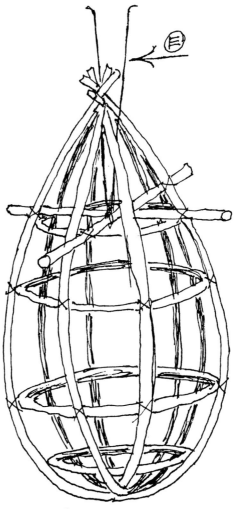

Step Eight Attach wire to E for later attachment to top ring.

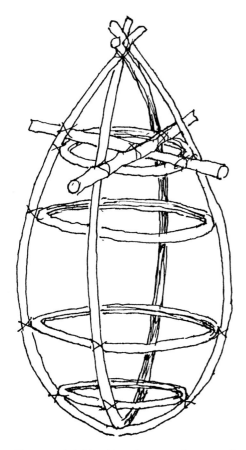

Step Seven Add inside rings as shown, then repeat tear drop stays until walls are as full as you desire.

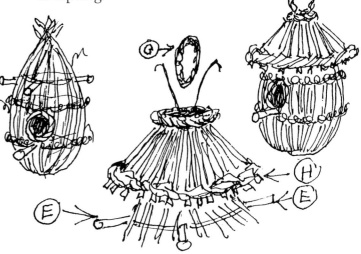

Step Nine Wire door and perch in place, then cut out door. Place roof over hanger wires and wire roof H to E. Tie hanger wires to G. Add small vines to outside for decorative trim.

Thatched Yurt

Asian nomads developed a distinctive round house that was collapsible and featured a domed or conical roof. This design lends itself beautifully to the use of natural materials, and is sure to enhance your outdoor site.

Materials List

> 3/8" x 6" dia. Plywood
>
> 8   3/8" x 2-1/2" x 5-3/4" Bark-faced
>   pine slats
>
> 1/2" x 18" Green twig, de-barked
>
> 1-1/2" dia. x 20" Bundle of straw
>
> 3/16" x 10' Grapevine
>
> 12' Thin vine or twine
>
> Tie wire

Step One Drill eight 3/16" holes around the perimeter of the 6" plywood circle, equidistant and 3/8" from the edge. The eight slats can be split off of a pine log to a thickness of 3/8"–1/2", then trimmed into 2-1/2" x 5-3/4" rectangles. You may gently whittle and sand the bark for a rounded look if you wish. Drill two 3/16" holes in each slat, about 3/4" from each short edge.

Step Two Weave a 6" dia. wreath and a 7" dia. wreath out of grapevine. The larger wreath surrounds the bottom rim of the bucket, while the smaller wreath fits inside the top rim. Using thin vine or twine, attach each slat to the plywood circle through their matching holes and around the larger wreath, wrapping your way around the rim. Lash the tops of the slats to the smaller wreath in a similar way. Cut the door hole between two slats with a coping saw, then tack a strip across the threshold cut from pine scrap.

Step Three With a sharp knife or hatchet, split the 18" twig into quarters 7-1/2" into one end. Fan these out into rafters and wire them securely to the bucket rim. Each rafter should extend 1" over the rim. Wire the remaining grapevine to the rafter ends to form eaves, then continue spiralling it up to form a conical frame, wiring it to the rafters as you go.

Step Four The bundle of straw surrounds the post, then fans out over the roof frame. Hold it in place with rubber bands around the post, then tie and wrap with thin vine or twine from the top down. Tie it down through to the frame as you spiral out over the straw, then around the eaves. Clip off the rubber bands. Trim the excess straw around the eaves with heavy scissors. A top loop can be woven as a wreath through a hole drilled through the post top for hanging.

Mosaic Twig Treehouse

This woodsy cottage belongs up in the trees amidst breezy boughs. It can be sized to suit many species of birds, and decorated with whatever patterns your twigs inspire.

Materials List

2	1 x 10" x 15" Wood planks
	1 x 10" x 10" Wood plank
2	1 x 8-1/2" x 10" Wood planks
2	3/8" x 9" x 13" Plywood
	Assorted twigs
28	1" dia. x 9" Bamboo
2	Tin cans
	10'–16' Multi-pronged trunk post
	Glue and assorted nails

Step One The chamber can be constructed out of most any 3/4" stock, preferably rough-sawn for a rustic look. Cut the roof peak out of both 10" x 15" planks at once leaving 10" corner edges. Cut an entry hole in one of these.

Step Two Glue and nail the 8-1/2" x 10" side planks to these to form the walls, lapping the larger planks over the smaller ones. Let dry, then glue and nail the 10" x 10" base plank to the bottom edges.

Step Three The shape of the twigs you find may help determine the patterns you add to the walls. The distinctively curved corner braces used on the front of this house are two halves of the same twig, carefully sawed in half. The fence pattern and door frame are split twigs cut and bent to fit, then tacked into place. Pre-drilling the nail holes will prevent splitting the twigs. A Y-shaped twig is glued into a hole drilled below the door for the perch.

Step Four The remaining walls can be decorated with twig mosaics. You may want to sketch a pattern on the wall before tacking the larger split twigs on to outline a particular shape, such as a star. Smaller twigs, perhaps of contrasting color, can then be cut to fit inside and around the outline and tacked into place.

Step Five If you plan to permanently attach your house to a post, install a lag screw through the floor and into the post before affixing the roof. If your post is multi-pronged, top nail the other flush-cut branches through the floor as well.

Step Six Cut 9" lengths of bamboo between the knuckles and split them in half. Pre-drill and nail a row of upturned halves on each plywood roof panel. Then pre-drill and nail rows of downturned halves over these, lapped like a tile roof.

Step Seven Pre-drill and nail the roof panels on top of the chamber. Open and flatten two tin cans. Bend them lengthwise to conform to the roof ridge, then pre-drill and nail them in place.

Thunderbird Tipi

Who's to say that certain native species wouldn't want to emulate the habitats of their human counterparts. A child could have lots of fun making and decorating this piece, then waiting to see who sets up camp.

Materials List

	1 x 9-3/4" dia. Pine base
7	1/4" x 15"–16" Dowels
	1/4" x 6" Dowel
	1/4" x 2-1/8" Dowel
	1/4" x 1-3/4" Dowel
	11-1/2" x 23" Canvas
	String
	Painter's caulk
	Glue

Step One After cutting the circular pine base, drill seven 1/4" holes about 5/8" from the edge. They should be somewhat evenly spaced, about 1/2" deep, and angled slightly toward the center. They can be widened as necessary to accommodate the tipi poles.

Step Two Make diagonal cuts on one end of each of the seven poles, plus the 6" dowel. This creates a more natural effect. You may even prefer to use straight branches instead of storebought dowels.

Step Three Glue three of the poles into somewhat evenly spaced holes, and tie them together with string about 4" from the top, before the glue dries. Glue in and tie the remaining four poles in the same manner, then the 6" dowel that supports the top flap. Squirt glue all around the top lashing to secure the juncture. Let dry.

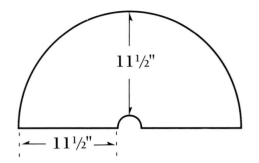

Step Four Cut a semicircle from the canvas as shown in the diagram. Save the scrap. Try wrapping the canvas around the poles, check for fit, and trim as necessary. There should be ample canvas touching the base to glue a seam.

Step Five Run a bead of glue around the base where the canvas skirt will rest. Run beads of glue down the outside of each pole and around the top lashing. Lay the canvas gently around the frame, and gently press it down over all the glue seam. Run a wide bead of glue inside the overlapping edge, then press it gently closed. Let dry.

Step Six Opposite the vertical seam, cut a 1-1/4" x 1-3/4" oval door, 2" from the bottom. Cut a 3" x 4" triangular flap from the scrap canvas, then glue it over the 6" dowel and onto the tipi wall. Cut a 1" x 2-1/2" panel of scrap canvas, then glue it as a V-shaped awning over the door hole. Let dry.

Step Seven Indent one end of the 2-1/8" dowel with a round file. Glue and nail the 1-3/4" dowel to this end to form the perch. Drill a 1/4" hole in front of the door, and glue it in place.

Step Eight Caulk the entire apex of the tipi, including the flap, as well as the door awning, vertical seam and base seam. Let dry. Prime and paint the entire piece with exterior grade paint. Designs can be painted on with hobby enamels. A feathered spear and other toy accessories can be added.

Bat House

Bats aren't birds, but mammals that can devour 500 insects per minute! They're harmless to humans, yet becoming endangered. A house this size can sleep a colony of up to 30 bats. This is a fun project for kids to help with.

Materials List

2	*1 x 12 x 15" Pine*
2	*1 x 12 x 9" Pine*
	1 x 10-1/2" x 15" Pine
2	*1 x 12 x 13-7/8" Pine*
	1 x 4 x 34" Pine
	1/2" x 14" x 25" Plywood
	Glue and assorted nails
	2-1/2" Bolt and nut

Step One You may want to use cedar for the box (painted blue in the photo) instead of pine, for better weather resistance. First cut 3/4" dado grooves lengthwise into the 12 x 9" side panels. There should be two 3/16" deep grooves on 3" centers to channel the inner partitions. Next, cut 3/16" deep grooves about 1" apart, lengthwise across one of the 12 x 15" panels (not shown in photo). Do this again with both 12 x 13-7/8" partition panels.

Step Two Glue and nail the 12 x 15" panels to the 12 x 9" sides, butting the corners, with all grooves facing inward. Glue and nail the 10-1/2" x 15" roof snugly on top. All seams should be tight to prevent leaks. Let dry.

Step Three Cut a 21" length of 1 x 4 for the tree mount. You may wish to jigsaw a bat head outline at one end and tail at the other, as in the photo. Bevel cut the remaining 13" of 1 x 4 as a mounting shim. Glue and nail the shim to the center of the tree mount, bevels up. Glue and nail the box to the center of the shim. This double seam can be reinforced with a 2-1/2" bolt through all three boards up toward the lid (not shown in photo).

Step Four Paint both partitions and the box interior flat black. Glue and nail the partitions into the dadoed grooves. They will be flush with the bottom of the box (unlike the photo, which has an angled roof).

Step Five Cut a bat silhouette from 1/2" plywood. Paint it well to seal the laminations. Paint the entire structure as you wish, then glue and nail the bat emblem proudly on the house.

Bats in the Belfry

Here's an elegant way to control your insect population, even if your neighbors think you're a little batty. Try mounting this in a shady spot near a garden.

Materials List

4   *1 x 11-1/4" x 24" Pine*
2   *1 x 10-1/2" x 14-1/2" Pine*
    1 x 10-1/2" x 10-1/2" Pine
4   *13-1/2" Triangles of 1/4" plywood*
    54" of 1-1/2" Decorative molding
    Floor flange
    1/2" x 3/4" x 10-1/2" Pine
    Bell
    Lathe-turned spire
    Glue and assorted finishing nails

Step One Each of the wall panels could be solid 1 x 12, two planks of 1 x 8, or 3/4" plywood. The overall dimensions can also be varied, along with corresponding adjustments for interior panels. After cutting the four wall panels, use a jigsaw to cut the window openings. The flat bottom sill should be 8" below the top edge. Mark the semi-circular arc with a compass. These windows measure 6" x 6", and should be 3/8" off-center.

Step Two Cut the two interior panels of solid 1 x or 3/4" plywood to fit snugly inside whatever sized chamber you're building. These can be inserted and nailed into place as simple butt joints or into dado cut grooves. Since these panels will partition the three sleeping compartments, be sure to rip cut horizontal grooves on both sides to facilitate the bat's foothold. Grooves that are about 1/8" deep and wide should be spaced 1–2" apart, and should be cut on the facing interior walls also.

Step Three Cut the square panel that forms the roof of the compartment to fit, either butted or dadoed into place. A standard 1" floor flange can be screwed onto the center of this panel. This will accommodate a 1" steel pipe, threaded at the top end, which can be used as the mounting post. The method used here utilized a 1-1/4" dowel post which is inserted into a 1-1/4" hole cut halfway into the roof panel. It is stabilized by a 3-1/4" square block with a 1-1/4" hole. The block slips down the dowel and is glued into place, flush with the bottom edge of the interior panels, into which it snugly fits. Use a hole saw to cut the holes.

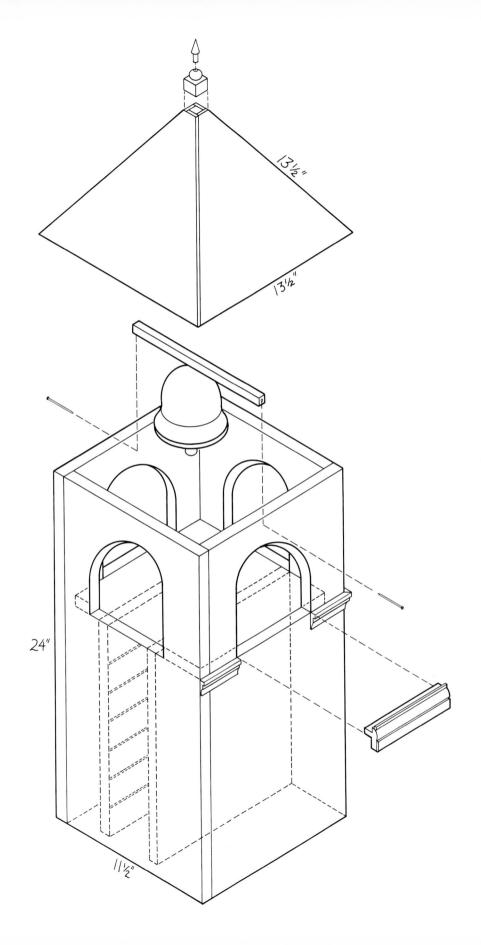

13½"

13½"

24"

11½"

Step Four Join the wall panels one corner at a time with glue and nails. Before attaching the last wall panel, insert the roof panel and secure it with glue and nails. Join the last wall, let dry, then sand all corner seams.

Step Five Insert the two interior panels, and secure them with glue and nails. Rip cut the 1/2" x 3/4" pine bell support, then cut a length to fit the top inside of the belfry. Find an old bell, or turn one from wood on a lathe like this one. Attach it to the support, then install the assembly with glue and nails.

Step Six Measure and cut the decorative molding to form the four cornices. It is wise to cut the miters first, hold them in place to mark the window edges, then make the straight cuts. Glue and nail them into place along a pre-marked horizontal line. The four sill moldings can be cut from the same molding and turned upside down, or from different molding. Cut and install these in the same manner.

Step Seven Cut the four 13-1/2" equilateral triangles that form the roof from 1/4" plywood. The edges that will join can either be miter cut or bevel cut for butt joints. If you choose to insert a block (as shown in the photo), bevel cut the top corners to fit. Otherwise, you can simply drill a hole in the finished roof to accept a dowel spire. To join the roof, run a bead of glue or silicone sealant on one upper edge of each panel, then lean them together and let dry. The seams can be reinforced by lightly tapping small brads into the joints, or gluing dowels or beveled strips into the inside seams.

Step Eight The spire can be lathe-turned, composed of doll house fittings, carved, or a sharpened dowel with beads threaded over it. Whatever its size and shape, it will be glued and nailed into a corresponding hole at the apex of the roof. This roof has a faux copper finish, but the color scheme is up to you. The finished roof assembly is glued and nailed atop the belfry. The top wall edges can be beveled for a stronger glue seam if you wish.

Honeymoon Hideaway

The urge to hole up in this birdie bunga-
low will prove irresistible to the nesting
instincts of all true love birds. And you
won't mind cleaning up after each mating
season using the handy pull-out drawer.

Materials List

2	*1 x 5-1/2" x 9" Pine*
	1 x 7-1/2" x 8" Pine
	1 x 6-3/4" x 8" Pine
	1 x 3-7/8" x 5-1/2" Pine
2	*1/2" x 7-5/8" x 12-3/4" Plywood*
	1/4" x 4" x 6" Plywood
3	*1/4" x 2-3/8" x 5-1/8" Plywood*
	1/4" x 2-1/2" x 3-1/2" Plywood
2	*5-7/8" 1/4-Round molding*
	1/4" Lath scrap
	1/4" x 3" Dowel
2	*Eyescrews*
	Glue and assorted nails

Step One Cut tapered bevels on both long edges of the 3-7/8" x 5-1/2" base block at 80°. Cut an 80° bevel on one short edge of each of the 5-1/2" x 9" side panels. Cut a tapered bevel at 60° on the opposite short sides.

Step Two Mark and cut the elongated pentagons from 1/2" plywood, following the diagram. In one pentagon, cut a 1-5/8" hole upper center with a hole saw. Then cut the bottom third off, 4" from the bottom, for the drawer panel.

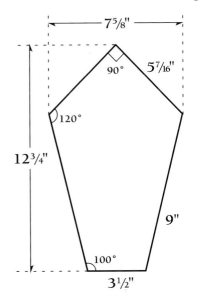

Step Three Glue and nail the whole pentagon to the base and sides, then join the upper pentagon section to this assembly. Glue and nail the 8" pine roof panels with a butt joint, then glue and nail the roof to the top of the chamber.

Step Four Cut 80° tapered bevels on both long edges of one 2-3/8" x 5-1/8" plywood panel (drawer bottom). Cut an 80° bevel on one long edge of the other two panels (drawer sides). Taper cut the 2-1/2" x 3-1/2" plywood (drawer back) so that the bottom edge measures 2-5/16". Glue these panels to the lower pentagon face, forming the drawer. Reinforce with brads after the glue is dry.

Step Five Cut the 1/4" lath scrap into 1/2" widths for fence and shutter slats. The same can be used for cross pieces. Cut picket points on the fencing, and attach as you wish. The windows can be painted on. Cut more scrap for the cross piece under the front gable after mitering and attaching the 1/4-round. The signs are also cut from lath scrap, glued and tacked into place.

Step Six Cut a crescent moon from the 4" x 6" plywood, paint it white, then glue and tack it to the back gable. Install the two eyescrews on the roof ridge, unless you prefer to post mount this house. Drill a 1/4" hole 1" below the entry hole. Cut a 2-1/4" length of dowel and glue it into place.

Step Seven The remaining 3/4" dowel is used to attach the miniature birdhouse, which is an optional feature. It is cut from 1/16" stock and glued on. The entry hole is drilled into the block, with a nail for the perch.

137

New England Town Hall

Here's a taste of colonial Americana at its finest. This architectural relic of early democracy could host a variety of species—even partitioned as a house for martins. And as with the old town meetings, you are free to interpret the consensus of this design.

Materials List

	1 x 12 x 22" Pine base
	1 x 12 x 20" Pine ceiling panel
2	*1 x 12 x 16" Pine walls*
2	*1 x 12 x 9-3/4" Pine walls*
	1 x 8" x 8" Pine
2	*1/2" x 9-3/4" x 20-1/4" Plywood roofing*
5	*1-1/4" x 11-1/4" Dowels*
	1/4" Plywood or solid stock
	1/8" Solid stock scrap
	2-1/2" x 2-1/2" x 10" Pine
	1-5/8" x 1-5/8" x 6-1/2" Pine
4	*1/2" Wooden beads*
	Roof shingles
	Bell

Step One First, cut the base, the four walls and ceiling panel from 1 x pine. The ceiling panel should be cut with a 45° bevel on both long sides to fit the roof panels. Use a jigsaw to cut all the door and window openings in the wall panels. If you choose to make this a martin house, construct inner partitions from 1/4" plywood to create between 8–12 cubicles in a bi-level configuration. Cut your doors and windows accordingly. Refer to the chart on pages 14 and 15 to accommodate other species.

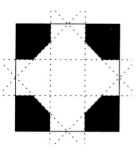

Otherwise, wall up all the openings except one front door with scraps of 1/4" plywood. Then glue and nail this structure together as shown in the exploded view drawing. Let dry.

Step Two Cut the 1 x 8" x 8" pine panel diagonally into two right triangles. Then cut both roof panels from 1/2" plywood. The top ridge seam can be miter cut or lapped with a butt joint. The eaves can be cut with a 45° bevel so as not to detract from the bottom tier of shingles. Glue and nail this roof assembly into place, starting with the triangles. Let dry.

Step Three Cut eight 1-1/2" squares from the 1/4" plywood or solid stock. Bevel cut the top edges, then use a hole saw to cut 1-1/4" holes through their centers. Insert the four 1-1/4" dowels into these blocks, and glue them into place to form the front portico.

Step Four To accommodate the spire, cut two grooves across the roof ridge, toward the front, 2-1/2" apart and to a depth of about 1". Using a coping saw, cut out a 2-1/2" square through the roof panels. Make this opening as snug a fit as possible for the 2-1/2" square spire base.

Step Five The spire is the crowning glory, whether you copy this one or free-form your own. This 2-1/2" square base rests on the ceiling panel. The belfry is opened up at the top by making a series of 3" cuts down from the top, then chiseling out the center (see illustration). Cut and chisel the straight angles before the diagonals.

A mitered 1" skirt of 1/4" stock is added just beneath this opening, and capped with beveled and mitered strips of 1/4" stock. Decorative cuts may be added before assembly. The mitered upper fascia is cut from 2" strips of 1/4" stock, including arches cut with a coping saw.

The 1-5/8" square upper spire is bevel cut to a point. Arched panels of 1/4" stock are glued and nailed around the bottom edge, then framed by long rectangular strips of 1/8" stock. 5/8" circles of 1/8" or 1/4" stock can be applied to these. Use a 1-1/4" eyescrew with glue to secure this upper assembly to the center of the 3-7/8" square of 1/4" stock that forms the ceiling plate. A small bell is attached to the eyescrew. Glue and nail all this to the four prongs of the spire base. Mitered 5/8" strips of 1/4" stock form the notched rails. Wooden beads adorn the corners, attached with glue. Dowels can also be used to secure the balls into the rail corners.

This entire structure is firmly secured into the roof assembly with glue. The roof/spire seam should be caulked with waterproof sealant.

Step Six All the remaining trim on doors, windows, roof gables, etc. is cut from 1/4" stock to fit, then glued and nailed into place with small brads.

Step Seven Cut four 3/4" mitered strips of 1/4" stock to form the front and rear roof edge caps, then glue and nail into place. The shingles can either be purchased ready-made as doll house trim, or cut from solid 1/8" stock. Apply successive beads of silicone across both roof panels, and apply each tier of shingles from the bottom up. Every other row is staggered and filled with half shingles on each end. You can paint the structure traditional white or as you wish to enhance the trim.

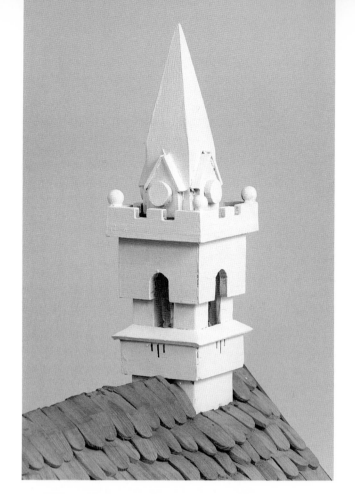

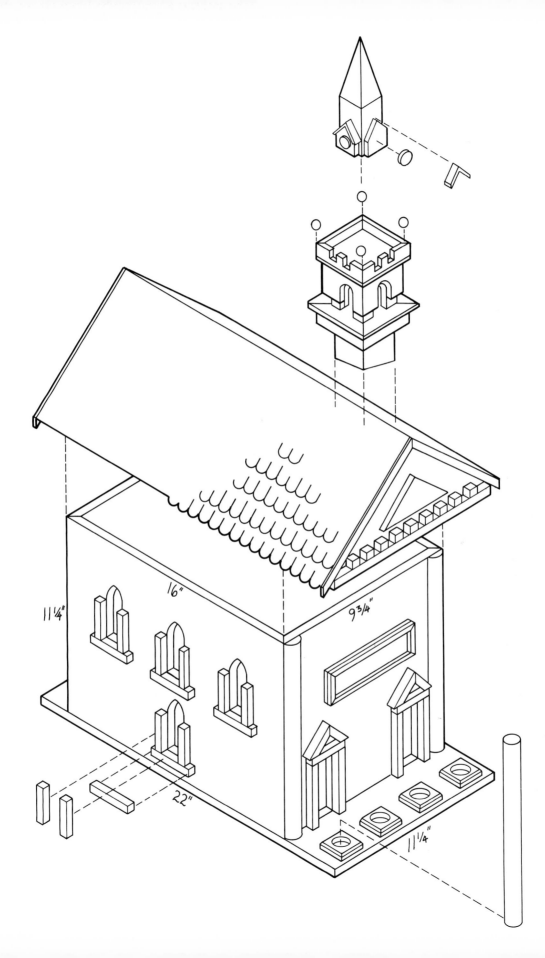

16"

11¼"

9¾"

22"

11¼"

Credits

Projects designed and constructed by:

Ron Anderson
(pages 74, 94, 108)

Don Daniels
(pages 56, 112, 121)

Mark Dockery
(pages 53, 70, 79, 96, 100, 128, 132, 136)

Mike Durkin
(pages 78, 80, 82, 84, 86, 98, 102, 105)

Harold Hall
(pages 119, 120)

Bobby Hansson
(pages 50–52, 126)

Michael Hester
(page 72)

Claudia & Bob Osby
(pages 53, 88, 92, 114, 116, 130)

Ralph Schmitt
(pages 59, 62, 64)

Fox Watson
(pages 67, 138)

Project design assistance by:

Thom Boswell
(pages 72, 74, 79, 82, 86, 88, 92, 98, 102, 114, 116, 130, 132, 136)

Gallery displays courtesy of:

Blue Spiral I, Asheville, NC
(pages 30, 31, 33, 36, 38, 44, 48)

Photography location courtesy of:

The Wright Inn, Asheville, NC
(pages 103, 139, 142)

Bird feed consultant:

Sally L. Coburn

Artist's Directory

Ron Anderson
115 Sue Ann Court
Sterling, VA 22170

Don Bundrick
P.O. Box 84
Tallulah Falls, GA 30573

Carol Costenbader
34 Deerhaven Lane
Asheville, NC 28803

Don Daniels
P.O. Box 939
Locust Grove, OK 74352

Mark Dockery
8 Busbee View Road
Asheville, NC 28803

Mike Durkin
c/o I. Ellis Johnson School
815 McGirts Bridge Rd.
Laurinburg, NC 28352

Marshall Fall
Rt. 1, Box 291-B
Hendersonville, NC 28792

Debra Fritts
385 Waverly Hall Circle
Roswell, GA 30075

Harold Hall
1203 Lake Martin Drive
Kent, OH 44240

Bobby Hansson
P.O. Box 1100
Rising Sun, MD 21911

Michael Hester
244-B Swannanoa River Rd.
Asheville, NC 28805

Mana D. C. Hewitt
947 Laurie Lane
Columbia, SC 29205

Bryant Holsenbeck
2007 Pershing Street
Durham, NC 27705

Barry Leader
122 West High Street
Elizabethtown, PA 17022

Bruce Malicoat
129 E. Vates Street
Frankenmuth, MI 48734

Claudia & Bob Osby
P.O. Box 976
Brevard, NC 28712

Charles Ratliff
183 New Avenue
Athens, GA 30601

David Renfroe
407 Big Pine Road
Marshall, NC 28753

Ralph Schmitt
75 Broadway
Asheville, NC 28801

Randy Sewell
38 Muscogee Avenue
Atlanta, GA 30305

Susan Starr
1580 Jones Road
Roswell, GA 30075

Paul Sumner
5721 N. Church Street
Greensboro, NC 27405

Fox Watson
50 Greene Drive
Black Mountain, NC 28711

West Olive Folk Art
8370 160th Avenue
West Olive, MI 49460

Index